Charlotta P. Einarsson

Beckett's Drama
Mis-Movements and the Aesthetics of Gesture

SAMUEL BECKETT IN COMPANY

Edited by Paul Stewart   ISSN 2365-3809

1   *Llewellyn Brown*
    Beckett, Lacan and the Voice
    With a foreword by Jean-Michel Rabaté
    ISBN 978-3-8382-0819-0
    (Paperback edition)
    ISBN 978-3-8382-0939-5
    (Hardcover edition)

2   *Robert Reginio, David Houston Jones, and Katherine Weiss (eds.)*
    Samuel Beckett and Contemporary Art
    ISBN 978-3-8382-0849-7

3   *Charlotta P. Einarsson*
    A Theatre of Affect
    The Corporeal Turn in Samuel Beckett's Drama
    ISBN 978-3-8382-1068-1

4   *Rhys Tranter*
    Beckett's Late Stage
    Trauma, Language, and Subjectivity
    ISBN 978-3-8382-1035-3

5   *Llewellyn Brown*
    Beckett, Lacan and the Gaze
    ISBN 978-3-8382-1239-5

6   *Paul Stewart &David Pattie (eds.)*
    Pop Beckett
    Intersections with Popular Culture
    ISBN 978-3-8382-1193-0

7   *Andy Wimbush*
    Still: Samuel Beckett's Quietism
    ISBN 978-3-8382-1369-9

8   *Lucy Jeffery*
    Transdisciplinary Beckett
    Visual Arts, Music, and the Creative Process
    ISBN 978-3-8382-1584-6

9   *Charlotta P. Einarsson*
    Beckett's Drama
    Mis-Movements and the Aesthetics of Gesture
    ISBN 978-3-8382-1298-2

Charlotta P. Einarsson

BECKETT'S DRAMA
Mis-Movements and the Aesthetics of Gesture

Bibliografische Information der Deutschen Nationalbibliothek
Die Deutsche Nationalbibliothek verzeichnet diese Publikation in der Deutschen Nationalbibliografie; detaillierte bibliografische Daten sind im Internet über http://dnb.d-nb.de abrufbar.

Bibliographic information published by the Deutsche Nationalbibliothek
Die Deutsche Nationalbibliothek lists this publication in the Deutsche Nationalbibliografie; detailed bibliographic data are available in the Internet at http://dnb.d-nb.de.

ISBN-13: 978-3-8382-1298-2
© *ibidem*-Verlag, Hannover-Stuttgart 2024
Alle Rechte vorbehalten

Das Werk einschließlich aller seiner Teile ist urheberrechtlich geschützt. Jede Verwertung außerhalb der engen Grenzen des Urheberrechtsgesetzes ist ohne Zustimmung des Verlages unzulässig und strafbar. Dies gilt insbesondere für Vervielfältigungen, Übersetzungen, Mikroverfilmungen und elektronische Speicherformen sowie die Einspeicherung und Verarbeitung in elektronischen Systemen.

All rights reserved. No part of this publication may be reproduced, stored in or introduced into a retrieval system, or transmitted, in any form, or by any means (electronic, mechanical, photocopying, recording or otherwise) without the prior written permission of the publisher. Any person who does any unauthorized act in relation to this publication may be liable to criminal prosecution and civil claims for damages.

Printed in the EU

For Ishrat Lindblad who told me to trust the authenticity of my own voice.

Let "found" or "made" mean as they work here as Beckett finds and makes us. Once we are "made" in Beckett's way, we say "oh yes," that always "was," we always "were" that way. But this "was" is retroactive. Only afterward does that seem to have been there before. Imagination makes and then something "was." How imagination works this way defines this "made," this "found," and "was." ... But you will have noticed that when I rejected an old concept of "imagination," I had something else to point to, instead. I called on you to let the word mean as it worked. I said we could let "magination" mean how Beckett wrote and what his characters do to us.

EUGENE GENDLIN (1985)

It is one thing for an artist to lack talent of vision and thus to make mistakes or make poorly through lack of skill, or time. But it is another to do what Beckett did: to mismake *on purpose*, to mismake *by design*—and to do so not to denigrate oneself, or one's audience, nor even to reconnect with a child or a savage within, but from the belief that such mismaking is in the interest of art and will shape its future.

LELAND DE LA DURANTAYE (2016)

Table of contents

List of Abbreviations XI

Preface XIII

Acknowledgements XV

Introduction 1

Chapter 1   Up 31

Chapter 2   Sideways 83

Chapter 3   Down 139

Conclusion 191

Bibliography 205

Index 215

List of Abbreviations

TN I　The Theatrical Notebooks of Samuel Beckett, Vol I
TN II　The Theatrical Notebooks of Samuel Beckett, Vol II
TN III　The Theatrical Notebooks of Samuel Beckett, Vol III
TN IV　The Theatrical Notebooks of Samuel Beckett, Vol IV

Preface

This book is a revision of my thesis, "Mis-Movements: The Aesthetics of Gesture in Samuel Beckett's Drama" (2012, Stockholm University), which focused on the significance of the idiosyncratic movements and gestures that Beckett's characters perform, *viz*- mis-movements. My interest in mis-movements was generated partly by phenomenology and partly by my previous experience as a dancer. Going back to revise this text more than a decade later has entailed travelling back in time to recall what I was trying to convey but could not then explain. It has also entailed identifying and unpacking ideas merely implied in the thesis, once again facing the limits of my own thinking. Yet, then as now, it is precisely such thinking from the edges of one's ideas that makes the carrying forward of ideas possible.

The phrase 'carrying forward' is taken from Eugene Gendlin's 'new phenomenology' (2004). According to Gendlin, the process of carrying forward is "a deliberate way to think and speak with what is more than categories (concepts, theories, assumptions, distinctions . . .)" (2004, 127). It is a way to think from that which exceeds the words we use and so it is a way to think with "the excess" that constitutes "our situated experiencing in the world" (Gendlin 2004, 28). The excess or felt sense is *always already* meaningful even as we cannot describe it at first, let alone explain it. Yet, "[i]f we do not have the felt meaning of the concept, we haven't got the concept at all–only a verbal noise. Nor can we think without felt meaning" (Gendlin 1997, 5–6). Thus, it is only because the felt sense exceeds language that it is possible to know and feel *more than* one is able to say. The process by means of which experience arrives to be conceptualized necessarily involves carrying felt sense forward, and in Gendlin's phenomenology this important insight is rendered as an ellipsis comprising five dots "(…..)" (1997, xi).

In revising my thesis, then, I have been working with the assumption that mis-movements mean something *more than* and *other than* what I previously was able to say. At the point in time when I was writing the thesis, the concepts I used seemed appropriate enough to the task of investigating mis-movements, but my understanding of those concepts did not quite capture my felt sense of their significance. As a result, my thinking about mis-movements remained a kind of *knowing without ta concept*. In fact, whatever conclusions there were in the thesis, I owed to my supervisors, most notably to Ishrat Lindblad, but also to Matthew Feldman and to Richard Begam, who generously agreed to read the thesis in its final stages. Revising the text has therefore involved thinking from old ideas in ways that imply new ideas. The difficulty is merely knowing when to stop thinking, writing, and editing etc. Words are essentially incomplete and, perhaps while striving to convey senses, using them pushes one to produce *more than* one intended: more and new perspectives, ideas, openings, difficulties, complexities, intricacies etc. Indeed, carrying forward never stops, and on that note, '…..'.

Stockholm 21st November 2023
Charlotta Palmstierna Einarsson

Acknowledgements

This book has been long in the making and there is simply no way for me to thank all of those who have inspired my thinking and so contributed to shape the book.

That said, I owe the opportunity of getting it published to specific individuals, namely to Matthew Feldman, who suggested that I should revise my thesis for publication; to Jonathan Bignell and Ulrika Maude, who both kindly agreed to endorse my book proposal in 2017; to Paul Stewart who, in his capacity as editor for the Beckett in Company Series, accepted it; and to Jessica Haunschild at *ibidem* Verlag for her kind and sustained support in the long process of revision. Thanks also to Christoph Ohlwärther and the editorial team at *Ibidem* Verlag for proofreading and indexing the book.

I also owe a very special debt of gratitude to my former supervisor Ishrat Lindblad, to whom this book is dedicated. Ishrat, you were and remain a guiding light, not merely for your erudite, sincere, and honest perspectives on all matters academic, but also for your mindful, considerate, and wise approach to life. Thank you for the loving kindness and attention you always found time to give in moments when I needed it most. Thanks for showing me the way to critically challenge my own ideas. I remain forever in your debt.

Many thanks also to my friends and colleagues Vicky Angelaki, Helen Asklund, Beyza Björkman, Michalea Castellanos, Elisabet Dellming, Carina Hermansson, Lena Jadekrantz, Marina Ludwigs, Raffaella Negretti, Anita Rakoczy, Anna-Pya Sjödin, Sonia York-Pryce, and Pieter Vermeulen. I am lucky to have you around.

Thanks to my friends Anne Sandblad, Tina Sandvik and Guiditta Arnese. You are in my heart.

Thanks Lena Haag, for introducing me to Wagner.

Thanks to the ETHER team led by Maggie Kubanyiova, Angela Creese, and Parinita Shetty. I am very grateful to have been invited into your encouraging and supportive circle.

Thank you, Cintya Andrea Floriani, for inspiring me to think about diversity and for inspiring me to 'be like water'.

Thank you, Annette Balaam, for inspirational conversations on Beckett's multiverse.

Thanks Jane Bennett and William Connolly for coming to the Autonomy Conference at Stockholm University in 2016. Your generous open-mindedness remains an inspiration.

Finally, to my family, pets included: you have helped me tremendously in thinking about the ideas presented in this book. The walks, the talks, the coffees, the support, the distractions (…..). Thanks for always being there for me. Much love.

Introduction

This book examines the incongruous, often highly formalised movements of the body in Samuel Beckett's drama, which I have labelled 'mis-movements' (Einarsson 2009; 2012). The body in Beckett's theatre is relentlessly made to break with what would appear to be more realistic modes of comportment. For instance, the idiosyncratic walking that many characters display exemplifies a kind of moving that draws attention to its own execution, as well as to the body as the locus of these activities, see for instance Krapp's "*laborious walk*" in *Krapp's Last Tape* (*TN III* 3:14), Clov's excessive, "*stiff, staggering walk*" in *Endgame* (*TN II* 3:12), and May's slow pacing and turning in *Footfalls* (*TN IV*, 292). Elsewhere, I have chosen to label such conspicuous moving 'mis-movement' (see Einarsson 2009, 14; 2017, 16).[1] By that term, I have sought to describe the function of physical movements in Beckett's plays as a means to foreground the body in order to problematize the concepts of perception and meaning-making and, finally, as a way to entirely resist comprehension. Mis-movements in Beckett's drama, I have suggested, should be understood as sensuous rather than intelligible manifestations of Beckett's poetic theatre (see Einarsson 2017 38, 65, 114, 120). In this book, however, I examine Beckett's use of mis-movements, not merely as part of a strategy to escape the confines of meaning in language, but as an instrument of artistic expression that upholds intellectual freedom.

In a sense, the use of mis-movements constitutes a phenomenological, heuristic solution to the problem of presentation and representation that Beckett explicitly addresses already in the early

---

[1] Examples of movements and gestures in this book are taken from *The Theatrical Notebooks*, volumes 1–4. According to the typographical standards of these editions, "[t]ext between square brackets [ ] has been added to the original English text. Text between pointed brackets { } has been revised. A pair of angle brackets < > indicates that a section of text has been cut from the original English text" (see *TN I*, 6).

1930s.[2] Notably, however, the mis-movements that Beckett's characters perform in his early drama are different from the mis-movements that characters perform in his middle and late dramas, and I connect this shift to their rhetorical function in performance. If initially mis-movements afford Beckett with a solution to attack and undermine language (cf. his oft-cited letter to Axel Kaun), then over time, mis-movements become poetic devices that solicit an almost ethical call to engage with the characters' embodied situations, which seem driven by need rather than accident. I have previously suggested that mis-movements could be approached as 'emergent or 'ontogenetic' phenomena, that is, "phenomena that are dependent on the techniques that produce them (for example, isolation, stasis, fragmentation, *dys*-appearance)" (Einarsson 2017, 169). Here, however, I return to address such ontogenetic phenomena, *viz*. mis-movements, as more precise experiences than the words used to describe them. Moreover, in Beckett's drama, I shall move on to suggest, and especially his late drama, the combination of mis-movements into patterns on a higher level of abstraction constitutes a poetic logic whereby the performance context is reconfigured from a context for interpretation to a context for aesthetic experience, a poetic logic that also holds the seed to intellectual freedom.

The question of how mis-movements arrive to be meaningfully grasped in the context of performance opens a variety of perspectives on the interconnections between sense and sense-making such as, for instance, the role of memory in experience or the question of how embodied experience is meaningfully grasped as an encounter. Taken as a whole, there is a high level of integration between the different parts that make up Beckett's drama, and looking at mis-movements therefore open a range of perspectives on the interaction between various phenomena as key to sense-making. Looking specifically at the embodied conditions for experiencing mis-

---

[2] See Beckett's article "Recent Irish Poetry" published 1934 under the pseudonym 'Andrew Belis' (Knowlson 1996, 180), and reprinted in *Disjecta* (1983).

movements in the context of Beckett's drama, however, I argue that mis-movements are instrumental to Beckett's reconfiguration of the performance context, and so that they are key to Beckett's development as director of his own drama. But I also suggest that the aesthetics of gesture in Beckett's drama safeguards an ethics of knowing. Indeed, that it affords a creative solution to the predicament of expression with aesthetic, as well as rhetorical and ethical implications. In the process of explaining such claims, I shall be referring to some of Beckett's plays to illustrate and exemplify my points. My aim, however, is not to discuss individual plays or explain the significance of the body in individual performances. Rather, it is to approach Beckett's stage directions from the perspective that they tacitly convey Beckett's transformation as a playwright, and that mis-movements are key to this transformation.

To this effect, I shall be engaging with Eugene Gendlin's process model of thinking, Gregory Bateson's ecological criteria for mental process, William James's and John Dewey's pragmatic aesthetics, and Mark Johnson's embodied aesthetics, all of which open perspectives for rethinking the interpretative frame of performance as ecology, and specifically with reference to the effects produced by mis-movements within this context. However, also Drew Leder (*The Absent Body*, 2009) and Sara Ahmed (*Queer Phenomenology*, 2016) afford useful perspectives on the issue of interpretation in the context of Beckett's drama. What Gendlin, Bateson, James, Dewey, Johnson, Leder and Ahmed (to name but a few,) arguably have in common, is an understanding that thinking cannot be separated from embodied experience, nor concepts, feelings, attitudes etc., from the contexts in which they occur, or from the phenomenal experiencing body. The interconnections between body and mind theorized in their work, respectively, will therefore help me shed light on the significance of mis-movements in Beckett's drama, and on the significance of the aesthetics of gesture for the process of understanding Beckett's innovative stage presentations.

Furthermore, my discussions of mis-movements in this book are aligned with studies that pay attention to the body in Beckett's drama, with studies that acknowledge the specificity of embodied experience for the event of interpretation, and with studies that acknowledge the dynamic and open-ended nature of interpretation. My focus on mis-movements should also be seen to participate in an ongoing re-evaluation of the recurrent motifs of the substance of thought, and on the relation between perception and cognition in Beckett's creative and critical work (see for example, Daniel Koczy *Beckett, Deleuze and Performance*, 2018, and Tim Lawrence *Beckett's Critical Aesthetics*, 2018). Clearly, Beckett's work affords fertile ground for studies seeking to understand the grounds on which drama continues to be a relevant conduit for human experience, and critical writings derived from such perspectives have therefore inspired my work in this book, as I hope to inspire others to probe into this rich field of research.[3]

Premises

To pave the ground for my discussions I begin with a tautological description of the role and function of the body in Beckett's drama: if the stage-directions collected in *The Theatrical Notebooks of Samuel Beckett* detail idiosyncratic movements and gesture (*viz*. mis-movements), then such idiosyncratic movements and gestures (mis-movements) must have specific functions within the context of performance.[4] This simple premise underlies the

---

[3] For instance, Beckett's reconfiguration of the subject-object relation invites consideration of the intersection of scientific and humanistic reasoning, as well as considerations of the third meaning-type of imagery that accompanies conceptualisations of ideas (whether auditive or visual), or the kind of theory welded in practice. Indeed, following Beckett in revisiting the foundations for perception, thinking, and meaning-making may entail rethinking the kind of questions asked within different contexts, illuminating the commonalities and differences between epistemologies, thereby paving the ground for multi- and interdisciplinary dialogues.
[4] Bateson's definition of a tautology is that it is "a body of propositions so linked together that the links between the propositions are necessarily valid" (2002, 78).

discussions in this book. Yet, somewhat paradoxically, it also underlies the propositions that I shall ultimately arrive at, namely that neither the aesthetics of gesture in Beckett's drama, nor the poetic logic of Beckett's strategic use of mis-movements, has anything to do with the concrete body in performance. Even though the stage directions are key to understanding the aesthetics of gesture in Beckett's drama, the specific movements that they detail are not relevant *per se*. Admittedly, different mis-movements will always generate different interactions, and so ostensibly it does matter which mis-movements are being foregrounded. Yet any performance adhering to the poetic logic of mis-movements (even if it emphasizes 'new' mis-movements,) would bear the mark of Beckett's creative vision, which arguably derives from the understanding that our habitual tendencies to grasp meaning in language obliterate creative, holistic, and even artistic perception. It also derives from realizing that curiosity is that mood of attention within which perception is homed. Indeed, if the issue of perception is key to understanding the poetic logic of mis-movements, as described in the stage directions, then mis-movements are key to perception. Mis-movements liberate spectators to see the world differently. But mis-movements also invite spectators to think differently about the potential meanings perceived. That is, mis-movements invite spectators to re-connect with embodied experience as that realm wherein new modes of thinking about the world emerges—modes of thinking that propose themselves, as it were, as if already there to be perceived, as afterthoughts to experience, and as occurrences to be carried forward into the future. Consequently, any performance that operationalizes Beckett's aesthetics of gesture by attending to mis-movements would be adhering to an underlying poetic logic that solicits intellectual freedom.

Doting

Beckett's meticulous attention to the body in performance is noteworthy. As evidenced by the careful descriptions of the characters' gestures and postures in the stage directions, Beckett dotes on the body, and even his prose is unparalleled in rendering chaotic physical experience idiosyncratic shape. As an artistic practice, Jane Bennett explains, 'doting' is, "a stylized mode of encounter, in real time and face-to-face with things. But doting is also a particular kind of linguistic description. It solicits a language-practice that shapes and elevates—writes *up*—lived impressions" (2020, 65–66). Discussing the way Walt Whitman practices doting, Bennett warns that doting may easily be warded off as an essentially aesthetic practice, one that merely foregrounds sensation over sense (2020, 68). However, according to Bennett, Whitman does not merely practice doting to foreground sensation: he also dotes to highlight the material chosen for artistic creation, specifically to 'rescue' it from "the status of pure passivity" (2020, 68). For example, in "Song of the Open Road", "stones (and paths, curbs ferries roofs)" are revealed to "add a twist" to the poetic speaker's perception of the world (2020, 68).[5] The practice of doting brings out new and different qualities and meanings. That is, doting brings out new and different images, which could be seen to transform the reader's understanding of the world.

Importantly, however, Whitman also dotes to bring perhaps more sinister aspects of the world to the fore. Thus, the "attention to detail" in "I Sing the Body Electric", according to Bennett, "shamelessly shines a light on the wondrous quality of the human bodies on display", ostensibly "in lieu of an overt repudiation of the moral horror of a slave auction" (2020, 69). Even as Whitman could be seen to "favor an inspirational over a polemical rhetoric", the "contrast between the beauty of bodies and the horror of the social situation", as well as the attention to the "exquisite senses, life-lit eyes, pluck and volition" of the bodies on display, effectively "links the value of each body-soul to the inestimably great worth of the 'diffuse float' from which each has 'cohered'" (Bennett 2020, 70). More than merely rescuing the human body from being reduced to "an

---

[5] A few lines earlier Bennett explains that in Whitman's poetry "[p]ave and promenade, clinks and jokes, metal badge and excited crowd, impassive stones and exclaiming women—each is worthy of dote" (2020, 66).

unremarkable, instrumentalized 'matter'", therefore, the poem "augment[s] and vitalize[s] the abolitionist argument", specifically by invoking "the presence of a *material kind of (a)personal sympathy*" (Bennett 2020, 70). In targeting the "negative feelings and forces" at work in the deeper layers of the fabric of society, Whitman's poetry should thus be seen to "enact an affective alchemy ... aimed at enlivening the will to keep going in dark times and exploring the ways in which *indirect* responses to social evil can supplement the tactic pf head-on opposition" (see Bennett 2020, 70–71). As Bennett convincingly shows, and even if it were to be defined as a matter of paying careful attention to the complexities of perception, doting qualifies as a disruptive, implicitly political, practice (2020, 69–72), one that could be seen to inspire readers to stay in discomfort and revaluate preconceived ideas.

Interestingly, much of what Bennett says about Whitman's practice of doting on the body could also be said about Beckett's use of mis-movements, which similarly seems to be a disruptive aesthetic practice that qualifies as, perhaps, implicitly political, specifically in its calling attention to perception and judgement. Indeed, if you want people to see the world differently, you cannot merely tell them to do so, but must show them a different world. Without seeking to overstate the similarities between Whitman and Beckett, I nonetheless maintain that Beckett's doting resembles Whitman's in that it places an ethical demand on us to experience the human body from the perspective of "curious sympathy" (cf. Bennett 2020, 71). A disruptive aesthetic practice, Beckett's careful attention to mis-movements in performance rescues the body from the shadows of consciousness to which it has been relegated by language (Einarsson 2017, 181), and 'adds a twist' (cf. Bennett) to the spectators' perception of the world. Indeed, mis-movements, as the tools of doting, afford encounters, between performance and audience, between text and context, between fictionality and reality, and between mediated and unmediated presentations that prompt spectators to reckon with their own reactions and responses. In what follows, I shall therefore move on to approach the question of the role and function of mis-movements in Beckett's drama from the perspective that a Beckett performance (or indeed any performance,) is an ecological system, comprising *more than* merely the dramatic text, a situation that also has profound implications for the possibility of interpretation.

Beckett and philosophy

The ways in which characters mismove in Beckett's drama reveals a thematic concern with lived experience. Still, according to James Knowlson, Beckett treated the plays as purely 'dramatically structured material', and generally avoided discussing the philosophical resonances, ambiguities, or possible interpretations of his work (2003, 103). Notwithstanding, references to movements and moving in Beckett's drama have often been taken as emblematic of Beckett's interest in philosophy (see for instance, John Fletcher, "Samuel Beckett and the Philosophers", 1965; Stanton B. Garner, Jr "'Still Living Flesh': Beckett, Merleau-Ponty, and the Phenomenological Body", 1993; and Dermot Moran, "Beckett and Philosophy", 2006). In the early stages of Beckett criticism, scholars also noted the influence of Schopenhauer, Descartes, Berkeley, Bergson the pre-Socratic philosopher Democritus, but also the influence of other authors, most notably Dante.[6] Pivotal figures in this

---

[6] In 1961, Martin Esslin also launched the idea that Beckettian drama was "absurd", taking the term from Albert Camus's writings (Pattie 2000, 114). However, even as the absurdist notion of the world seems "akin to the existentialists" (Esslin qtd in Pattie 2000, 114), Esslin does not equate Beckett's drama with existentialist philosophy: "While these parallels may be illuminating, we must not go too far in trying to identify Beckett's vision with any school of philosophy. It is the peculiar richness of a play like *Waiting for Godot* that it opens vistas on so many different perspectives. It is open to philosophical, religious, and psychological interpretations, yet above all it is a poem on time, evanescence, and the mysteriousness of existence, the paradox of change, and stability, necessity, and absurdity" (Esslin 2001, 61–62). In suggesting that Beckett's first drama "does not require an external justification for its meaning, but [...] creates its effects, as a poem does, by the careful use of the form itself", Esslin thus

period of criticism are, for instance, Ruby Cohn who, in *The Comic Gamut* (1962) uses the theories of Bergson to discuss the significance of laughter in Beckett's work, and Hugh Kenner who in "The Cartesian Centaur" (1959), presents an influential argument, subsequently developed by scholars tracing the significance of the prosthetic device and technology in Beckett's drama, including Cohn, namely, that Beckett's drama could be understood within a Cartesian framework. Interestingly, while Kenner identified many references to body-mind dualism in Beckett's work, he was also a forerunner in identifying its limits (Morot-Sir 1976, 34). Thus, Edouard Morot-Sir maintains, "without saying so specifically", Kenner "suggests an anti-Cartesianism with Beckett's works showing the contemporary doom of the Cartesian expectations" (1976, 34). The perspectives that open out from Kenner's article are undeniably relevant to the current development in Beckett studies towards embodied experience, but also to the present study's concern with mis-movements.

Cartesian reverberations

Indeed, it seems inevitable that a concern with the mind enfolds a concern with the body as the locus of experience, as well as with the interaction between mind and body. In "Philosophical Fragments in the Works of Samuel Beckett" (1964), Ruby Cohn comments that "Cartesian echoes sound through" Beckett's work in phrases as well as in characters' penchants, desires, and interests (34–35). However, she continues "[f]ar more telling than these incidental reminiscences, is the fact that all Beckett's work paradoxically insists upon and rebels against the Cartesian definition of a man as 'a thing that thinks', insists upon and rebels against the knowledge that is confined in consciousness" (Cohn 1964, 35). Picking up on Cohn's observations more than a decade later, Morot-Sir adds that "[t]he true Beckettian problem concerns 'that things which thinks'—in other

---

foreshadows the discussion of meta-theatricality in Beckett criticism (Pattie 2000, 115).

words, its consciousness, not in itself and its glorious power of self-awareness, but in its precarious link with the body and the latter's successive 'stages of decay'" (1976, 36). Arguably, Cohn and Morot-Sir prefigure contemporary interest in Beckett's thematic concern the significance of the body and embodied cognition for understanding his work. And their ideas could also be seen to serve as the background against which the concerns of this present study should be read. Of course, neither discuss the body as such—the mood accompanying literary criticism in the 1960s and 70s did not endorse the body's participation in meaning-making. Yet in lifting the body, that is in discussing philosophical theories on the interconnections between mind and body (Cohn),[7] and in surveying the contemporary field of Beckett criticism with reference to its Cartesian and anti-Cartesian proclivities (Morot-Sir),[8] both Cohn and Morot-Sir could be seen to predict a change to come, namely critical interest in the "versions of embodiment" in Beckett's work (McMullan 1997).[9]

In targeting the relationship between body and mind as a topic worthy of attention Morot-Sir and Cohn could thus be seen to point the way forward, and many seem now follow their lead. For example, in *Postcognitivist Beckett* (2020), Olga Beloborodova approaches the body in Beckett's drama within the framework of extended cognition, which is part of the "4E" approach to cognition.[10]

---

[7] For instance, Cohn identifies and examines references to Occasionalism as discussed by Arnold Geulincx and Nicholas Malebranche.
[8] According to Cohn, Beckett's attitude to Descartes is ambiguous, post *Whoroscope* (1930) "Descartes himself does not reappear in Beckett's work", and Morot-Sir's concern is to defend Anglo-Saxon criticism against the denigrating accusation of being Cartesian readings, which has been launched by French critics who claim to have moved on to Existentialism(Morot-Sir 1976, 30–32); and he does so specifically by pointing at Hugh Kenner, Frederick J. Hoffman, and Ruby Cohn (1976, 32–35).
[9] Notably, as Rita Felski points out, literary criticism is always accompanied by a mood, which, as it were, "bridges the gap between thought and feeling" (2015, 21).
[10] "The four E's of 4E cognition initialize its central claim: cognition does not occur exclusively inside the head, but is variously embodied, embedded,

The extended perspective on cognition maintains that "the mind does not reside exclusively in the head, but rather extends into the world in a continuous and constitutive way" (Beloborodova 2020, 1). With reference to Beckett's work, Beloborodova maintains that earlier Beckett scholars have failed to give an account for the "extended fictional minds" that appear in Beckett's work, whether in the prose or in the drama, precisely on account of a Cartesian bias (2020, 2). In Beloborodova's analyses, moreover, Beckett's fictional minds are characterized by interaction. They are hybrid cognitive systems enfolding "external cognitive artefacts (such as rocking chairs, notebooks, or language)" (Beloborodova 2020, 59). Importantly, however, according to Beloborodova, these hybrid cognitive systems do not support the characters: "the Beckettian fictional mind remains just as lost, confused, and unreliable, fumbling in the dark against all odds to make sense of the world" (2020, 59). Yet, even if Beloborodova's understanding of the body's participation in cognition in Beckett's work differs from the one I am presenting here, which takes interaction as key to sense-making, the description of the "organic" type of cognition that emerges in Beckett's work seemingly refutes the Cartesian mode in favour of an interactive model of cognition. Put differently, Cartesian dualism insufficiently captures the continuity between body and mind that emerges in Beckett's work, a continuity that embodied perspectives are more apt to explain.

Even more recently, Amanda Dennis's book length study *Beckett and Embodiment: Body, Space, Agency* (2023), examines the "radical interrogation of agency" in Beckett's work (9), specifically through the lens of phenomenology and embodiment initiated in the works of Ulrika Maude (*Beckett, Technology and the Body*, 2009), Anna McMullan (*Performing Embodiment in Samuel Beckett's Drama* 2010). According to Dennis, "Merleau-Ponty's thinking anticipates theories of material agency that underpin contemporary efforts to rethink relations between the human and the nonhuman" (2023, 11). Thus, she

---

enacted, or extended by way of extra-cranial processes and structures" (Rowlands qtd in Carney 2020, 77).

proposes that "Beckett's hybrid bodies, vital landscapes ad parodies of anthropocentrism may anticipate and inform efforts to reimagine the rapport between the human and the nonhuman environment" (2023, 13). Reading the body in Beckett's work through the combined lenses phenomenology, ecology, and new materialism, Dennis, like Beloborodova targets interaction as key to Beckett's 'hybrid bodies', and argues for a reconceptualization of the "abject, decrepit body in Beckett" (Dennis 2023, 15). And, even as my understanding of the role of interaction for meaning-making differs slightly from their accounts, both Beloborodova's and Dennis's studies show why embodied experience remains a useful starting point for revaluating not merely implicit references to Descartes in Beckett's work, but a whole range of conceptualisations of the body-mind complex as they emerge in Beckett's work.

Indeed, embodied approaches resonate with the focus placed on the interconnections between body and mind in this present study, although the main aim of this study is not to outline the nature of the body-mind connections appearing in Beckett's work, but rather to approach the body in Beckett's drama as an artistic tool, and to consider the effects of this tool on audiences. More to the point, my aim in this study is to show the relation between Beckett's reconceptualizing of the performance context and the shift in Beckett's development as a playwright. In so doing, I shall be addressing Beckett's concern with mis-movements as a poetics that could be seen to safeguards interpretation and freedom of mind. With these concerns in mind, I approach the body in Beckett's drama (*viz*. mis-movements,) as a poetic device with rhetorical effects, and I also consider aesthetic experience as the foundation for ethical discernment. Taking off from the idea that the strategic use of mis-movements in performance constitutes an artistic response to the predicament of expression, then, the present book addresses Beckett's heuristic solution to this predicament in three chapters dealing, respectively, with ecological (Chapter 1), phenomenological (Chapter 2), and aesthetic (Chapter 3) aspects of mis-movements. Each chapter also suggests directions both for the process of approaching its subject as a relevant element of performance, and for discussing its effects.

Anti-Cartesian reverberations

As already suggested, to many of Beckett's earliest critics, his emphasis on the mechanisation of the body seemed decidedly Cartesian in nature. Still, scholars have also maintained that the emphasis on Cartesian elements in Beckett's work has pre-empted other perspectives (Mooney 1982, 218). In contemporary criticism Cartesian readings of Beckett have also been increasingly challenged, for instance, as discussed above, by Olga Beleborodova, who argues that Beckett studies today generally construe Beckett as anti-Cartesian (2020, 16–18). Yet Beloborodova is not the first one to maintain that reading Beckett as a closet Cartesian is a mistake. Decades earlier, Michael E. Mooney (1982) lists seven important Cartesian studies on Beckett, proposing that the Cartesian studies, which "so dominate critical response to Samuel Beckett" since the publication of Kenner's article, have been no more than refinements of the very same idea, and this had led to a situation where "the importance of presocratic and sceptical thought in his work" has been overlooked (214, *fn*1). According to Mooney, "Beckett's fiction beginning with Murphy can be better understood by reference to the presocratic philosopher, Democritus of Abdera and to Sextus Empiricus' scepticism" (Mooney 2018, 215), a claim that has since been corroborated by Matthew Feldman, who similarly derives Beckett's concern with the relation between perception and knowledge to his reading the presocratic philosophers, and who concludes his argument for the relevance of addressing presocratic influences in Beckett's work by suggesting that "[p]erhaps, then, by "going backwards contextually—both in philosophical history and in the genesis of Beckett's art—new ways of advancing in Beckett Studies may visible" (2006, *npag*).

Philosophical reverberations

Arguably, a concern with the body is integral to any philosophical perspective on the human condition. Thus, for instance, scholars who turned to existentialism could also be seen to have cultivated an interest in the interconnections with body and mind, not least since the existentialist argument coming out of Sartre's *Being and Nothingness* (1943) clearly paved the way for rethinking the ontological dimensions of embodiment. In "Still Living Flesh: Beckett, Merleau-Ponty and the Phenomenological Body", Stanton B. Garner lists several studies that have explored "the intricate relationship of Beckett's literature to the post-Husserlian philosophy of Heidegger and Sartre" (1993, 447),[11] before moving on to state his aim, namely to [reclaim, "the body for philosophy, in other words, phenomenology" as this "has relevance, not only for Beckett's plays, but for non-Beckettian dramatic texts and for theatre studies in general" (Garner 1993, 448). Garner's argument is directed at the contemporary effort "to reassess the relationship of his career to its twentieth-century philosophical and aesthetic contexts", since Beckett's death in 1989 (1993, 443). Most notably, his argument is pointed at those who attempt "to resituate Beckett's literary and dramatic canon within the theoretical milieu of poststructuralism and [who] find within his art an epistemological and linguistic critique closer to Derrida and Deleuze than to Sartre and Heidegger", and he includes among these, for instance, Steven Connor *Samuel Beckett: Repetition, Theory and Text* (1988), Lance St. John Butler and Robin J. Davis's edited collection *Rethinking Beckett: A Collection of Critical Essays* (1990), and Thomas Trezise's study of Beckett's prose *Into the Breach: Samuel Beckett and the Ends of Literature* (1990) (Garner 1993, 443)[12].

---

[11] Stanton B. Garner's list includes: "David H. Hesla, *The Shape of Chaos: An Interpretation of the Art of Samuel Beckett* (Minneapolis: University of Minnesota Press, 1971), especially pp. 167-207; Eugene F. Kaelin, *The Unhappy Consciousness: The Poetic Plight of Samuel Beckett* (Dordrecht: D. Reidel, 1981); and Lance St. James Butler, *Samuel Beckett and the Meaning of Being: A Study of Ontological Parable* (London: Macmillan, 1984)." (1993, 447, *fn11*).

[12] For Garner's more comprehensive list, see Garner 1993, 443*fn2*.

Even so, Garner points out, studies approaching the "phenomenological/existentialist Beckett" are once again gaining ground (Garner 1993, 443), a fact he attributes to the "theoretical richness of phenomenology" (1993, 444). Phenomenology, according to Graner, is frequently overlooked by scholars who are taken in by the intellectual dexterity of deconstruction but fail either to appreciate the affinities between phenomenology and deconstruction, or to acknowledge that "the Derridean critique presupposes a role for such concepts as presence and subjectivity, if radically revised and purged of their privileged, transcendent idealism" (Garner 1993, 445), or both. In Garner's words, "we must be careful not to underestimate the links that bind heresy to the very orthodoxy against which it rebels" (1993, 446-447). Yet, while this specific statement is made about Thomas Treizse's "repudiation of phenomenology" (Garner 1993, 446), it could be argued that Garner's claim hints more broadly at the relevance of taking a dialectical approach, on various issues. For instance, Beckett's 'attack on language', similarly merits a bifocal approach, one capable of enfolding *both* the body's complicity in linguistic meaning *and* its resistance to being rendered in language. Indeed, in Beckett's drama, the body is *both* present *and* absent, *both* meaningless *and* meaningful, *both* singular *and* universal; and taking such bifocal perspectives on embodied experience seriously is key the understanding mis-movements in Beckett's drama.

On a slightly different yet related note, scholars have noted the extent with which Beckett's characters are being moved in various ways, suggesting a more 'ontico-ethical', structural or philosophical basis for Beckett's attention to the body. For example, according to Ackerley and Gontarski, various philosophers' concern with movement in relation to metaphysical and ontological questions of Being, as well as with Being's relation with motion as an organising principle of the universe, are represented in Beckett's work in different ways, most noticeably in his early novels but also in his plays (2004, 384). For example, in *Krapp's Last Tape*, Krapp recalls drifting "with the punt ... into the stream" (*TN* 221) evoking Geulincx's notion of the boat in which "God moves the boat, but on it our deliberation is free" (Ackerley and Gontarski 2004, 385). And, in *Rockaby*, the woman who moves without moving could be seen to exemplify the notion of a prime mover, specifically as the stage directions specify that the woman is to remain "*completely still*", whereas the chair, "[*c*]*ontrolled mechanically without assistance from w*" (*CDW* 433). Such images recall Geulincx's *occasionalism*.[13] Moreover, as Hugh Kenner suggests, the "strange detachment with which Beckett's people regard the things their hands and feet do", is founded in the notion of "*Quod nescis quomodo fiat, id non facis* [Because you do not know how it was done, you did not do it]" (1973, 84). The body in Beckett's work has thus frequently been read philosophically in ways that move far beyond Cartesian dualism, most notably evoking the intrinsic interconnections between body and mind that could be seen to underpin human sense-making.

Methodological concerns

In recent decades, however, perspectives tracing the process of creation or mapping out historiographical detail have tended to take precedence over studies focusing on the formal, aesthetic, ethical, and many-minded perspectives opened out in Beckett's work, with the issue of methodology and "empirical corroboration" broached by Feldman in *Falsifying Beckett: Essays on Philosophy, and Methodology in Beckett Studies* (2015), looming large in the background (64). According to Feldman, who could be seen to inaugurate the archival turn, such a turn corrects more tendentious readings and furthers our understanding of Beckett's work, as well as our understanding of his development as a writer, in ways hitherto unprecedented (2015, 67). In readings with such explanatory power, the criterion of "empirical corroboration" arguably safeguards the criterion of "relevance"

---

[13] Everett Frost explains that Geliuncx is prompted by a desire to overcome or replace "Aristotelian scholasticism, church doctrine, or divine revelation with the autonomous individual as the prolegomena *[Sic.]* and ultimate authority not only for ontological certainty but also for the ethical conduct that Geulincx thought must follow from it" (2012, 293).

(Feldman 2015, 61). By contrast, readings that build networks merely based on associations made "in the mind of the critic", produce the irrelevant perspectives that ostensibly characterize "'critical theory'" (Feldman's shorthand for "'postmodernism', 'deconstruction', or 'poststructuralism'" 2015, 60), and so fail to meet the two criteria of relevance and usefulness.[14] The appreciation for detail and empirically substantiated claims, characteristic of archival studies, simply has more explanatory power than theories that build on "synthetic statements" (Feldman 2015, 69). Whether and where readings that, like my own, centre on reader-response and aesthetic effects, fit into this grid, I am not sure. Nor am I sure whether readings that see texts as reservoirs for cultivating and affirming individual and collective meanings fit into such a grid, either. Yet, I shall seize this opportunity to put in my two penn'orth.

I do not deny the relevance of archival studies as capable of providing nuanced, exhaustive analyses of Beckett's work, nor that the

---

[14] I am not sure whether all scholarly work produced under the remit of postmodernism, deconstruction and poststructuralism, deserves to be contrasted with archival studies (literary history, or genetic manuscript studies), but in, for example, Angela Moorjani's *Abysmal Games in the Novels of Samuel Beckett* (1982), Thomas Trezise's *Into the Breach: Samuel Beckett and the Ends of Literature*, and Steven Connor's *Samuel Beckett: Repetition, Theory and Text* (1988), Beckett's postmodernist strategies are seen as evidence that Beckett exhausts language to deconstruct notions of literary representation. Also, in *The Language of Silence* (1984), Leslie Kane writes that "Beckett's drama is characterized by a retreat from the word; physical, emotional and linguistic entrapment; stasis as dramatic structure, evocation of evanescence; the motif of waiting; and the centrality of time" (1984, 108). Finally, Richard Begam's *Samuel Beckett and the End of Modernity* (1996), which places "the theoretical argument over Beckett's status in modernity and post-modernity in context" (Pattie 2000, 195), and Carla Locatelli *Unwording the Word: Samuel Beckett's Prose Works After the Nobel Prize* (1990), which traces Beckett's transformation from "a gnoseological quest into a modern epistemological analysis, based on a critical, self-reflective use of language" (Locatelli 1990, 2), could be seen to approach Beckett's work from the perspective that Beckett's use of language signals the impossibility of communication. Whether these ideas are empirically corroborated or relevant, I leave for others to decide.

process of unearthing and corroborating various influences on Beckett's thinking and writing have generated much valuable insight into the interconnections between Beckett's life and work. Moreover, I understand Feldman's agenda to be more productive than merely castigating the "other thans" (see Dowd 2008, 378). Surely the aim is not to distinguish between "relevant" readings and readings with "less explanatory power", but to make a call for critical self-reflection *vis-a´-vis* the methods used to approach Beckett's creative work. Feldman claims on the one hand that the archival studies contribute to further understanding of the connections between Beckett's life and his work, specifically through presenting falsifiable and therefore scientific facts; and, on the other hand, that the 'other thans', that is non-archival, literary studies, apply methods that amount to nothing more than "'interior decorating'", motivated by "comparison or synthesis of otherwise disconnected subjects in the interest of adding to an understanding of *something other than Beckett*" (Feldman 2015, 71 *my* emphasis). According to Feldman, then, to see connections between seemingly unrelated phenomena is to present unfalsifiable connections, and so to falsify the connections one sees (see Feldman 2015, 71). Consequently, scholars who synthesise perspectives on Beckett's work merely end up producing 'headaches among their own overtones', whereas scholars who excavate the archives dig up hard, falsifiable facts. But why set up this dichotomy in the first place? I concur with Garin Dowd that Feldman's application of Popper's "two-fold demarcation" (2008, 375), fails to consider the effects of the "'fusion of horizons'" (Bruno Clément qtd in Dowd 2008, 385), inevitably taking place in literary criticism, for instance between reader and text, between text and context, or between body and mind. Moreover, I concur with Dowd that the very grounds on which Feldman criticizes scholars the 'other thans' are precarious, not least since those he castigates for having presented facts that were later to be corrected, most notably Linda Ben-Zvi, clearly fulfilled the criteria of presenting facts that are falsifiable (Dowd 2008, 381–382). Dowd's analysis of Feldman's argument thus convincingly illustrates why a discourse of justification bordering on scientism is problematic, but it also shows why Feldman's reasoning seems to be begging the question.

More to the point, I take the suggestion that there is "no dearth of theories in Beckett studies" (Feldman 2015, 72,) not a testimony of the lack of scholarly analytical rigor, but as an indication of the suggestiveness of Beckett's work. Consequently, I find Feldman's conclusion that "[w]hat is needed is a better appreciation of the academic working methods separating these two techniques, these two approaches", as well as the claim that the "lack of organising principles to distinguish between *types of theories*" (Feldman 2015, 72), unwarranted. Ideally, both theoretical, synthesising perspectives and archival, genetic, or material studies do both, that is they *both* uncover something more about the theory *and* about Beckett's work. Clearly, synthesising perspectives do not merely afford insight into 'other things than Beckett'. Rather, synthesising perspectives afford interaction that inevitably opens new perspectives, *both* on Beckett's work *and* on the theory or methodology within which Beckett's work is approached. Given the open-ended process of thinking, moreover, there must be more ways to support the relevance of one's claims than mapping them to authorial intention; and, whether synthesising perspectives seem relevant to Beckett's intention or not, there is no stopping the processes of association generated by Beckett's suggestive work. Clearly, too, it is very difficult to transcend one's own perspectives to objectively examine one's assumptions. I therefore take refuge in Stanley Cavell's insightful comments about the progression of his own thinking, as stated in the preface to *Must We Mean What We Say* (first published 1969): "Only in stages have I come to see that each of my ventures in and from philosophy bears on ways of understanding the extent to which my relation to myself is prefigured in my relation to my words" (2002, xxiv). Indeed, the process of thinking, whether on philosophy or on drama, unfolds slowly, sometimes in unexpected ways, and rarely do we 'hit the nail on the head' in our first, second, third, fourth etc., trials. Given that we are all immersed in the perspectives we try to transcend, 'failing better' seems the only methodological stance to take up. By contrast, the notion that we should only conduct relevant research, that is research that will succeed in advancing understanding, seems curiously circular in nature.

Finally, on the issue of use, Abraham Flexner's by now classic essay on the "Usefulness of Useless Knowledge" springs to mind. According to Flexner:

> curiosity, which may or may not eventuate in something useful, is probably the outstanding characteristic of modern thinking. It is not new. It goes back to Galileo, Bacon, and to Sir Isaac Newton, and it must be absolutely unhampered. Institutions of learning should be devoted to the cultivation of curiosity and the less they are deflected by considerations of immediacy of application, the more likely they are to contribute not only to human welfare but to the equally important satisfaction of intellectual interest which may indeed be said to have become the ruling passion of intellectual life in modern times.
>
> (Flexner 1939, 545)

Flexner's argument is compelling, not only because it locates the activity of investigation in curiosity and so acknowledges the affective roots of human thinking, but also because it emphasizes the collective structure of research and diminishes the criterion of application. Indeed, there is no saying what may happen when ideas take flight. For whatever it may be worth, therefore, it is in the spirit of collaboration that the ideas put forward in this book should be understood.

Beckett and the body

Encouragingly, outside the scope of archival studies, the body's participation in meaning-making has increasingly been recognized in Beckett criticism, as discussed above, along with phenomenological and embodied perspectives on his work. As Ulrika

Maude points out, Beckett's emphasis on the body is a literary effort to "cast light on embodied experience" that "can be read as one of the most serious inquires […] in literature", comparable to Merleau-Ponty's effort to do the same in philosophy (2009, 5, 137). Admittedly, Beckett's presentation of the body evokes metaphoric meanings and "[m]ost of Beckett's work, and especially his late work for the stage, remains utterly unintelligible unless read metaphorically to signify a fundamental problematic of the human condition" (Wynands 2007, 84–85). In *Back to Beckett*, Ruby Cohn thus notes that *Acte sans paroles I* and *All that Fall* both use falling as a metaphor for the "human condition […] Each play adheres to its genre and exploits that genre to make a metaphysical implication" (1973, 158). Only, the problem with such interpretations is, as Maude also reminds us, that "the discursively produced body takes precedence over, if not eclipses, the flesh" (2009, 2). I take Maude's caution to heart. Beckett's literary effort is akin to Merleau-Ponty's phenomenological exploration of embodiment as involvement that extends beyond language or linguistic discourse, although my interest in mis-movements takes place on the cusp of the experience/content divide, which seems to open between those who address either what it means to experience a work of art or what a work of art means. More to the point, I am interested in interaction as generative of whatever meanings that could be seen to emerge in the context of performance.

With reference to my own concern with the body in performance, I thus find the more recent development in Beckett criticism, which focuses on the importance of the body in Beckett's work, especially relevant. For example, Hannah Simpson's work on neurodiversity (2018) sheds light on the interaction between spectator and performance more broadly, and her work on embodied cognition and disability (2021) illustrates the relevance of re-evaluating the stage directions.[15] In "A Bodily Haunting: The Woman's Wordless Scream

---

[15] According to Simpson, there are "undetected indicators of disability in the scripts, including mobility impairment, automatic speech, stuttering, and memory deficiency" (2018, 26–27).

on Samuel Beckett's Stage", Simpson maintains that "the performed scream returns embodied trauma to embodied expression in *Not I* and *Happy Days*" (95). Simpson's examination of the significance of the "the wordless scream" (2023, 96), is an exploration into the nature of embodied experience that reveals the body and mind to be intertwined in experience. Importantly, too, Simpson's interest in the experience of trauma as represented onstage, while not specifically targeting those organic dimensions of embodiment that could be seen to underlie the social body, opens fruitful perspectives on embodied experience in Beckett's drama.[16]

Also, Amanda Dennis's excellent book length study, *Beckett and Embodiment: Body, Space, Agency* (2023), contributes to the recent wave of embodied perspectives on Beckett's *oeuvre*. Placing Beckett's bodies in relation to Merleau-Ponty's phenomenology, Dennis suggests Beckett's representations of the human body as intertwined with the environment (2023, 209), testifies to his essentially phenomenological understanding of human situatedness. This is not to say that the Beckett's focus on embodied cognition has previously gone unnoticed. As discussed above, several important books—for example, Anna McMullan's *Performing Embodiment* (2010), Ulrika Maude's Beckett, *Technology and the Body* (2009), Yoshiki Tajiri *Samuel Beckett and the Prosthetic Body* (2007) and Olga Beloborodova's *Postcognitivist Beckett* (2020), have emphasised the intrinsic interdependence between body and mind in Beckett's work. Earlier, and highly perceptive contributions to Beckett criticism that emphasise the importance of Beckett's dramatic practice also include Jonathan Kalb's *Beckett in Performance* (1989), which covers both the theoretical and the practical implications of Beckett's theatre practice, and Rosemary Pountney's *Theatre of Shadows: Samuel Beckett's Drama 1956–76* (1988), which seeks to explore Beckett's evolution as a playwright through focusing on Beckett's structuring and patterning

---

[16] The wordless scream, says Simpson, is a "form of spectral embodiment, giving voice—and, by extension, body—to unarticulated trauma." (2023, 96).

of the plays as a director. Tribute is also due to Lois Oppenheim's seminal work, *Directing Beckett* (1994), in which several highly distinguished Beckett directors contribute with records of their experiences. More recently, finally, Nicholas E. Johnson and Jonathan Heron's *Experimental Beckett* (2020) convincingly address the ways in which Beckett's drama experiments with the formal aspects of performance when they place Beckett's formal innovations in conjunction both with the cultural and historical context of specific performances, and with Beckett's own understanding of his work, as expressed in his critical writings.

The current re-evaluation of the body in Beckett, then, comprises a variety of perspectives, many of which take issue with previous scholarship's tendency to downplay the physical embodied self, in favour of a more philosophically 'dis'-embodied, linguistic sense of self, thereby ignoring the body's participation in language, despite the fact that the connection between body and mind in Beckett's work was there the whole time, waiting to be written about. Yet, current research into Beckett's attention to the body also engages with embodied theories of cognition and language, which although they derive from phenomenological theories of experience, have developed into the new research field on Embodied Cognition (Rosch 2016, xivii). This newer strand of Beckett criticism, inaugurated by McMullan and Maude, and continued by Dennis, Simpson and Beloborodova to name but a few, convincingly shows why the visceral dimensions in Beckett's work is worthy of critical attention and why embodied perspectives are relevant to further understanding of Beckett's work, but also why examinations into this key aspect of Beckett's work has had to wait until a period when new technological development and new insights into the body-mind complex has been assimilated into the critical fabric. Importantly, then, it is on the strength of insights gained in recent decades both within the field of embodied cognition and in Beckett studies, that I argue that mis-movements in Beckett's drama operate on an aesthetic level, enfolding both visual and auditive elements of performance, thereby connecting non-verbal and verbal realms of experience.

Beckett as critic

Encouragingly, Beckett's own critical writings on art and literature could be seen to support, not only embodied perspectives on his work, but also the assumption that mis-movements serve an important function in the context of performance. Over the years, scholars have probed Beckett's critical writings for evidence of an aesthetic creed that would be applicable to his creative *oeuvre*. Admittedly, to seek authorial sanction in this way may seem wrong in that it seemingly goes against Matthew Arnold's famous directive, namely that "it is the business of the critical power […] 'to see the object as in itself it really is'", which is a creed that has been guiding modern criticism ever since its emergence in the early twentieth century (Leitch et al., *Norton* 809). However, as Mary Bryden suggests, "Beckett's early essays on, and reviews of, the writing of others do provide privileged insights into the evolving viewpoints which were to underlie some of his later fictional writing" (1998, 5), and—one might add—also his dramatic works. I therefore believe, with Bryden, that the selection involved even in the act of writing criticism speaks "(more voluminously than volumes) of the seer, in equal measure to the seen" (1998, 5). I also believe that Beckett's criticism should not be ignored as one explores his creative work. Even though it might be problematic to use the author as an authority on his own work, Beckett's comments about his own or other artists' work help towards an understanding of his creative use of the body in performance, and his use of mis-movements. More recently, Tim Lawrence has also convincingly shown a constructive way of understanding Beckett's creative processes by applying Beckett's comments about his own or other artists' work, particularly in letters to friends (see *Samuel Beckett's Critical Aesthetics*, 2018). Finally, since Beckett ended up directing his own plays, it is possible to regard him as an interpreter of his own texts, and thereby justifiable to quote him as one among many Beckett critics.[17]

---

[17] In *Disjecta,* Ruby Cohn gives a comprehensive overview of Beckett's critical writings covering roughly the years between 1928, when Beckett left

The corporeal turn

The shift in Beckett's drama towards an increasingly aesthetic and visual theatre happened in the mid 1960's as "Beckett began officially to take charge of staging his own plays" (Gontarski *TV IV*, xv); a move that included paying attention to a variety of extra-linguistic aspects of performance (Gontarski *TN IV*, xvi). Picking up on this claim, I have previously traced the progressive corporeal turn in Beckett's drama towards a theatre of affect and suggested that Beckett's attention to the body in performance has created a situation where his drama prompts audiences to "forge attachments with the stage presentations beyond the level of language" (Einarsson 2017 1). In such presentations, I have maintained, the aesthetic object is experiential rather than referential (2017, 41), and the corporeal turn therefore comprises a new rationale for artistic creation; one that foregrounds sensing over sense-making, specifically through the emphasis on the body in performance. In *A Theatre of Affect*, I thus suggested that Beckett's corporeal turn entailed an increased focus on "the experiences of spectators/readers" (Einarsson 2017, 141), which in turn meant that his notion of text changed (Einarsson 2017, 58). I also tentatively divided Beckett's corporeal turn into three stages, "viz. the 'material' (1953–1962), the 'organic' (1962–1975), the 'atmospheric' (1975–1983) (Einarsson 2017, 84–85), and suggested that these three phases to essentially overlap chronologically with the

---

Dublin for Paris and two years of exchange studies, to the mid-1950s, at which time Beckett had stopped writing critical texts. The mid-50s also marks the point from which Beckett was able to live on his royalties, a fact that perhaps help him close the door to other sources of income. In later years Beckett would downplay the importance of his critical texts, suggesting these were the result of on the one hand financial need, and on the other, a wish to promote his poor painter friends. Ultimately Beckett stopped engaging in critical writing altogether and while it may be assumed that this is partly due to a more stable financial situation, it is also plausible that he grew increasingly weary of explanations, and that he stopped writing criticism himself because he considered this task to be an offence against the work of art as an aesthetic phenomenon, as suggested by Lois Oppenheim (2003, 66).

conventional periodisation of Beckett's drama into his early, middle, and late drama (Einarsson 2017, 84). And as descriptions of mis-movements in Beckett's stage direction continue to change, in each directorial phase (viz. material, organic, or atmospheric), Beckett also seems to stage mis-movements slightly differently.

Beckett's corporeal turn signals his transformation as a playwright, a shift that takes place over decades. In actual practice, however, the corporeal turn breaks down into three functional stages overlapping with the progressive development in Beckett's writing, "from a concern with the material conditions of the expression, towards a focus on organising and structuring this material, and finally towards the effect of the dramatic presentation: its mood and atmosphere" (2017, 85). Initially, mis-movements appear as anomalies to undermine language yet over time they emerge as technologies that implicate spectators in processes of meaning-making (Einarsson 2017, 83). Gradually, the clownish and the slapstick elements invoking laughter disappear, most notably through Beckett's own directorial decisions, and in the later plays they have been replaced by a stronger emphasis on the formal structure of the stage-presentations, which now more consistently resemble the "static 'tableaux'" that Beckett chose to "give concrete form" to the waiting points in his first play *Waiting for Godot* (*TN I*, xiii). Ultimately, in the atmospheric phase, mis-movements allow for a dialectic between stasis and continuity, failure and success, knowledge, and ignorance, but they also involve the audience in acts of meaning-making. Thus, even as mis-movements continue to be epistemological frames to perception, in the first phase they seem designed to be seen (aesthetically perceived); in the second phase they seem designed to be felt (experienced); and in the final phase, somewhat paradoxically, they seem designed to be used to carry linguistic meanings forward. Importantly, as Beckett became increasingly involved in the process of staging his own drama, his insight into the ways in which a performance depends on context seems to have grown and the distinctions between early, middle, or late (or material, organic and atmospheric) therefore do not hold with reference to the versions of the texts presented in *The Theatrical*

Notebooks, Vol. I-IV. In fact, the process of writing new work that could be seen to implement new insights into the event of performance, is parallel in time to the process of going back to revise older work. The corporeal turn in Beckett's drama is therefore concomitant with Beckett's creative examination of the artistic expression more broadly.[18]

As the discussions in this book hope to reveal, however, the poetic logic of Beckett's meticulous attention to the body in performance does not rely on stage directions being followed. As Anette Balaam maintains, "[it] is now an accepted fact within Beckett studies that in his role as director and writer Beckett made changes and cuts in production that were never reproduced in the printed texts" (2019, 24). Clearly, Beckett frequently modified and altered his plays in the process of directing them and he was also open to the fact that his plays would necessarily transform with each performance. The poetic logic of Beckett's aesthetics of gesture therefore has nothing to do with notions of originality or with artistic control, but with producing the necessary conditions of possibility for perceiving things more clearly, as well as with the realisation that there is no escaping the illusions that we are all complicit in creating.

---

[18] Tim Lawrence has convincingly argued that Beckett's desire to cast off the veil of language underwent a transformation as he gradually shifted into writing in French. Referring to Pim Verhulst and Dirk van Hulle (qtd in Lawrence 2018, 82, *fn7*), Lawrence also observes that Beckett wrote in French long before his first creative post-war work in French was published and that the process of casting off the veil of his first language therefore was both longer underway more comprehensive than has previously been noted (Lawrence 2018, 81–82). Indeed, the process of change in Beckett's writing was ongoing rather than sudden, as has been convincingly demonstrated by the archival turn in Beckett scholarship, yet I would want to add that the process did not merely relate to language but enfolded also other aspects of the creative expression, not least the use of the body onstage.

Beckett in context

Considering the above, it is perhaps not surprising that Beckett's work has also transgressed into other genres and inspired artists working in various genres. Maybe on account of the musicality of his drama (see Gontarski *TN IV*, xvi; Horst Bollman qtd in Knowlson 1996, 489, 283; Knowlson and Pilling 1979, 283; Cohn 1987, 16; Esslin 1987, 174), but perhaps also on account of the way Beckett stages the body in performance, that is on account of "the deliberately aesthetic effect of these moments of movement" (see Starte 2014, 179). As Josephine Starte observes, "[d]ance has certainly been influenced by Beckett, and it is important to note that a relationship between Beckett and dance is acknowledged by dancers and choreographers" (2014, 178). For instance, in 1998 the choreographer Maurice Béjart create the piece "L'Heure Exquise: Variations on a theme by Samuel Beckett 'Oh, les beaux jours'", for the dancers Carla Fracci and Micha van Hoecke (Genetti 2011, 53), and inspired by Beckett's play *Happy Days*. And Marina Kotzamani reports that, in Greece, Beckett's influence is noticeable in the work of "three major visual artists: Nikos Navridis, Alexandras Psychoulis, and Nikos Alexiou, who work with new technologies or combine new and traditional mediums, such as handicraft" (2009, 34). According to Kotzamani, the fact that these artists "explore Beckett's theatricality in original, unpredictable ways, [is] attesting to the classical value of his work" (*Ibid.*). It would be impossible to try to present an exhaustive survey of the great variety of artists and critics that have been influenced by Beckett's creative reconfiguration of the stage presentation. Yet, as I have discussed above, the field of Beckett studies has been expanding since the 1960s and is "still finding new directions today can be overwhelming" (Oppenheim, 2004, 3). Correspondingly, the influence of Beckett's creative output on contemporary artists continues to proliferate.

Objectives and limitations

Indeed, art is often perceived to have the power to change people's thinking. More specifically, according to Hans-Ulrich Gumbrecht, one of the reasons people turn to art is that it has this capacity to bring us closer to ourselves (2004, 49). Having said that, it is beyond the aim and scope of the present study to account for individual responses to mis-movements. Instead, my aim is to outline the 'what', 'how', and 'why' or mis-movements, that is aspects that go into outlining a tentative itinerary of Beckett's aesthetics of gesture. My main claims in this book relate to a) the nature of Beckett's drama, which is the topic of chapter one, b) the role and function of mis-movements, which is the topic of chapter two, and c) the poetic logic of Beckett's aesthetics of gesture, which is the topic of chapter three. Beckett's drama, I maintain, is not an object but a dynamic, organic, performing ecology. Just like any communicative event, it inevitably changes with every context and so no one performance will ever be exactly like another. Still, there is a poetic logic to be traced in Beckett's drama, one that pivots on mis-movements as interfaces, openings, or interactions, setting the mood of performance. The issue of responsiveness arguably underlying Beckett's reconfiguration of the performance context, however, is central to the discussion in the third chapter as well as in the conclusion, which outlines an exploratory itinerary of the aesthetics of gesture in Beckett's drama.

Broadly speaking, then, the issue of responsiveness is central to the main argument in this book, not least since its underlying premise is the assumption that mis-movements have a specific function within the context of performance—namely, to rob spectators of their habitual strategies of interpretation. This is not to say that spectators do not arrive at interpretating mis-movements. It is merely to suggest that Beckett seems to have been keenly aware of the numbing effects of habit and the 'affects of power'[19] that influence

---

[19] The phrase 'affects of power' is taken from Rick Roderick in the lecture series "Nietzsche and the Postmodern Condition" (1991). URL: http://rickroderick.org/.

perception and our understanding of what it means to be a thinking human being. More than merely conspicuous, mis-movements are important frames to stage spectator perception, which is also why they are so meticulously described in the stage directions. Yet the stage directions should not be taken as a key to the process of staging Beckett's drama. They are a testimony of Beckett's development as director, signaling that the function of mis-movements and the rationale of the aesthetics of gesture, is to guide the spectator's perception towards the event of performance as an experience with ethical implications. If the ability to judge with prudence is a function of language, then it is vital that language does not harden into a wall of consensus, beyond which preconceived meanings are allowed to circulate unchallenged. Indeed, where habit is allowed to take precedence over imagination, evaluating the meaning or value of expression amounts to confirming or maintaining the *status quo*, and the aesthetics of gesture in Beckett's drama challenges this idea. My aim is therefore not to identify and explain the potential meanings of mis-movements: it is to address mis-movements as a solution to Beckett's artistic dilemma, *viz.* the predicament of expression, and to examine this solution on phenomenological and aesthetical, but also rhetorical and ethical grounds in the communicative context in which they appear, namely in performance.

Chapter 1   Up

I begin my discussion of mis-movements and the aesthetics of gesture in Beckett's drama by considering the performance context as a frame for communication, a frame in which different modes of presentation reflectively reveal the constitutive force of perception. Within the context of performance, Beckett's strategic use of mis-movements is an essentially heuristic solution to the predicament of expression (albeit the notion of solution is perhaps imbued with a sense of finality that ill befits his creative effort). The main questions that propel the discussions in this chapter are a) what characterizes Beckett's innovative drama, and b) how do mis-movements fit into Beckett's creative reconfiguration of the stage presentation? In the process of examining these questions, I address the consequences of Beckett's creative use of mis-movements by linking it to Eugene Gendlin's process model for thinking, which he characterizes as a 'new phenomenology of carrying forward' (2004). Notably, Gendlin's method "is not an analytical or intellectual process"; rather it is "a process in which you make contact with a special kind of internal bodily awareness [which he calls] *felt sense*" (1978, 11). More to the point, therefore, I approach Beckett's drama as a performing ecology that fulfils the criteria for experiencing change, not as new concepts, or ideas, but as "a deliberate way to *think and speak with* what is more than categories (concepts, theories, assumptions, distinctions . . .) (Gendlin 2004, 127). In short, watching a Beckett drama is to be engaged in a sustained response to change, tentatively defined as something *more than* the words used to describe it.

To scaffold my discussion in this chapter, however, I take off from Gregory Bateson's six "criteria for mental processes", presented in the fourth chapter of *Mind and Matter*, "Criteria of Mental Process" (2002, 85–119).[20] According to Bateson, "phenomena which we call

---

[20] Bateson's criteria of the mind stipulates that the following conditions apply for the mental process:

thought, evolution, ecology, life, learning, and the like occur only in systems that satisfy" a set of specific criteria for the mind (2002, 86). Thus, "to think about thinking", we need to come to terms with the idea that "mental process is always a sequence of interactions *between* parts" (Bateson 2002, 86), and we also need to recognize that what "the receiver (e.g., a sensory end organ) responds to is a *difference* or *change*" (Bateson 2002, 89).[21] In fact, "our sensory system–and surely the sensory systems of all other creatures (even plants?) and the mental systems behind the senses (i.e., those parts of the mental system inside the creatures)–can only operate with *events*, which we call *changes*" (Bateson 2002, 90). To address change is therefore to rethink our understanding of how meaning emerges in the world, and in this process, many of the conventional explanations may? seem redundant.

Notably, the issues that seem to have propelled Beckett's creative use of mis-movements—the problem of representation or expression, for instance—overlap with issues of intellectual freedom and the ethics of interpretation, specifically with reference to their explanatory principles. The twentieth century was a period when "intellectual freedom [was] threatened from many directions" (Polanyi and Prosch 1977, 3). By analogy, Bateson maintains that "the presupposition or premises of thought upon which all our teaching is

---

(1) *A mind is an aggregate of interacting parts or components.*
(2) *The interaction between parts of the mind is triggered by difference*, and difference is a nonsubstantial phenomenon not located in space or time; difference is related to negentropy and entropy rather than to energy.
(3) *Mental process requires collateral energy.*
(4) *Mental process requires circular (or more complex) chains of determination.*
(5) *In mental process, the effects of difference are to be regarded as transforms (i.e., coded versions) of events which preceded them.* The rules of such transformation must be comparatively stable (i.e., more stable than the content) but are themselves subject to transformation.
(6) *The description and classification of these processes of transformation disclose a hierarchy of logical types immanent in the phenomena.*
(Bateson 2002, 86)

[21] By analogy, Mark Johnson maintains that "meaning is relational", and it is only by comparing similarities that we may perceive change (2008, 10).

based are ancient and ... *obsolete*" (2002, 203). According to Bateson, the epistemologies that no longer serve our needs include:

> a. The Cartesian dualism separating 'mind' and 'matter.'

> b. The strange physicalism of the metaphors we use to describe and explain mental phenomena—'power,' 'tension,' 'energy,' 'social forces' etc."

> c. Our anti-aesthetic assumption, borrowed from the emphasis which Bacon, Locke, and Newton long ago gave to the physical sciences, *viz.* that all phenomena (including the mental) can and shall be studied and *evaluated* in quantitative terms.

> (Bateson 2002, 203)

The premises Bateson lists have been absorbed into the very fabric of our thinking and talking about the world, and so the problems we identify, as well as the solutions we come up with, are inevitably tainted by our habitual complicities with such premises. Yet, Bateson maintains, the "latent and partly unconscious epistemology –which such ideas generate is out of date in three different ways" (2002, 203). Firstly, "because they lead to greed, monstrous over-growth, war, tyranny, and pollution"; secondly, because these "premises are obsolete in that systems theory, cybernetics, holistic medicine, ecology, and gestalt psychology offer demonstrably better ways of understanding the world of biology and behaviour" (Bateson 2002, 204); and thirdly, because "in the aftermath of Darwinian evolution ... [and] as a base for *religion*, such premises ... became *clearly intolerable and obsolete* about 100 years ago" (Bateson 2002, 204). In short, those metaphors produced by Cartesian dualism, the 'metaphors we live by'—to borrow a phrase from Mark Johnson and George Lakoff—combine with scientism to muddle our systems of thinking, and we must therefore begin to rethink our belonging to the world and find new ways to express our understanding of the performing ecologies we belong to.

Admittedly, Bateson's concern is not with drama, but with any ecological system that could be seen to regulate itself, and so his examples include "ecosystems such as a seashore or a redwood forest" (2002, 104). Yet, on the assumption that a performance is a self-regulating system, Beckett's drama could fruitfully be approached as a performing ecology. Indeed, any performance is a whole that predicates on the audience's sustained attention to how all elements in performance combine to make it thus. A performance, then, is a self-regulating system within which change appears as leverage points that can be identified and possibly intervened with, something Beckett seems to have discovered through his involvement with the staging of his work. It is therefore not so much that he changed the nature of performance as that he noticed the way live performances work and adapted his mode of presentation to such a mode of becoming. Considering this, the issue of intellectual freedom is strikingly useful to understanding Beckett's exploration of the dramatic medium, yet the problem of intellectual freedom goes deeper than merely historical context. It goes to the embodied roots of cognition. The issue of meaning, what it is and how it may be produced, is therefore not straightforward, is not primarily the product of language but of ideology, and ideology changes with time. Given that problems, definitions, solutions etc., are context-bound, my discussion of mis-movements in Beckett's drama takes the historical context into account although my aim is not to try to map Beckett's progressive artistic development to the publication of specific dramas. It is merely to acknowledge that the intellectual roots of Beckett's drama, which I take to be essentially Socratic in their emphasis on intellectual freedom, are *both* intellectual *and* embodied.

In proposing this perspective, I do not deny that Beckett's plays could also be seen to explore the mood emerging in post-war Europe, arguably a transformed world, as for example Emilie Morin

(2018) and James McNaughton (2018) have shown.[22] Perhaps, in the wake of WWII, it was necessary to reclaim the insight of what it means to be human as part of figuring out how to come to terms with the trauma of war. Adhering to the perspectives that open up from the archival turn, both James McNaughton and Emilie Morin maintain that Beckett's work is deeply in touch with political issues, and that occasion, relation, and correspondence may, at least tentatively, have incited Beckett's aesthetic imagination. Admittedly, several changes to society in the late 19th and early 20th centuries open human experience to a variety of moods commonly associated with fear of death, anxiety, and a sense of the meaninglessness or absurdity of life. Beckett's drama therefore seems as topical today as in the 1950s, perhaps because of the questions it asks or perhaps because of the ways in which it thematizes moods or perspectives that could be seen to limit or condition human experience of the world—among those, a sense of the mood of absurdity, fragmentation, isolation, and anxiety, which is to say moods presumably derived from existentialism. Yet, as Rick Roderick points out, among the reasons for why existentialism became so popular was the "both frightening but also exhilarating" recognition that "your life becomes your own construction" (URL: http://rickroderick.org/303-sartre-and-the-roads-to-freedom-1993/). Indeed, Sartre's understanding of freedom entails the recognition that meaning is fluid rather than preordained and fixed and so it paves the way for a new paradigm of interpretation. As Hazel E. Barnes writes in the introduction to Sartre's *Search for a Method*, "[i]t is not true that man is unknown, but only that we have not yet had at our disposal the proper instruments for learning to know him. … What is needed is a new kind of Reason" (1968, xi). Thus, if the search for meaning derives from the destruction of conventional values associated with modernity, then Beckett's exploration of various moods associated with existentialism could perhaps also be understood to engage in a

---

[22] Emelie Morin, *Beckett's Political Imagination,* Cambridge University Press, 2017, and James McNaughton, *Samuel Beckett and the Politics of Aftermath,* 2018.

re-transvaluation of all values whereby the road to freedom is explored in response to the changes to society in post-WWII Europe. Indeed, Beckett's emphasis on dread, anxiety, solitude, meaninglessness has a Nietzschean streak, and the primary experiences of the characters in the drama seem related to the primary experiences in Beckett's own life. In fact, even Beckett's identity as a freedom fighter could be linked to such a process of self-(re)creation.

However, even if reading Beckett historically as a political author generates highly valuable insights into his work, thematically as well as historically, it does not shed light on what goes on in the pragmatic communicative context of performance. Thus, while I agree that Beckett's drama presents ways to be human in the wake of the destruction of values previously taken for granted—and even if I agree that Beckett's drama could be read against the transformation of society— my discussion of it addresses solely its effects in performance. And in this context, Beckett's effort, seemingly, is not to recover those same values that have been destroyed, but to produce the conditions of possibility for thinking differently, a process that inevitably would generate new knowledge and new meanings. And the shift in Beckett's creative work that seems to pave the way for intellectual freedom is perceptual rather than intellectual. In this chapter, then, I shall move on to argue that mis-movements in Beckett's drama are effects of systemic change designed to produce a shift of perception in audiences. Indeed, perceiving Beckett's drama as a performing ecology makes it possible to approach mis-movements, not as symbols but as effects of systemic change, a shift of perspective that has consequences for how spectators arrive to make sense of them in performance and to this effect, Batson's criteria of mind propose a useful framework.

Performing Ecology

The first of Bateson's criteria, maintains that "A Mind is an Aggregate of Interacting Parts or Components" (2002, 86). By analogy, and although my focus here is on mis-movements, Beckett's drama underwrites the equivalency between all elements of performance, verbal and non-verbal. This is evident in for example *Footfalls* and *Not I*, but also in *Act Without Words I*, "Act Without Words II" and "Quad", to name but a few, where the movements that the characters perform constitute the total of interaction (Beckett, *CDW* 41, 47, 289). That said, the assertion that mis-movements are integral to the whole performing ecology should not be taken to mean that Beckett has invented some kind of body language such that there are specific meanings that adhere to specific gestures in the play. Rather, the way the body is staged in Beckett's drama speaks to an understanding of performance as a particular mode of communication, one in which interpretation is central and emerges as interaction between fictionality and reality.[23] Having said that, there is no significant difference between attending to fictional and real contexts. As human beings, we cannot help attending to things, and whether we are attending to a character in a work of fiction or to a real-life person we meet on the street, our evaluations are intrinsically connected to the rhetorical criterion of relevance.[24] In Beckett's drama, the actions that characters perform may therefore be interpreted in (at least) two different ways: either "as performance or as a 'real' event in the characters' fictional lives" (Kalb 1989, 35). But there is also a third option, namely, to see mis-movements as real events that audiences experience. The latter assumption implying that the fictional mis-movements stand out to perception on account of failing to achieve whatever real, conventional purposes associated with

---

[23] This is not to deny that there are many real-life situations of communication where gestures have been standardised to convey specific meanings. For example, in sign language, specific meanings accompany specific gestures, and in different social situations, different groups share a common understanding of what a certain posture or physical response, such as nodding or shaking one's head, may mean.
[24] In this I follow Richard Walsh, who maintains that "the point of theorizing fictionality is not … to inform or enable the interpretation of fictional texts, or to refine the apparatus of literary study …; it is a more abstract inquiry into the conditions of significance that make these activities conceivable and worthwhile" (2007, 3).

them (for instance conventionally walking should take you somewhere,) and that audiences tacitly associate such movements (even in fictional contexts), with real failings.

Considering the above, attending to mis-movements in performance is essentially entering a conscious relationship with them as objects for experience that transcend the fictional. Such a perspective casts new light on the predicament of expression that preoccupied Beckett, as well as on his use of mis-movements as a tentative solution to this predicament. In taking this approach, I follow Richard Walsh, who "seeks to characterize fictionality in discursive terms" (2007, 52), although, admittedly, I take his perspective slightly out of its context. Walsh posits fictionality as "a feature of communicative rhetoric rather than a quality of certain objects of representation" (Walsh 2007, 52).[25] According to Walsh, fictionality therefore "resides in a way of using language", yet I expand this perspective to also include ways of using mis-movements in the context of performance. If the "distinctiveness" of fictionality, "consists in the recognizably distinct rhetorical set invoked by that use" (Walsh 2007, 15), then to frame (some of) the movements that Beckett's characters perform as mis-movements, is to take them as fictional based on their mode of appearing for perception in the context of performance, namely as idiosyncratic and so distinctive. Notably, however, it is the spectator's mode of approaching movements as idiosyncratic that singles them out as mis-movements, not the actual movements. At the same time, it is only by appearing as

---

[25] According to Walsh, "[a]ll narrative is fictional, and in that very restricted sense fictive ... [yet] fictional narrative has a coherently distinct cultural role, and [so] a distinct concept of fictionality is required to account for this role (Walsh 2007, 15)." If "the logical priority of fabula and sujet" should be inverted, then "sujet is what we come to understand as a given (fictional) narrative, and fabula is how we come to understand it" (2007, 68). Thus reconfigured, fabula is "a function of the process of interpretation", and so "always relative to and contingent upon both a given sujet and a specific act of interpretation" (2007, 68). Importantly, by making fabula's relation to sujet a matter of interpretation, Walsh can show why any narrative event "is constituted by the discourse, under a mode of interpretation" (2007, 57).

conspicuously fictional, specifically on account of failing to achieve functions tacitly associated with them, that mis-movements become real events to be experienced. Admittedly, the claim that interpretation produces fictionality risk collapsing into relativism, but Walsh's additional point that interpretation always takes place in a context provides a way out of the dilemma (see Walsh 2007, 26).[26] Yet, the implications of Walsh's inverted order of story and narrative are far-reaching, not least with respect to the predicament of expression. Notably, with reference to mis-movements, the notion that fabula, in this case mis-movements, is the result of interpretation and so implicitly part of the effect of the narrative structure, means that the very process of meaning-making is not a matter of retrieving something lodged in the poetic image but of creating it, and so perception becomes an act of creation rather than an act of interpretation. And the notion that mis-movements afford creative acts is helpful for understanding their function in the context of performance. On such an assumption, to pay attention to mis-movements in Beckett's drama is already to single them out, to create them as real experiences to be reckoned with and considered in the larger whole that is the performance. In other words, it is the fictionality of mis-movements that singles them out or foregrounds them in the storytelling context of performance as *real* experiences, notwithstanding that to make sense of such experiencing, audiences must tap into their embodied sense of what it means to move (walk, stoop, turn, fall etc.).

The fact that Beckett's drama could be seen to blur the borders between fiction and reality has of course not gone unnoticed in previous scholarship, although the function of the body in this respect has not been sufficiently addressed. Still, as Oppenheim observes, the "collapsed distinction between the imaginary representation of reality and reality itself—the 'theaterreality'— [...]

---

[26] By analogy, also Bateson's claims that a context comprises a "weaving of context and of messages that propose context" (Bateson 2000, 275)

became increasingly important in Beckett's middle and late dramatic works" (2003, 68). And while Oppenheim's emphasis on the theatricality of the texts aims to explore the role of the director for the creative exegesis of staging the drama, she also observes that Beckett's dramatic work truly "existing off the printed page and in the theatre" (2003, 2). By analogy, the pun embedded in the title of Ruby Cohn's book, *Just Play*, refers precisely to the tension between the mediated and the unmediated reality that Beckett, in his role as author-director, so fruitfully explored. "Beckett's plays", writes Cohn, "are just play for precise performance. They are play as opposed to unmediated reality, but play is its own mode of reality" (1980, 3). Moreover, Oppenheim's claim that "performance, by its very nature, is, [...] a mediated presentation of unmediated experience", the unmediated experience necessarily belonging to the audience (1997, 1), is supported by McMullan, who maintains that Beckett's drama "draws on a phenomenological understanding of both being and performance" (McMullan 2010, 10). Thus, although far from any claim to verisimilitude or 'vraisemblance', an unadorned stage, barely lit, a tape recorder, a mound, or a couple of trashcans and a wheelchair, may be enough to suggest a context for Beckett's characters in which real embodied experience take precedence over intellectual achievement, precisely on account of the ways in which mis-movements appear to be breaking with the conventions of the real-life purposes associated with certain movements (for instance walking,) and precisely on account of the fact that such purposes would have gone unnoticed, had the characters not mis-moving.

The body in performance is always important but Beckett's exploration of the dramatic presentation involves the realisation that even the most insignificant movement or gesture has relevance on the stage. The actor and director, Pierre Chabert, explains that Beckett works the body, both as author and director; "[h]e approaches it—just as he approaches space, objects, light and language—as a genuine raw material which may be modified, sculpted, shaped and distorted for the stage" (1982, 23.). The notion that the body is raw material, Chabert suggests, should therefore be taken quite literally in equal measure to "the raw materials of the painter or sculptor" (ibid.). Formal aspects of composition and organization are at the centre of choreography, and Beckett's writing could in this sense be seen to share an affinity with dance since mis-movements call attention to the fictionality of gesture in the context of performance. Indeed, Beckett's attention to the body and to the combination and organization of physical movements into patterns is even reminiscent of a choreographer, to whom the body is the raw material par excellence.[27]

As he came to direct his own work, Beckett also came to realize the extent to which a text changes in the process of becoming a performance: "Once Beckett began directing himself in 1967, staging became a full extension of his creative process" (Gontarski 2004, 201). For Beckett, no play was ever fully created until it was staged in performance (Gontarski 2002, 204). Consequently, as James Knowlson points out in the introduction to *The Theatrical Notebooks, Volume I* (henceforth *TN I*), Beckett's Schiller Theatre production, combined with the revisions made to the text in the San Quentin production (1984) —which Beckett took care to note down,— "may be regarded as a new version of *Godot*, shorter, tighter in structure, and visualized much more clearly in theatrical terms, as well as being, in our view, aesthetically more satisfying" (Knowlson *TN I*, xii). Of course, at the time when Knowlson wrote this (1993), the implications of research into the embodied mind were merely nascent. Nevertheless, Knowlson's observations hint towards a richer, more nuanced understanding of the complex entanglements between mind and body, fiction, and reality, which condition the aesthetics of gesture in Beckett's drama. The version of *Godot* printed in *TN I* thus takes

---

[27] Interestingly, the many instances of walking, falling, turning, reaching etc., that occur in Beckett's work, whether in the prose or in the drama, seems to coalesce with the interest in everyday gestures that choreographers, especially in the US, displayed in the 1960s, where the desire to "break the boundaries of movement", which occupied many of those "working in the post-Cunningham era", has remained an influential artistic aim in modern dance (Kassing, 2017, 218).

both the audience's experience of the event of theatre and the stage craft involved in producing such experience into consideration.

In *Godot*, the plain setting "*A country road. A tree. [A stone.]/ Evening*" (*TN I*, 9:1–2), combine with the characters' terse commentaries to create atmospheric and emotionally charged stage-images where everything or nothing seems important: speech, silences, mis-movements, and not least immobility, which is specifically part of a "waiting motif – repeated at twelve strategically chosen points, or *Warstellen*, throughout the play in other static 'tableaux' (as Beckett also sometimes called them)" (*TN I* xiii). Notably, too, at the end of Act I, when the characters remain immobile even as they state they shall leave (*TN I*, 50 :1550-64), their immobility becomes part of a larger structure of interconnected parts, involving not merely immobility, but also other movements repertoires such as—for example—the hat routine (*TN I* 65: 2119–2137). In such presentations spectators are invited to move beyond merely attending to dialogue. Indeed, as John Calder suggests, the audience "should find its initial fascination with this new non-naturalistic, sometimes balletic and mimetic drama, gradually turning into curiosity and the desire to know more, as it begins to realize the symbolic quality of the play" (2001, 91).

That said, it could also be argued that, in the *TN I* version of *Godot*, the characters' mis-movements correspond to what Alex C. Purves describes as "embodied repetition recalled by habit" (2019, 16): In *Homer and the Poetics of Gesture* (2019), Purves examines the *Odyssey* from the perspective that kinaesthetic memory provides the foundation for our understanding of the patterns that bodies produce in the poem (2019, 5). According to Purves, gestures "makes memory within the poem".[28] That is, "[t]he structure of habit is useful, indeed crucial, insofar as it allows us to re-embody the past, to draw the past back into our bodies and thereby engage in action" (2019, 16). Purves's source is Henri Bergson, who similarly maintains that "the body is a centre of action, the place where the impressions received

---

[28] Purves quoting Gillian Beer, "End of the Line." *The Guardian* January 12, 2007.

choose intelligently the path they will follow to transform themselves to action" (2005, 138). And, when memory "is prolonged into nascent action ... [in] truth it no longer *represents* our past to us, it *acts* it, and if is still deserves the name of memory, it is not because is conserves bygone images, but because it prolongs their useful effect into the present moment" (Bergson 2005, 82).[29] Thus, (mis-) movements and gestures have the capacity to activate habitual or ingrained action sequences, and the "embodied repetition recalled by habit affects not only the actor but also the reader and listener of the poem" (Purves 2019, 16). The regimes that control an individual's *habitus* derive from ingrained habits of self-regulation imposed on us since infancy. And as embodied beings, we are sensitive to such embodied meanings, leading anyone who breaks those unspoken rules to inevitably attract attention, whether on the stage or in real life.[30] Hence Theodore Adorno's claim that art is both "aesthetic and *faits sociaux*" (1997, 328). Arguably, then, the characters' mis-movements in *Godot* could be seen to express the characters' *habitus, viz.* their physical orientation in life, as confirmed by Beckett own comments that "Estragon is on the ground; he belongs to the stone. Vladimir is light; he is oriented towards the sky. He belongs to the tree" (qtd in *TN I*, xiv). Clearly, too, the attention to bodies that mismove could fruitfully be read as critique of social convention created by aesthetic means.[31] Viewed

---

[29] It should be noted that Bergson here seems to be criticising our tendency to apply an *if-then*-logic to account for the causality between past and present. logic is a poor model of causality" (Bateson 2002, 55). That is "causality don't work backwards", and so there seems to be interesting parallels between Bergson and Bateson specifically with respect to their critique of logic and time.

[30] The habitus is "a subjective but non-individual system of internalized structures", which emerges as directions and orientations common to all members in a certain "class (or group)" (Bourdieu 2014, 60). Even if not "all practices and schemes" that emerge within a group are "impersonal and interchangeable", it is still the case that what is commonly referred to as "'[p]ersonal' style", is "never more than a deviation in relation to the style of a period or class" (*Ibid.*)

[31] If everything we do is subsumed in the Bourdieusian notion of *habitus*, then actors will inescapably colour their characters with aspects of their

thus, mis-movements seemingly have a social dimension, not least since the characters' physical comportment open metaphorical readings of social status, mental health and various other notions associated with dominant views of what constitutes acceptable or unacceptable social behaviour.

Yet to read mis-movements as symbolic of the characters' social status our as integrated habits is to miss out on their more subversive properties. Rather than confirming our habits and presuppositions, mis-movements challenge us to examine such practices. Admittedly, as Bateson explains, human beings are primed to use a repertoire of "notoriously rigid" habits of interpretation, in order to be as efficient as possible in dealing with propositions that "have general or repetitive truth", which is to say propositions "of a relatively high order of abstraction" (2000, 275). Thus, we are hardwired to perceive certain meanings, all the while disregarding others. Efficacy or competence, in this context, "consists precisely in *not* re-examining or rediscovering the premises of habit every time the habit is used" (Bateson 2000, 274). Indeed, over time we have all "developed a *habit* of not examining" our habits (Bateson 2000, 275). However, mis-movements seem designed to challenge precisely our 'habit not to examine habit', specifically by returning audiences to a pre-reflective realm of aesthetic experience. Viewed thus, the textual notes that accompany *TN I* reveal Beckett's emphasis on the aesthetic dimension of the stage presentation. The explanation of the added instruction—'looking up'—at the end of Act I (see *TN I*, 50, 1566–1571), is a case in point:

---

own bodies. Even if actors do their best to avoid contaminating a character with their own manners, "the preservation of affect and experience in gesture" (see Purves 2019, 23) necessitates that individual emotions and earlier experiences and events are always inscribed into our physical repertoire of movements, like indelible frames that shape, structure and predict our interactions. In fact, this may be why we prefer some actors in some roles over other. The precision with which the stage-directions sculpts Beckett's characters could therefore also be understood to counter the excess of *habitus*.

1568—*(Looking up)*. Added. These contrasting looks are paired with corresponding looks at the end of Act II to contrast the endings of the two acts. As parts of the final images of the *Warstelle* at the curtain they are important. They were first suggested and rejected in *Schiller nb.*, *Page 31*, but they were later incorporated in the San Quentin text. In the Schiller Theatre version, at the end of Act 2, Vladimir and Estragon look for a long time at each other then turn back fronts for these lines. At the end of Act II, they merely stand looking in front without exchanging a look. The absence of the look at each other suggests a diminishing interaction but still in the context of their interdependency. In the version here, at the end of Act II, the names of the speakers are simply exchanged as they deliver each other's lines and actions of Act I. There is a greater depiction of disparity, inter-changeability, recurrence with change, activity, inactivity, and varying dejection and optimism. The fact that they still look in different directions also implies that their differences are inherent rather than incidental.

(*TN I* 145, item 1568)

The characters' coordinated gestures (looking up and down at intervals) invite aesthetic perception of the patterns that emerge in performance ('recurrence with change'), and so they offer a route to perceive beyond the confines of habit. Yet, the textual note also emphasizes the effects of such aesthetic structuring, namely "a greater depiction of disparity, inter-changeability, recurrence with change, activity, inactivity, and varying dejection and optimism" (*TN I* 145, item 1568). The coordinated mis-movements described in the textual notes therefore do more than merely tear at the veils of language, habit, or culture: they are the very means through which Beckett's drama becomes an aggregate of interacting parts and components, all of which contributing to the play as a whole, and in a manner that could be fruitfully compared to Bateson's description of a performing ecology as a system of integrated parts that produce change by means of a "weaving of context and of messages that propose context" (Bateson 2000, 275)

Over time, Beckett veers toward a more complex visual and auditive paradigm, where every aspect of staging—direction, scenography, lighting—is written into the dramatic text. In the late plays, the stage directions even target the pitch of voice. For example, in *Come and Go,* the characters' voices are instructed to be as "low as compatible with audibility" (*TN IV* 211). Sometimes Beckett omits dialogue altogether—for instance, in *Quad* (1982), *Nacht und Träume* (1982), and *What Where* (1983)— but, in all Beckett's carefully orchestrated pieces, the body nonetheless remains key. Other characteristics of the late plays are a lessening of props, a diminishing and restricting of light, colours, and a reduction of the playing area. Indeed, as Eric Tonning suggests, Beckett's pursuit of an abstract language produces "a continuous dialectic between an emphasis on formal schematisation and the reduction of a realist background, and efforts to compensate for the resulting losses of expressive force by utilising new technical possibilities" (2007, 15). The impulse to concentrate and restrict the expressive elements of the theatrical space, noticeable already in *Godot,* therefore becomes more effectively realized in Beckett's later drama. Even so, the process of reduction appears to have been gradual, beginning with a frustration with language and eventually leading to carefully choreographed pieces in which all elements of performance interact.

Mis-movements as efficient differences

The second criterion Bateson identifies concerns the notion that "The Interaction Between Parts of Mind Is Triggered by Difference" (Bateson 2002, 89). As stated above, the analogy between Beckett's corporeal turn and Bateson's criteria for mental process predicates on the assumption that Beckett's drama is a performing ecology. Not only are there complex interactions between all elements in performance, but performance *qua* performance also predicates on consistent adjustments, calibrations and regulations that happen in the event of performance. In short, a performance is a living organism and Bateson's ecological perspective illuminates not only the ways in which difference emerges from the interactions between staged parts, but also the interconnections between audience and performance. I therefore connect this criterion with the ways in which mis-movements, as coded difference, trigger interaction in the context of performance, for instance between characters and characters, and between spectators and play. Mis-movements hint at new ways to think about how meaning is produced in the context of performance. If a performance is a holistic context, which is to say an ecology of interacting parts enfolding characters, audiences, actors, props, lighting, theatrical space, auditorium, stage, historical context etc., then Beckett's corporeal turn entails reconfiguring this context from a context in which interpretation takes place, to a context for aesthetic experience. Thus, by means of repetition mis-movements, as ephemeral manifestations, gradually transform into patterns of significations, metamorphosising into poetic images that appear within the continuum of the dramatic work (Einarsson 2017, 59).

In the context of Beckett's drama, mis-movements are the means through which change appears. Taken in isolation mis-movements mean nothing, yet within the whole of performance they accrue significance as patterns that spectators may recognize and to some extent predict. Yet, even if mis-movements could be seen to connect spectators to the event of performance as an experience of change, the impasses that the characters endure, their physical immobility and their fragmented argumentations have frequently been interpreted as metaphors for "circularity" in the sense of stasis (*TN 1* xxii). Indeed, the "unchanging is imperceptible unless we are willing to move relative to it" (Bateson 2002, 90), an observation that brings Beckett's complaint about the dulling effects of habit to mind. According to Beckett, habit dutifully performs the "continual adjustment and readjustment of our organic sensibility to the conditions of its worlds" (1999, 28). Habit prevents the human being from perceiving or experiencing 'life', as it were, but importantly the function of habit is also to safeguard against the: "[s]uffering [which] represents the omission of that duty" (1999, 28). Yet, as discussed above, mis-movements tend to challenge habitual, preconceived strategies of interpretation, precisely on account of inviting audiences to engage creatively with the stage presentation.

Admittedly, however, it is "very difficult to detect change because along with our sensitivity to rapid change goes also the phenomenon of accommodation" (Bateson 2002, 91). The fact that stillness or immobility is overwhelmingly present in *Godot*, thus indicates the deadening effects of habit and the explicit symbolism inherent to this physical and 'mental' deadlock that spells 'waiting for Godot' must therefore duly be acknowledged:

> Estragon and Vladimir are certainly non-knowers and non-can-ers. They try to hang themselves; but they cannot. They try to leave the spot; but they cannot, detained as they are by their hope that eventually Godot will arrive. Even at the end of the play, they do not leave the stage, although the Boy has told them that Godot will not be coming that night: *'They do not move'*.
>
> (*TN 1* xix)

However, as Pierre Chabert has pointed out, and as Kalb explains, even immobility holds the seed of motion:

> Just as there is an intrinsic tension between silence and words, so there is an intrinsic tension between immobility and movement. Words emanate from silence and return to it; movement emanates from immobility and returns to it. All movements, all gestures move, so to speak, within immobility, are a victory over immobility and have a value in the tension they maintain in relationship to immobility.
>
> (Kalb 39-40)

Thus, although the characters' manifestations of stasis and immobility in the play may be seen to target the theme of stasis, they also present the counterpoint of stasis, namely change.[32] Moreover, change is also what connects characters to place. For instance, in *Godot*, Vladimir observes that "things have changed here since yesterday" (*TN I* 54: 1694). That is, Vladimir notices difference (in himself, in Estragon, in the tree etc.,) and this is also why he knows that they must continue waiting for Godot, whereas Estragon, who does not recognize anything, not the tree, not the spot, not his shoes, not Pozzo and Lucky, is the one suggesting they should leave.

As coded effects of change, mis-movements are key to honing spectators' attention towards such aspects of performance that do not normally fall under the remit of interpretation. Thus, if conventionally spectators approach a performance context as a context within which to interpret linguistic messages, then the characters' mis-movements signal that meaning in this context occurs on a different level, namely on the level of aesthetic experience. To this effect, seemingly, Gontarski maintains that Beckett's plays "do not represent or realize a world of actuality ... but offer images that make us feel in their affect the movement of existence, its flow, becoming, durée" (2015, 164). More recently, Annette Balaam's examination of Beckett's virtual worlds also confirms Gontarski's claim, all the while adding to its

---

[32] Similarly, in *Endgame*, "movement and immobility, beginning and end, life and death and absence and presence are shown to be intrinsically intertwined. The audience as well as the characters arrive at the moment the action ambiguously slows down seemingly to end. At this point in the play, both characters and spectators alike are struck by the fact that something has already taken place. The play, of course, has taken place, but there is also a change to be noticed among the characters. The final tableau of the play, where Clov, is standing "impassive and motionless, his eyes fixed on HAMM till the end" (133), echoes the opening tableau, where Clov stands "[m]otionless by the door, his eyes fixed on HAMM" (92). The significance of Clov's immobility [therefore] changes during the play so that by its end, immobility is pregnant with a meaning and significance that it initially did not have and which now also casts new light also on the opening tableau [...] Something has taken its course, and change has suddenly appeared to be noticed" (Einarsson 2009, 119–120).

potential implications (2019). According to Balaam, the recognition that "this world is not a fixed thing, but continuously comes into and out of being in varying degrees of cohesion along a continuum" means that we are intrinsically part of creating it (2019, 21). Thus, we are responsible for the world we create, just as audiences are consistently part of the meanings of Beckett's drama. The question of what we can expect from Beckett's virtual worlds, then, is very much a question of the degree to which spectators recognize the event of performance as a context for perceiving and producing change. And to this effect, mis-movements are instrumental. Mis-movements emerge as deviations incongruences, gaps, inconsistencies that call attention to change, specifically on account of the impossibility of stasis, immobility, and fixed meanings. Yet, importantly, mis-movements also promote such adjustment of perception that is required for change to be perceived.

A new paradigm for interpretation

The issue of how change appears in the context of performance therefore leads me to consider Bateson's third criterion, which stipulates that "Mental Process Requires Collateral Energy" (2002, 93). This criterion maintains that interaction must be energized by something, and I connect this idea to the notion of interaction between audience and performance. Nominally, a "*context* is a set for a certain class of response" and any breach in the "weave of contextual structure" will disrupt the patterns of interaction proposed by this context (Bateson 2000, 275). Put differently, as already been suggested above, context comprises a "weaving of context and of messages that propose context" (Bateson 2000, 275), and Beckett's drama should therefore be conceived of as a performing ecology, comprising all elements of performance.

However, within this ecology, mis-movements also comprise interruptions (whether of habitual modes of appropriating linguistic meanings or of habitual modes of interpretation,) and the process whereby patterns of interaction are disrupted produces what Bateson calls a "double bind" (2000, 271), which is to say an "experienced breach in the weave of contextual structure" (2000, 276). Given that Beckett's drama could be seen to deliberately challenge spectators to calibrate their responses, the double bind theory seems to afford a productive analogy for the rupture in interpretative context caused by mis-movements in Beckett's drama. Admittedly, the analogy is not perfect. Bateson's double bind theory was originally developed to explain the forms of coercion, for instance cognitive dissonance and confusion, that generate trauma and suffering (Bateson 2000, 206–207). According to Batson the double bind requires a set "necessary ingredients" such as, for example, "two or more persons", of which one is "the 'victim'", involved in a situation where the victim is repeatedly subjected to the traumatic experience, which includes a "primary negative injunction", a "secondary injunction conflicting the first", and a "tertiary injunction prohibiting the victim from escaping the field" (Bateson 2000, 206–207). None of these necessary ingredients of course apply in the context watching Beckett's drama, in which case audiences are neither repeatedly subjected to the experience (unless they want to,) nor prohibited from escaping, should they prefer. The demand placed on audiences to interpret Beckett's drama is also not comparable to a traumatic experience, which is concomitant with the way in which the double bind theory is theorised for instance in trauma theory or psychology. Nonetheless, the double bind analogy highlights why placing audiences in a situation where they must struggle to negotiate their place in their ecology of performance, paradoxically, produces the kind of confusion that seems a necessary ingredient for the creative production of change, merely by breaking the conventional patterns of interaction.

Notably, it was precisely because it ruptured the context for interpretation that *Godot* radically transformed and altered audience expectations of what could be put onstage. Producing "near riots among a good many highly sophisticated audiences in Western Europe" (Esslin 2001, 19), the play presented nothing to be recognized, no readily identifiable 'tragic' heroes and no psychologically invested plot. James Knowlson reports that *Godot* received "very mixed" reactions (1996, 349). While "[m]ost of the reviews were good and the play gained distinguished admirers, among them Jean Anouilh, Armand Salacrou, Jacques Audiberti, and Alain Robbe-Grillet … its success was [not] assured [until] it became controversial" (Knowlson 1996, 349–350). Indeed, Kenneth Tynan pointed out, Beckett's first drama "forced people … to 're-examine the rules which [had] hitherto governed the drama'" (qtd in Knowlson 1996, 350). Clearly, then, *Godot* could be seen to disrupt the paradigm for theatrical performances. The literary critic Vivian Mercier famously wrote:

> Its author has achieved a theoretical impossibility—a play in which nothing happens, that yet keeps the audiences glued to their seats. What's more, since the second act is a subtly different reprise of the first, he has written a play in which nothing happens, twice.
>
> (1994, 29)[33]

In writing *Godot*, then, Beckett seems not only to have invented a new mode of conveying experience to spectators, but he seems also to have produced a shift in their understanding of what to expect from a drama.[34] In his first staged play, Beckett was already projecting the direction that his drama would take towards affect (Einarsson 2017, 180–181), and Bateson's claim that the "double bind theory is concerned with the experiential component in the genesis of tangles in the rule or premises of habit" (2000, 276), provides a helpful tautology for such development. Because, if "to act or be one end of a pattern of interaction is to propose the other end (Bateson 2000,

---

[33] "As far as I know, Mr Beckett may never have been back-stage in his life until "Godot" was first performed. Yet this first play shows consummate stagecraft. Its author has achieved a theoretical impossibility—a play in which nothing happens, that yet keeps the audiences glued to their seats. What's more, since the second act is a subtly different reprise of the first, he has written a play in which nothing happens, twice" (Mercier 1994, 29).

[34] Indeed, as James McNaughton observes, "if the degree to which a play is any measure, *En Attendant Godot (Waiting for Godot)* exerts a curious subversive force" (2019, 183).

275), then already *Godot* suggests that the significance of mis-movements to produce affect, is to produce openings in the fabric of performance, which also pave the way for rethinking the context for interpretation. To the extent that mis-movements produce experiential breaches in the "weave of contextual structure" (Bateson 2000, 276), then, they could be fruitfully compared to what Bateson calls "transcontextual syndromes" (2000, 276), which is to say situations in which the conditions for one context no longer holds for the larger *"context of contexts"* (Bateson 2000, 277). [35] Thus, in the context of performance, if mis-movements produce frustration or bewilderment, then in so doing, they also produce necessary conditions for transformation and change, whether with reference to the meanings we create or to the strategies by means we approach the performance context.

Moving up a ladder of abstraction

To address the ways in which mis-movements transform in the context of performance, I shall now move on to Bateson's fourth criterion, which states that "Mental Process Requires Circular (or More Complex) Chains of Determination" (Bateson 2002, 96). I connect this criterion to the transformation that mis-movements

---

[35] To illustrate his point, Bateson reports on a situation where a female porpoise in captivity was subjected to repeated instances of 'double binds', as the trainer decided that she should learn to present a new trick every time she came on stage. Thus, producing the same trick did not generate a reward. The porpoise suffered a great deal until she understood what was required of her, and the trainer must comfort her repeatedly to sustain their relationship. Ultimately, however, the porpoise "put on an elaborate performance including eight conspicuous pieces of behaviour of which four were entirely new—never before observed in this species of animal (Bateson 2000, 276–277). Thus, Bateson concludes, "[t]he story illustrates … two aspects of the genesis of a transcontextual syndrome: "First that severe pain and maladjustment can be induced by putting a mammal in the wrong regarding its rules for making sense of an important relationship with another mammal. And second, that if this pathology can be warded off or resisted, the total experience may promote creativity" (Bateson 2000, 278).

undergo within the space-time of performance. As spectators learn that the performance is a context for aesthetic experience, mis-movements gradually appear as descriptions for interaction. Mis-movements code difference and the predicament of expression therefore finds a tentative solution in the use mis-movements as phenomena that produce change. However, by dint of being repeated, mis-movements also produce patterns that transform into information *about* mis-movements. The difference between attending to mis-movements as mis-movements and attending to mis-movements as patterns, is, to retain the analogy with Bateson's system analysis, a difference in logical typing (see Bateson 2002, 39).[36] Initially mis-movements emerge as individual instances of incongruous physical actions, yet through repetition they transform into physical action sequences, namely, patterns, and Bateson's fourth criterion helps me explain this transformation in terms of differences between discrete mis-movements and the patterns that mis-movements produce.

As individual phenomena, mis-movements correspond to what Bateson labels "divergent sequences" (2002, 37), which is to say phenomena that are unpredictable. There is simply no way of determining what mis-movement will come next or to guess what an individual mis-movement means, based merely on one occurrence. Through repetition, however, mis-movements gradually transform into what Bateson labels "convergent sequences" (2002, 40), which is to say phenomena that are predictable. The shift from individual to class therefore entails a shift in logical typing (2002, 106–119).[37]

---

[36] Admittedly, Bateson does not talk about Beckett's work, whether drama or prose, he is describing an engine, yet his description of how change is registered is suggestive of what goes on also with mis-movements, not merely in *Footfalls,* but also in, for instance *Godot, Come and Go, Footfalls, Rockaby, Play,* etc. As mis-movements are repeated, spectators are prompted to compare mis-movements to mis-movements, which is equivalent to comparing change to change, and in this process a change in "logical typing" occurs.

[37] According to Bateson, "phenomena provoked by logical typing have fascinated thinkers and fools for many thousands of years" (2002, 108).

Importantly, however, to talk about interaction as a transformation or shift in logical typing, we need a syntax capable of capturing the relationships between things and people. Our habitual way of talking about relationships, Bateson maintains, is lopsided (2002, 94). It tends to take merely one side of the relationship into consideration. This 'old syntax' corresponds to what Bateson calls billiard-ball physics and predicates on a set of assumptions about the nature of interaction that Bateson argues are inherently misguided:

> Billiard-ball physics proposes that when ball A hits ball B, A *gives* energy to B, which responds *using*, this energy that A gave it. That is the old syntax and it is profoundly, deeply nonsense. Between billiard balls, there is, of course, no 'hitting or 'giving or 'responding' or 'using'. Those words come out of the habit of personifying things and, I suppose, make it easier to go from that nonsense to thingifying people—so that when we speak about the 'response' or a living thing to 'external stimulus,' we seem to be talking about something like what happens to a billiard ball when it is hit by another.
>
> (Bateson 2002, 94)

The idea that energy is transferred from billiard ball to billiard ball, says Bateson, is problematic as it "makes the total relationship into one of partial mobility on each side" (Bateson 2002, 95). This way of talking is an example of the 'old syntax', which is embroiled in a habit of personification, but which importantly also hides the fact that energy is not merely given from one object to another, but energy is "already available in the respondent, in advance of the impact of events" (Bateson 2002, 95).

To further illustrate this point, Bateson refers to the relationship between a faucet and the water that flows from its head. The flow of water is controlled by a "switch", which is the point of connection whereby these two systems are interconnected. To forget this point of connection, Bateson argues, is to fail to acknowledge that in "life and its affairs, there are typically two energetic systems in interdependence: One is the system that uses its energy to open or close [which in Bateson's example is] the faucet or gate or relay; the other is the system whose energy 'flows through' the faucet or gate when it is open" (Bateson 2002, 95). The difference between an 'old' and 'new' syntax, then, "is the difference between talking in a language which a physicist might use to describe how one variable acts upon another and talking in a language about the circuit as a whole" (Bateson 2002, 100). Arguably, even if Bateson's example concerns the relationship between billiard balls, or water and piping, and my discussion concerns mis-movements, the insight that we may need a different syntax to describe interaction is important. Not only does the billiard-ball analogy illustrate why a metaphorical use of language tends to distort meaning, but it also affords a description of events that considers *both* how energy is distributed between interacting phenomena, *and* the fact that "only difference can trigger response" (Bateson 2002, 95). In short, the new syntax combines the insight about energy sources with the second generalisation in Bateson's list, namely the criterion that interaction is triggered by difference. Applied to the context of Beckett's drama such a new syntax would make it possible to attend to the hierarchies of meaning produced as mis-movements shift logical typing in the whole circuit of performance. In addition, it would make it possible to think about the role and function of mis-movements as coded effects of change that trigger a different mode of interaction between spectator and stage presentation, one capable of releasing spectators from the yoke of linguistic interpretation.

To give this idea a bit of context, I turn to the stage directions for *Footfalls*, which detail the movements of woman (MAY) walking a narrow strip of floor (*TN IV* 275: 1–21). According to Beckett, everything in the play evolves from this image: "[t]he walking up and down is the central image... [t]he text, the words were only built up around this picture" (Beckett qtd in Asmus 1977).[38] In the stage directions, the relationship between walking and its effect is specified—through 'clearly audible rhythm'—and the same goes for the relationship between the stage lighting and its effects—the 'stage is in darkness' but for a 'strip', 'downstage, parallel with front', which 'fade up to dim on strip' as the play begins. Maintaining the analogy with Bateson's example, then, the meticulous stage directions could be seen as the switch—that is "the pathway for the passage of energy which originates elsewhere" (see Bateson 2002, 95), the combinations of actions sequences (feet and sound, movement, and immobility, but also light and dark,) could be seen to comprise a faucet, if the metaphor is permitted. Correspondingly, the play that unfolds in the context of performance is analogous to Bateson's example of the water. Commenting on the meaning of the word 'switch', Bateson observes that the concept "is of quite a different order from the concepts 'stone,' 'table,' and the like" (Bateson 2002 101). A switch is nominally part of a circuit, and as such it "*does not exist* [*sic.*] when it is in the on position" (Bateson 2002, 101). Thus, Bateson explains, a switch has "a special relation to *time*. It is related to the notion 'change' rather than to the notion 'object'" (2002, 101). By analogy, whereas the stage directions connect action to performance, they have no influence over the flow of the play in performance, nor over the actual enactments of the action sequences since these are done by the actors. Even if the textual notes that accompany the stage directions specify the exact moments when the woman's voice (V) says 'May' and so interrupts her walking, and "[a]ccording to Beckett's assistant, Walter Asmus, 'The first "May" comes on the fourth step while May is walking from right to left, the second "May" comes on the eight step" (*TN* IV, 285, item 78–84), these descriptions are not the stuff of sensation. The stage directions are thus geared towards the changes

---

[38] SB qtd in Asmus "Practical Aspects of Theatre, Radio and Television", rehearsal notes for the German première of Beckett's *That Time* and *Footfalls* at the Schiller-Theater Werkstatt, Berlin, directed by Beckett, *Journal of Beckett Studies*, No. 2, Summer 1977.

that emerge in performance but, given that their function is analogous to that of a switch, they disappear when the performance begins and what appears instead are the changes afforded by the unfolding of the play in the context of performance.

However, to account for the transformation that mis-movements undergo in the space-time of performance, one must also take the spectators' experiences into consideration.[39] May's walking may first strike spectators as unusual, but as the play progresses, spectators will automatically take this image as the baseline against which the effects of difference emerge. The sound of May's feet as she walks, or the silence when she stops walking, now produce difference on another level, and such difference, "which is usually a *ratio* between similars, has no dimensions. It is *qualitative*, not *quantitative*" (Bateson 2002, 93). With reference to how spectators arrive to make sense of May's walking, it makes no sense to count the number of her steps or the number of times she stops walking. Such aspects of performance belong to chronological, objective time (*Chronos*), as the structure within experience takes place. Instead, it is the rhythms, lines, paths, directions etc. that emerge from her walking and stopping that matter, and these are of a different order than the actions performed since they relative to qualitative time (*Kairos*). Indeed, "differences that make a difference" (see Bateson 2002, 92), are "*not* substance" (Bateson 2002, 93). They are information. In Bateson's words: "difference which makes a difference is an idea. It is a 'bit, a unit of information" (2000, 272). Rhythms, directions, lines etc. are of a different qualitative order than the actions that produce them. The process of analysing such sequences must therefore entail taking more than merely their quantitative value into account. By analogy, questions pertaining to May's past are similarly redundant. The issue of whether it is her mental condition that causes her to walk, or if her mental condition is caused by her walking, cannot reveal the nature of the encounter

---

[39] Cf. Bateson's claim that the focus on energies must be combined with the second criterion, which stipulates that interaction is triggered by difference (2002, 89; 95).

proposed by the image of walking. The subtle change that happens as May continues to walk her strip of floor must be taken in terms of a description of the relations that open in performance between spectator and stage image. Importantly, experiencing those relations is of a different order than cause-and-effect descriptions can account for. It is an encounter that prompts attention to the relation *between* the sound of feet falling *and* listening to the sound of feet falling, as well as a relationship *between* walking *and* walking. And, as Bateson explains, when causal systems become circular, that is when spectators begin to compare walking to walking, then walking (as an individual mis-movement) disrupts the lineal logic of language. The fact of May's walking being idiosyncratic is no longer the cause for its effect because the logical typing of walking has transformed. May's walking is no longer an instance of something incongruous, *viz.* a mis-movement. No longer a conceptual idea, it has become an encounter that connects walking to stopping, sound to silence, audience to performance and past to present. The poetic logic of Beckett's careful stage directions is thus to connect verbal and non-verbal realms of experience.[40]

Consequently, the issue of how spectators make sense of May's walking has nothing to do with the stage directions. Keeping the distinctions between individual and class in mind, there is a difference between talking about mis-movements on the level of individual phenomena and talking about the patterns that mis-movements produce in the context of performance, *viz.* the "circuit as a whole" (see Bateson 2002, 100). And it is important to keep these distinctions in mind. One must not "confuse individual with class" (2002, 40). The means used may disappear in the encounter with change, which is in the present, yet—as Bateson maintains—the reason that history is unpredictable into the future is precisely because

---

[40] Notably a shift in logical typing may take place also in the dialogue. For instance, the last line in *What Where* (1983), when the voice of Bam (V,) a mirror reflection of Bam, states "I switch off". The performative statement means that the flow of performance has come to an end. But the issue of what happens to the flow of information is another matter: "Make sense who may" (*TN IV* 414: 199).

individual entities (human or non-human) play such important roles. To say that it does not matter who was the instigator for a trend because that something would have trended anyway, or to say that something was unavoidable, makes no sense (Bateson 2002, 40). Of course, "it *does* matter who starts the trend. If it had been Wallace instead of Darwin, we would have had a very different evolution today" (Bateson 2002, 40). By analogy, it *does* matter which mis-movement is emphasized in the stage directions. Walking produces different differences than stooping, falling, or turning. But it is not the number of repetitions of mis-movements that produces those aesthetically significant patterns. Rather, patterns are latent in phenomena that unfold through repetition *as* patterns, and as Bateson explains, "*a ration between two quantities* is already the beginning of a pattern" (2002, 49). In the event of performance, spectators will therefore encounter mis-movements *both* as divergent *and* convergent phenomena. That is, although a mis-movement may seem incongruous or even absurd the first time it appears, as it is repeated, spectators will begin to compare it to itself, and so begin to see various effects of difference.

The careful organization of mis-movements in performance therefore teaches spectators to reconfigure the performance context as a context for aesthetic experience. And, moving up the ladder of abstraction, spectators will turn to the *effects* of mis-movements as relevant, and this is also how the predicament of expression finds a tentative solution in the use mis-movements as phenomena that produce information about change. In short, mis-movements produce the shift in logical typing necessary to perceive change. But once such a shift in logical typing has occurred, then perceiving mis-movements is tantamount to encountering interaction as it unfolds in the present, *between* sound and silence, walking and walking, sensation, and sense. Importantly, therefore, a comparison between Bateson's circuits and wholes and Beckett's use of mis-movements in performance, illustrates how Beckett's drama reconfigures the context of performance, from a context for interpretation to a context for aesthetic experience.

Against mapping

The sections above have suggested that the coded effects of mis-movements comprise patterns, for instance rhythmical or visual, appearing in the context of Beckett's drama through mis-movements, and that such patterns emerge to be experienced. As Bateson explains:

> the difference between effect and cause when both are incorporated into an appropriately flexible system ... is the primary premise of ... transformation or coding. Some regularity between effect and cause must be assumed, since otherwise we would not be able to distinguish between effect and cause, yet granted such regularity we can go on interminably to classify relationships between cause and effect.
>
> (Bateson 2002, 102)

An upshot of spectators' caring about them, mis-movements are incomplete and ambiguous expressions producing a conduit for body-based meanings that are not reducible to the material of bodies. Correspondingly, as Sarah Ahmed explains, a "path is made by the repetition of the event of the ground 'being trodden' upon ... we walk on the path as it is before us, but it is only before us as an effect of being walked upon" (2006, 16). The path, then, is an effect of our taking it, rather than its cause. To address this idea, I turn to Bateson's fifth criterion, "In Mental Process, the Effects of Difference Are to Be Regarded as Transforms (i.e., Coded Versions) of the Difference Which Preceded Them" (Bateson 2002, 102), partly to discuss how mis-movements afford a space where linguistic and embodied meanings coalesce and partly to address the implications of such presentations.

Mis-movements function within the context of performance to the end of refiguring both the aesthetic object and the act of interpretation itself. By means of mis-movements, Beckett seems to have found a method for undermining conventional language, or conversely for adding non-verbal communication, all the while returning the spectator to experiencing both the non-verbal and the verbal. To engage with mis-movements is therefore to momentarily abandon the hermeneutic stronghold of interpretation. No symbolic meanings are attached to mis-movements and nor can mis-movements be correctly interpreted. Primarily a means to sharpen spectator attention, mis-movements are contextually bound. They do not refer to anything outside of the context in which they appear, and the meanings of mis-movements cannot be expressed in terms of their status as conventional symbols or metaphors. Rather, mis-movements produce the necessary conditions of possibility for encountering change, thereby forming new habits for thinking about meaning. Whether the potentialities generated by mis-movements tend towards interpretative autonomy, or towards the end of meaning, they emerge in the context of performance as coded effects (or transformations) of the difference that preceded them.

In a sense, mis-movements could be seen to produce machinic desire (Deleuze), that is desire that cannot be reduced to material form, philosophical ideas, or historical context. Machinic desire does not comprise of material bodies but takes place the plane of incorporeal transformation, for instance as attunement or attachment, and tapping into the machinic quality of mis-movements would therefore entail appreciating that "what appears to empty space is … a virtual whole, a nothing full of potentialities, including all possible actions and movements" (Gontarski 2015, 163–164).[41] The fact that mis-movements do not stand *in* for anything makes them conspicuously different from language, which is famously characterized by absence. Contrary to language, mis-movements are

---

[41] Importantly, the notion of 'machinic desire' is not limited to the material of which it is composed. Machines are not collections of things, but rather particular arrangements of desire. The effects of connectivity would, from this perspective, reveal something about the mind capable of producing it *viz.* a machinic desire attuned to connections. One way to tease out an assemblage, according to Deleuze and Guattri, is therefore to ask, for each 'effect', 'what kind of machine would is capable of producing it?' And, given a certain machine, what can it be used for?' (qtd in Buchanan 2021, 63).

only meaningful in precisely the contexts in which they appear.[42] Watching a Beckett-play, spectators cannot but notice the characters' idiosyncratic movements, and—in so doing—are inevitably faced with the difficult task of trying of make sense of what seemingly lack significance, beyond being ostensive. By analogy, characters in Beckett's prose similarly display eccentric gestures and movements that could be seen to attract both the reader's attention, and the attention of other characters. Thus, in *Watt*, Watt's gait is described as a "high stamping mass" that impresses Lady McCann to the effect that she decides to throw a rock at him (Beckett 1953, 31–32). What provokes Lady McCann to strike out in such a manner is not specified to the reader yet Watt's incongruous walking puzzles her to the point of frustration. The reader, similarly is faced with having to assess a manner of moving that falls short of what would normally be expected: Watt's knees do not bend, not because they cannot bend, but because for some reason they simply will not bend, and Watt therefore propels himself by means of a balancing act involving stamping feet that produce a complicated rhythmic structure (Beckett 1959, 30–31). In reading about Watt's walk, readers cannot but go through the motions, unless of course they decide to skip the passage, and as Steven Connor reminds us, "[w]alking and telling are always closely connected in Beckett's work" (2014, 123). Watt's "funambulistic stagger" (a description illustrating both the unsteady quality of Watt's walking and its precision), thus comprises an example of how Beckett's attention to the body projects a context for the reader's kinetic meaning-making. Whether in the drama or the prose, then, characters are presented in ways that prompts spectators and readers to reckon with mis-movements that seemingly serve no rational purpose, other than to draw attention to the act of moving itself.

Yet, Mis-movements provoke spectators (and arguably readers) to reckon with non-conceptual presentations. The fact that

---

[42] This is also why deconstructive readings of mis-movements seem less helpful.

there is no connection between mis-movements and specific meanings— movements do not represent concepts in the sense that words do—make mis-movements non-propositional. However, as discussed above, the repetition of mis-movements inevitably creates patterns by means of which they begin to acquire meaning, and so the spectator is drawn into the performance context. Put differently, a performance is not a name for a specific type of action, but, again following Bateson, it could be described as "the name of a frame for action" (2002, 130), and within this frame mis-movements invite spectators to act differently. Indeed, as Stanton B. Garner explains, "Beckett stages his spectator as deliberately as he does his characters, consciously manipulating the experiential orientations of audience to stage" (1994, 81). In Beckett's experiential dramaturgy, then, audiences "are not detached observers, but rather are positioned as an inherent part of the performance, though individual spectators may resist or redefine that role in particular productions" (McMullan 2010, 13). And, as I hope to convey, mis-movements are instrumental in this process. not merely because they code abstract change but also because of the ways in which they destabilize the spectators' habitual strategies of interpretation.

The poetic logic of mis-movements is to undermine 'ordinary language use', as defined by Ludwig Wittgenstein in *The Blue and the Brown Books* (1958), and subsequently developed by Stanley Cavell in *The Claim of Reason* (1979). According to Juliet Floyd, who quotes Cavell, ordinary language, while a reservoir of implicit meanings, is also a potential threat to us as creative language users on account of its tendency to automatise expression. And the difference between automatism and creativity can be allegorized as "our tendency to self-mechanize' in musical terms" (Floyd, *Lecture* 2019, 11:20–11:32). Cavell illustrates the danger of reducing language to the sole purpose of generating images in the hearer—which is to say the danger of understanding of language as an automatized process—by referring to the *pianola,* the self-playing piano. That is, a machine-generated performance could be seen to reduce or human creativity or performance to something mechanical, (Cavell qtd in Floyd 11:32–

11.54). Paradoxically, we need to take off from the ordinary if we are to come to terms with the way images become meaningful, but if we give ourselves over to such perception and communication, we only arrive at silence. Among the unbearable costs to ordinary language use are therefore the loss of voice, the loss of creativity, the loss of authenticity of expression, and the loss intellectual freedom. Ultimately, what is at stake in ordinary language use is the limit of reason, which is not, Floyd explains, "reached in contradictions … or wrong philosophical theories, or mistakes or arguments. [But] in lapses of imagination, ill oriented ways of positing yourself with respect to the meaning of words, in something other than a half-way way" (Floyd, *Lecture* 13.15–13.33). We therefore need to recognize the intrinsic incompleteness of words and meanings and embrace the opportunity to act as 'response-able' interlocutors whose participation is necessary to complete the expression (see also Karen Barad, *Meeting the Universe Half-Way*, 2007). According to Floyd we should therefore be mindful of the fact that Cavell's philosophy urges us to break with the tendency to self-mechanize. Above all, we must abandon the idea of "completeness" and of finding words that perfectly match experience, because unless we give up on this idea, "we chain ourselves to false necessities. We give ourselves over to words all the way. We seek the last word in philosophy, particularly in analytic philosophy, and then we find we're done. We can't say anything. We're voiceless" (Floyd *Lecture* 09.33-09:54).

Such a perspective on the dangers of succumbing to the lull of the ordinary, I argue, is strikingly relevant to Beckett's oft-cited complaint with words. By contrast, the effects of mis-movements, for instance as rhythmic structures and paths, are dense with informational qualities that open paths—albeit incomplete ones—for creative thinking beyond ordinary language use. Mis-movements break out of the so-called natural world of given meanings, and this is also how they contribute to the liberation of spectators from the yoke of linguistic interpretation. The fact that mis-movements do not refer to anything outside of the context they appear therefore does not mean that they are meaningless. Meaning always emerges in context and is intrinsically part of perception itself, only mis-movements require spectators to recognize their own participation in creating meaning in the context of performance, and this is also how they undermine ordinary language use and open new paths for communication.

Reconfiguring the context for interpretation

Bateson's sixth and final criterion, finally, affords a perspective on the poetic logic of this situation. This criterion states that "The Description and Classification of these Processes of Transformation Discloses a Hierarchy of Logical Types Immanent in Phenomena" (2002, 106). And my assumption is that this criterion presents a model for understanding why mis-movements are not to be considered the causes of the effects produced. Indeed, "no message, under any circumstance, is that which precipitated it" (Bateson 2002, 106). To perceive the patterns of mis-movements as significant in some way, spectators need to already know that patterns are relevant. Again, as Ahmed reminds us, "[t]he more a path is used, the more a path is used" (2019, 40), but mis-movements invite spectators to take different paths. Given that the meaning of any message changes depending on context, spectators need to learn to take mis-movements into consideration, that is they need to reconfigure the performance context as a context for aesthetic experience. The question of what kind of knowledge is produced in the context of performance must therefore be reformulated. Only, the question is not what mis-movements mean, but how they are perceived in the context within which they appear, and how the respondents (*viz.* audiences) understand this context. Because the skill to distinguish one context from another "is the recipient's skill" (Bateson 2002, 43); therefore, unless a spectator is prepared to see mis-movements as qualitatively relevant elements of the coordinate structure of performance, the significance of mis-movements will remain hidden in plain sight. Notably, however, learning and adaptation is hierarchical, which is to say it happens on different levels of communication and necessarily involves trial and error and feedback loops, whereby first-order changes demand second-order changes that in turn will reduce the effort needed to achieve first-order change etc. (Bateson 2000, 274). Bateson again: "every circuit of causation in the whole biology, in out physiology, in our thinking, our neural processes, in our homeostasis, and in the ecological and cultural systems pf which we are parts—... conceals or proposes those paradoxes and confusions that accompany errors in logical typing" (2002, 102). To illustrate this point, Bateson refers to Goethe's "syntax or grammar in the anatomy of flowering plants, where each organ is determined by its contextual status" (2000, 274). By analogy, in the context of Beckett's drama, learning becomes a matter of reconfiguring the context for interpretation.

Interestingly, Beckett's own statements about art in many ways correspond to Bateson's criteria for mental process. In an oft-cited conversation with Georges Duthuit, Beckett states that he prefers "[t]he expression that there is nothing to express, nothing with which to express, nothing from which to express, no power to express, together with the obligation to express", over the pretence of adequate expression (Beckett 1983, 103). The topic of conversation is the specificity of abstract expressionism of Pierre Tal Coat, André Masson, and Bram van Velde—the latter, a friend of Beckett's—and the above quoted statement is therefore not about Beckett's own work. Even so, it reveals something about Beckett's attitude to the problem of artistic expression, namely that he is concerned with the nature of the relationship between mind and matter, and that he cannot accept the logic of "lineal thinking" (cf. Bateson 2002, 56) as a model for expression. According to Beckett, the artist obsessed with expression must consistently face "a kind of Pythagorean terror, as though the irrationality of pi were an offence against the deity, not to mention his creature" (Beckett qtd in "Three Dialogues", *Disjecta*, 1983, 145). Such a terror comprises the suspicion that the universe is not logic, that cause-and-effect relations do not exist, and that there is no orderly universe to understand. In such 'presence of unavailable terms', Beckett asserts, "the analysis of the relation between the artist and his occasion, a relation always regarded as indispensable" is no longer of interest since "if the occasion appears as an unstable term of relation, the artist, who is the other term, is hardly less so, thanks to his warren of modes and attitudes" (*Disjecta* 144). Rather, what we should concern ourselves with is the unstable and "acute *anxiety* [*Sic.*] of the relation itself" (*Disjecta* 145). In a letter to Georges Duthuit, Beckett writes about this anxiety with reference to his friend Bram van Velde's paintings:

> Whatever I say, I will appear to be enclosing him again in relation. If I say that he paints the impossibility of painting, the denial of relation, of object, of subject, I appear to be putting him in relation to this impossibility, this denial, in front of it. He is within, is this the same thing? He is them, rather, and they are him, in a full way, and can there be relations within the indivisible? Full? Indivisible? Obviously not.
>
> (Letter to Georges Duthuit, March 9, 1949, in Craig et al. 2008, 140.)

Beckett's claims may seem paradoxical, yet Bateson's criteria of mind provide a tautology for such a description of van Velde's art. Beckett is struggling to conceptualize the relation between subject and object, or even the idea of the artist, as somehow stable entities. In fact, he asserts that the idea of stability in connection with such concepts is redundant (*Disjecta* 144). And, arguably, Bateson would say that Beckett is right in problematizing the idea of stability. As Bateson explains, conventionally, the word stable "is commonly used syntactically as an adjective applied to a thing. A chemical compound, house, ecosystem, or government is described as stable" (2002, 57). However, such a syntax fails to appreciate the "range of mechanisms" that are implicated in the idea of stability, and which are at work on different levels of complexity—from the simplest level describing the quality of "relations of impact between the stable object and some other", such as "hardness or viscosity", to the more complex levels where a "whole mass of interlocking processes called *life* may be involved in keeping our object in a *state of change* that can maintain some necessary constants, such as body temperature, blood circulation, blood sugar, or even life itself" (Bateson 2002, 57–58). The point, then, as also Beckett seems to have realized, is that stability can only be defined "by reference to the *ongoing truth of some descriptive position*" (Bateson 2002, 58). Stability is "the result of continual changes in descriptions", and so statements about stability require labelling "by reference to descriptive proposition so that the typing of the word, *stable*, may be clear" (Bateson 2002, 58).[43] Stability, then, can only be perceived relative to change, making Beckett's comment about van Velde a call for more precise descriptions about the descriptive position referenced, even as this idea remains implicit in his claim. Lawrence confirms that:

> [b]y the time when Beckett began to formalise a theory of art built around notions of visual resistance and states of impossibility in his essays on the van Veldes, his fiction was already developing tropes out of non-appearances, failed and receding figurations.
>
> (2018, 80)

Beckett's own critical writings therefore seem to testify to his projection of a visual paradigm in which the work of art is simultaneously a phenomenon of disclosure and concealment, resistance and acceptance, negation and affirmation, whether of meaning, knowledge or truth. In Beckett's work, interaction is triggered by difference, as that which emerges through repetition. Yet,

---

[43] Importantly, Bateson explains, 'change' and 'stability' are not of the same logical typing, and so they could not be used to describe the same kind of relations (2002, 58). To exemplify the significance this idea Bateson refers to the French phrase attributed to Jean-Baptiste Alphonse Karr, "*Plus ça change, plus c'est la même chose*", a phrase that is frequently translated into English as 'the more things change, the more they stay the same' (Bateson 2002, 58).

in the years that separate Beckett's pre-war essay, "Les Deux Besoins" (1938), from the post-war piece on Henri Hayden, he came to realize that "to cast aside the veil it was necessary to assume another veil" (Leslie Hill qtd in Lawrence 2018, 82).[44] There is no escaping the fact that to create is to shape, and that to shape is simultaneously both to reveal and hide. Over time, Beckett's early desire to unveil perception through "an assault against language in the name of beauty", as expressed in the letter to Axel Kaun (Beckett 1983, 173), as well as his later recognition that habit, defined as an "impediment" (*empêchement*) to perception, thus gives way to a more nuanced understanding of the implications of the creative act.

Moreover, in his letter to Duthuit Beckett also refers to a previous conversation about the temporal and spatial dimension of van Velde's paintings (see *fn* 5, Craig et al. 2008, 141).

> To say that the painter, by spreading colour on a canvas, is necessarily setting out along the road of spatial and temporal references, seems to me true only for someone who has never stopped bringing them in in the form of relations, which is not the case for Bram" [van Velde].

(Craig et al. 2008, 141).

Concluding that he hopes to have "misexpressed [himself] aright", Becketts moves on to state that he seems to have gotten nowhere and that here seems no way out of the predicament of expression, but he also maintains that he will "hold on to this last appreciation, until the day comes when [he] shall not need another hand to hold in his wrongness" (Craig et al. 2008, 141). To understand Beckett's complaint here, I once again turn to Bateson's criteria for mental process. Importantly, Bateson points out, change is not "located in

---

[44] Leslie Hill, "Samuel Beckett (1906–1989): Language, narrative, authority," in *The Cambridge Companion to European Novelists*, ed. Michael Bell (Cambridge: Cambridge University Press, 2011), 394–409.

time or space" (Bateson 2002, 92). That is, even if we are geared towards difference *as* change, difference itself is not *in* the things we see; rather, it is the kind of information we *draw* from perception.

In Beckett's drama, then, change emerges *both* on the level where mis-movements emerge as efficient effects *and* on the level at which these effects shift logical typing by transforming into patterns. The process of registering such shifts in 'logical typing', however, does not require cognition: we need not understand a mis-movement to notice the effects it produces (for instance pattern, rhythm, or direction), and nor do we have to be aware that in so doing, we are attending to phenomena of a different order. Indeed, responding to mis-movements is not in the first place a matter of evaluating individual movements of gestures (even if it may entail this too), but about experiencing a unified whole, an entire situation, "pervaded by an all-encompassing quality that makes [it] what and how it is" (Johnson 2008, 73). Indeed, a performance is a system comprising various elements that interact, yet for it to maintain the truth of its proposition to be a performance, both those involved in performing and those involved in watching must continuously attune and calibrate such interaction, or it will end.

Upwellings

In this chapter, then, I have explained why Bateson's six criteria for mental process are useful to illustrate why Beckett's drama is a context for experiencing change. Change surges up in the context of performance by means of mis-movements, partly because mis-movements are different, and this is initially how they attract attention. However, through repetition, mis-movements also emerge to be *re-*cognized, and when this happens, spectators begin to compare mis-movements to mis-movements and so mis-movements transform into patterns, that is phenomena of a different logical order. On this level of communication, the original event of breaking with expectation no longer matters because now mis-movements produce circuits within which change may appear anywhere. Thus, mis-movements transform from being unexpected elements of change to seemingly predicable elements of continuity that stabilize the event of performance by giving it formal shape. On the one hand, then, mis-movements disrupt habitual perception and so produce change, but on the other hand they transform into patterns which produce the necessary conditions of possibility for predictable configurations. That is, mis-movements propose themselves in the form of visual and auditive images to be reckoned with in various, highly specific ways. However, perceiving the meaning of such images is not a straightforward process of mapping signifier onto signified, differentiating between presentation and representation. Indeed, as McMullan maintains, one should be wary of "anchoring meaning in 'Samuel Beckett' as any kind of stable signifier, coherent identity, or origin" (2010, 3). Any claim to meaningfulness in Beckett's plays must be framed by allusions to ignorance, ambivalence, and ambiguity, and in this context mis-movements similarly emerge to reveal the 'perhaps' that lingers between the something and the nothing, between meaning and non-meaning.[45]

    Importantly, however, the images that mis-movements produce are not meaningless, and the fact that they are so carefully staged testify to their significance. While real life may be completely arbitrary, drama is a mediated presentation of reality within which context all elements of performance are relevant. Indeed, even those elements of performance that appear by chance will be incorporated into the performance as spectators seek to combine everything they see and hear into a unifying whole. In the context of performance, mis-movements may first appear as idiosyncratic images that seemingly resist comprehension, but through repetition they begin to code the effects, *viz.* produce patterns, which will appear relevant to audiences simply on account of appearing in the context of

---

[45] On the Beckettian stage the notion that 'nothing is more real than nothing', a sentiment attributed to Democritus who "asserted that not-being (the Void) had an equal right with Being to be existent" (Ackerley and Gontarski 2004, 410), is arguably reflected in every situation.

performance. Mis-movements therefore invite consideration of images that lack concrete shape and consideration of the relations *between* and *around* such images. Notably, however, as patterns mis-movements do more than merely jolt audiences out of habitual strategies of meaning-making. The patterns produced by characters, such as walking, falling, rocking, stooping, or remaining immobile etc., encourage spectators to predict, project and anticipate beginnings, trajectories and ends. Located in-between the real (performance context) and the ideal, (the spectators' construction of the performance context as a whole,) mis-movements serve to refocus the spectator's gaze on aspects of the stage-presentation nominally deemed irrelevant such as, for example, the sound of silence in an auditorium or of feet falling. And the effect of such careful attention to the characters' physical behaviour is the reconstruction of the frames that condition interpretation.

Indeed, as John Thobo-Carlsen observes, Beckett's method to "represent [a] mocking attitude to words" (2001, 245), predicated on the layering of focal perspectives in his work. It is Beckett's frustration with language that leads him to "de-sign" the artistic expression (Thobo-Carlsen 2001, 250). According to Thobo-Carlsen, the method of de-signing could be understood through the lens of "Mikhail Bakhtin's theories of dialogism" (Thobo-Carlsen 2001, 245). This, as it points "to a fundamental obstacle or schism that is tied up with the relationship between thought and extension, mind and body, I and other, knowledge and experience, as well as displacement or exclusion from company, whether self-inflicted or not" (Thobo-Carlsen 2001, 246). However, the method for staging conflicting perspectives also implicitly speaks to the effects of mis-movements. That is, juxtaposing perspectives may reveal the instability of meanings (whether these meanings pertain to the social realm or experience or to deeper epistemological levels), which also underpins the strategic use of mis-movements. Both the effort to 'de-sign' and the use of mis-movements therefore speak to a poetic logic that takes the audience's experience of the presentation into consideration, and both 'de-signing' and mis-movements adjust spectator perception by prompting consideration of more than one perspective. Indeed, as Thobo-Carlsen maintains, the ensuing result of Beckett's method to de-sign is "a rhetorical dialogue of impotence" (2001, 247), which aims "to keep his promise from *Dream of Fair to Middling Women* of writing a book 'where the experience of my reader [...] shall be the menace, the miracle, the memory, of an unspeakable trajectory'" (Thobo-Carlsen 2001, 245). Such emphasis on audience experience in the statement holds a seed to understanding Beckett's *logoclasm* more broadly, and specifically mis-movements, as a heuristic solution to the predicament of expression.

However, a rhetorical theory about narrative also reveals that, even if texts are relevant, narrative meaning "*is not entirely about the text*" (Phelan 2017, *ix*). In fact, as James Phelan reminds us, "narrative is ultimately not a structure but an action, a teller using resources of narrative to achieve a purpose in relation to an audience" (2017, *x*). Viewed thus, the claim made in *Dream of Fair to Middling Women* (about the reader's experience,) could be seen to evoke an image of the context for reading as an amalgamation of the author, the narrator, and the audience. Yet so could the performance context. If audiences influence narrative to a greater extent than conventional narrative theory has previously noticed (Phelan 2017, 4), then it seems reasonable to take Beckett's emphasis on mis-movements in performance as a sign of his awareness of the extent to which audiences participate in the narrative of performance. By analogy, in *Bodied Spaces: Phenomenology and Performance in Contemporary Drama*, Stanton B. Garner explains:

> The locus of Beckett's theatre of the image remains the audience, that individual/collective 'third body' (along with the character and actor) of the stage's intercorporeal field. For Beckett stages his spectator as deliberately as he does his characters, consciously manipulating the experiential orientations of audience to stage.
>
> (1994, 81)

Beckett's experiential dramaturgy thus foregrounds mis-movements as the pre-linguistic and pre-conceptual realm of experience and so of meaning. It seems reasonable therefore to assume that this awareness grew out of his involvement in the staging of his own work, a fact that also makes it possible to address mis-movements as points of entry into the performance context. Given that an author's writerly efforts always include keeping various audiences in mind (Phelan 2017, *ix*), May's walking back and forth—for example—does not necessarily symbolize a linguistic idea (is not a metaphor), but an action designed to draw audiences into the event of performance, specifically through guiding their attention towards the sound of feet falling as coded effects of change, and towards listening to such coded effects of change in acts of attention. Similarly, Vladimir and Estragon's waiting in *Godot* does not symbolize human helplessness, but implicates audiences in the process of waiting, an experience that is highly specific, although it may be difficult to state precisely what it means. Admittedly, experiencing *something* is always already to grasp an idea, a sense of what that something *is*. But this does not automatically mean that all we do is to confirm what we already know. If that were the case, then experiencing, for instance a clash between (social) perspectives or between linguistic and non-linguistic elements of performance (as outlined by Thobo-Carlsen), would not be particularly captivating as it would entail encountering what we already know to be the same, namely social perspectives, linguistics meanings and notions about conflict. Importantly, experience is always something *more* or *other* than the actual event experienced, and this *something more* is what Gendlin terms "excess", or "our situated experiencing in the world, in situations with others" (2004, 128). To express the experience of our situatedness, words and concepts are undoubtedly useful. Indeed, Gendlin explains, "[a]pplying different categories does indeed bring forth phenomena" (2004, 128), Even so, he continues "the direct experiencing … always responds very precisely, … and always with more than what could follow just from our categories" (Gendlin 2004, 128). Experiencing mis-movements, we therefore always also experience something *more*, something that is not part of the mis-movement, something conceptually vague or "unfinished", to borrow Gendlin's terminology, but nonetheless something experientially significant. Arguably, the effort to capture that *something* in words is difficult. As Gendlin maintains, even "if you are willing to think with the 'excess' gain rather than leaving it behind", you will find that "it will not permit you to say most of the cogent things you can easily say. It will stay opaque, stuck and mum unless and until just certain sentences 'come' to open it" (Gendlin 2004, 128). Experience, according to Gendlin, is "an unfinished order that has to be taken along when we think" (Gendlin 2004, 128), and Gendlin's 'new' phenomenology therefore reverses the philosophical order or thinking and experiencing (2004, 128). That is, the implicit intricacy is of "a more *organic* order, a more *precise* and more demanding *kind* of order, a very finely *determined* order, very *different* from logic, yet responsive to logic" (Gendlin 2004, 130). What Gendlin describes as 'implicit intricacy' seemingly recurs in idioms such as 'actions speak louder than words', 'silence is golden', 'silence is louder than words', 'silence speaks when words can't', 'sometimes silence is a really good answer' etc. Yet it also resurfaces in Michel Polanyi's claim that "*we know more than we can tell*" (2009, 4). And, in the notion that words are insufficient to expression may seem paradoxical, that is in the paradox that Beckett targets in his oft-cited letter to Axel Kaun (1983, 171). However, the paradox that words are insufficient to express seems unravelled by theories that acknowledge the tacit dimensions of experiencing and thinking. Words often fail to express the meanings we sense perhaps for the very reason that what we feel is so much more precise than words allow us to express, and mis-movements, seemingly, are how Beckett manages to show this paradox, rather than tell it. Mis-movements are therefore, in part, how Beckett's 'poetry of the theatre' appears.[46] They are a means to complicate, contradict,

---

[46] In *Images of Beckett*, James Knowlson traces the origin of the expression 'a poetry of the theatre' to Jean Cocteau who is supposed to have written it as early as 1922 (2003, 107). It subsequently reappeared in *Theatre*, vol. I, preface to *Les Mariées de la Tour Eiffel* (Paris: Gallimard, 1948), p.45. (Knowlson, 2003, 153*n*).

undermine, qualify, and redefine semantic meaning. As poetic devices, they are applied on the assumption that perception and by extension knowledge, derives from the communicative situation, rather than predates it. Thus, in the context of Beckett's drama, mis-movements are designed to shake spectators out of their habitual interpretative strategies, by means of producing experiences that could be described as reservoirs for implicit intricacies, the experience of which are very precise, even as we often struggle to find the right words to express precisely what they mean.

That said, the obligation to express remains. Indeed, if we do not try thinking from such experiencing, then we risk getting out of touch with experience, and we also risk failing to notice that we are out of touch with ourselves, a perhaps more serious threat to thinking and to the prospect of communication than we care to recognize. Tracing his own thinking back to Emerson, Cavell maintains that what Ralph Waldo Emerson realizes, and what John Dewey seemingly fails to appreciate in Emerson's thinking, is that to be able to trust the authenticity of our own voices, we must learn how to focus on our own experiencing as a process of revelation:

> To believe your own thought, to believe that what is true for you in your private heart is true for all men — that is genius ... A man should learn to detect and watch that gleam of light which flashes across his mind from within, more than the lustre of the firmament of bards and sages. Yet he dismisses without notice his thought, because it is his. ... In every work of genius we recognize our own rejected thoughts: they come back to us with a certain alienated majesty. Great works of art have no more affecting lesson for us than this. They teach us to abide by our spontaneous impression with good-humored in exibility then most when the whole cry of voices is on the other side.
>
> (Ralph Waldo Emerson, "Self-Reliance" 1841)

In using words unthinkingly, we run the risk of failing to recover a sense of what we mean. Thus Clov's complaint in *Endgame* makes sense: "I use the words you taught me. If they don't mean anything anymore, teach me others. Or let me be silent." (*TN II* 24:804). By contrast, mis-movements challenge us to look elsewhere than language and to use words 'thinkingly' as we proceed to capture such non-verbal experiencing in words. As such, they are important vehicles to 'turn words against words'—to borrow Cavell's phrase. We do not merely think in words, but to think, we must also tap into those sensations that emerge in experience. And when words fail us, we search for better words. Indeed, the nature of our sensations are so precise that we may discard words because they do not fit. Thus, we may know *more than* we can say, as both Polanyi and Gendlin suggest, independently of each other.

The interdependence between experiencing and conceptualizing means that "experiencing and concepts (or symbols) are surely not two separate things that have come to be 'related'. Each is already implicit in the other. There is no 'unsymbolized experiencing' any more than there is 'pure logic'" (Gendlin 1997, xii). Importantly, too, "conceptual variety would be relativism if there were nothing else" (Gendlin 1997, xiii). Phenomenologically speaking, then, "every manifold of experience, however far extended, leaves open still closer and new determinations of things and so ad infinitum" (Husserl qtd in Gendlin 2004, 139). Even if mis-movements prompt us to think *from* experience, there is no saying what insights such thinking may produce. To claim that mis-movements produce change therefore is not to claim that they produce new concepts (although they may). It is to suggest that spectators arrive to make sense of change by *carrying* whatever embodied experience they find lodged in mis-movements *forward*. And while it is impossible to say how individual members make sense of mis-movements, it is possible to say something about the structure of experience that affords carrying forward the implicit intricacies entailed in experiencing. Only the 'old syntax' of cause and effect cannot meaningfully capture what is going on. What is needed is a syntax that allows us to follow the flow of experience as it envelops both the objects perceived *and* the perceiver.

Arguably, then, Bateson's criteria for mental process very much resembles Beckett's criteria for art. The predicament of expression, which is among Beckett's strongest concerns (Beckett 1983, 139), is a problem derived from perception as a form of epistemic failure, and—even though Bateson discusses self-regulating systems, and Beckett discusses art— Bateson's criteria for mental process are useful for understanding what is at stake in Beckett's creative solution to the problem of expression. The comparison of Beckett's drama to Bateson's criteria for the mind reveals that mis-movements (as coded effects of change), are designed to critique, or undermine the conventional epistemologies that condition thinking and talking about the interconnections between mind and world. Indeed, within the dynamic context of performance, mis-movements produce change *viz.* effects that emerge beyond words, namely in patterns, rhythms, sequences etc. and the poetic logic of mis-movements hinges on the reconfiguration of the performance context, from a context for interpretation to a context for aesthetic experiencing. In short, mis-movements are metamessages whose function is to teach spectators that the performance context is a context for aesthetic experience, and within the context of performance, change is process rather than psychological fact.

In this chapter, I have therefore compared Beckett's frustration with language and his emphasis on the predicament of expression, on the one hand to Bateson's commitment to rethinking the epistemologies that prevent us from realizing our complicity in the performing ecology of life, and on the other hand to Gendlin's 'new phenomenology of carrying forward' (2004), both of which reminds us of the importance of thinking with *more than* those categories and assumptions that usually form the basis of interpretation. In so doing, I have suggested that Beckett's solution to the predicament of expression paves the way for abandoning our foothold in symbolic thinking, at least in so far as it calls spectators to engage in aesthetic experience and in so far at it prompts spectators to recast the context for interpretation. That said, I do not deny that it is our capacity for symbolic thinking that makes it possible to break out of the prison house of language. The brain thinks in images, and—faced with images that are incommensurable with linguistic meanings—will begin to produce new images which may in turn become re-conceptualized in language. Indeed, as Gendlin explains, "any datum of experiencing––any aspect of it, no matter how finely specified—can be symbolized and interpreted *further and* further" (1997, 16). It is merely that our tendency to mistake the images we produce for reality makes us forget our participation in creating both the images and the reality we reference. Beckett's attack against words therefore does not do away with symbolic thinking: it merely exposes the inherently subjective nature of interpretation along with our participation in creating whatever meanings shape our understanding of the world. What seems to be at stake in Beckett's meticulously staged drama is our capacity as audiences to respond judiciously to aesthetic experience. Mis-movements cultivate a different mode of experiencing, one that does not rehearse conventional ideas but stays attentive to that 'gleam of light', which according to Emerson announces authentic thinking. Indeed, if aesthetic experiencing is an important aspect of intellectual freedom, then it is precisely because it entails trying to 'eff the ineffable', a notion that seemingly corresponds well to Beckett's stated artistic intentions. To think from aesthetic experience is therefore to strive to express "*more than conceptual* logic" (Gendlin 1997, xii). It is a process where "the *move* from one step of thought or speech to the next may come by a conceptual inference. Or there may simply be an interruption, a change to something else" (Gendlin 1997, xii).

    The analogy between Gendlin's process model of thinking and the potential effects of Beckett's drama is apt, yet I am not suggesting that Beckett's drama is therapeutical or instructive, only that mis-movements produce difference and that spectators are geared towards experiencing such difference as aesthetically relevant. Mis-movements invite us to think from *more than* their formal properties. They invite us to trace visual and auditive patterns that emerge in performance and to connect these patterns to the whole of the dramatic situation. Admittedly, this is not an easy task since whenever we try to refer directly to experience, we tend to resort to classification, categorisation, and explanation etc. that is, we end up using language to hide or foreclose what we experience. This is in part why it is so difficult to talk about mis-movements. Merely describing their formal properties does not suffice. Description is not explanation, and Beckett's meticulous stage directions do not tell us anything about the potential effects of the characters' physical comportments. Consequently, it is not their formal properties that matter most: it is their capacity to produce difference—*viz.* change in the context of performance—thereby guiding spectators towards taking *more than* merely words into account, that make mis-movements such useful tools for artistic expression. Mis-movements widen the scope of perception otherwise limited by the threshold of language[47], and this is how mis-movements arrive to implicate spectators in the ecology of performance that is Beckett's drama.

---

[47] As Bateson explains, "perception is always limited by threshold" (2002, 27).

Chapter 2   Sideways

In the second chapter, I place my focus on the complex notion of interaction, as intrinsic to the ecology of performance and as the path to experiencing, encountering and feeling. The material discussed in this chapter primarily comprises *Krapp's Last Tape* (1962), a play that has been categorized as belonging to Beckett's middle period, and specifically to the stage directions for the Schiller Theatre production of *Krapp's Last Tape* in 1969, which illustrate the effects of Beckett's careful attention to mis-movements in performance. But I also discuss *Happy Days* (1966), and one of Beckett's radio plays, *Embers* (1959), to elaborate on the implications of experiencing mis-movements *as* interaction. To provide a bit of context for these discussions, however, I begin by walking you through a personal experience——merely a short side-tour that serves as an introduction to the chapter's concern with various aspects of the phenomenology of mis-movements as interaction in the context of Beckett's drama.

Beckett and Wagner

A couple of years ago, the event of my fiftieth birthday coincided with a performance at the Royal Opera in Stockholm of Wagner's *The Ring of the Nibelung* (WWV86), directed by Staffan Valdemar Holm, and featuring the Swedish Dramatic Soprano Nina Stemme in the role as Brünnhilde. The full four cycles[48] were performed within the space of one week and amounted to sixteen hours of opera to be savoured, or endured, depending on your disposition or mood. Sixteen hours of opera is a considerable volume. Some might say it is beyond what one would be able to digest. I decided the time was ripe for a challenge and asked a friend, an experienced Wagner afficionado, who had watched the *Ring* (both the

---

[48] *The Rhinegold (Das Rheingold), The Valkyrie (Die Walküre), Siegfried, and Twilight of the Gods (Götterdämmerung)*

full cycle and the separate dramas) several times and listened to it more times than she could remember, if she wanted to go. She was delighted to join me. Luckily as it turned out. I am not sure I would have stayed the full sixteen hours had she not been there to support me. Yet, she also helped me prepare for the experience, if that makes sense, by summing up her understanding of Wagner's *Ring* as, primarily, an emotional experience. Wagner's *Ring* she said, 'is mainly for the emotionally crippled'. 'For us' (apparently, she included herself in that crowd,) 'Wagner is a supreme experience. But for those more in touch with their feelings, it may be too intense, perhaps almost unbearably so. It is by far the most visceral, emotional, and intense opera experience you may have; it combines all art forms, but it is its quality of aggregated sensory assault that makes it is such an important outlet for those of us who cannot express our own feelings'.[49] Needless to say, perhaps, my first experience with Wagner proved her right. I would not dare to presume anything about anyone's emotional status, let alone mine or hers, but we stayed the full cycle of four performances, and the *Ring* turned out to be an emotional marathon, but in a good way. It took its toll on my entire body. Not only because the acts lasted at least two and a half hours without intermission—after *The Rhinegold* I anticipated nothing less—but because everything, the music, the coordinated visual effects, the poetic stage images etc., touched my senses. The cycle was a visceral experience. It was also a time machine, evoking memories of previous existence, not merely on account of the weird number of times that I recognized *'that tune'* but also because of the emotions that the performance evoked. Admittedly, I had not until then realized just how profoundly Wagner must have influenced composers around the world. I had of course been told that 'Wagner is an important inspiration for many composers, listen, for instance, to John Williams's music', but I had not realized that listening to Wagner for the first time would entail a stroll down memory lane. It seemed to me that I could recognize

---

[49] Lena Haag in conversation. The wording in quotation marks denotes my recollection of her statements, but it is not an exact rendering of it.

almost every melody. Or rather, the music comprised fragments of melodies and I felt I had already heard them all. Yet in the moment of recognition, I was also thrown into past moments and so my experience of Wagner became mixed up with vague memories of past existences. Thus, the *Ring's* assaulted my senses. It entailed encountering something that touched me although I could not precisely say why, could not remember why. Sitting in the audience, you have no time to intellectualize how you feel. You simply feel *something*, and only with hindsight will you, perhaps, recognize the nature of *that* something. The encounter, then, is primary, its potential meanings, secondary. Yet, the temporality of such experiencing indicates that, on some level, knowing is a mode of recognition of past meanings that seizes you in the present and projects you into the future.

The event of encountering Wagner's *Ring* encapsulates many of the things that I have been trying to explain about mis-movements in Beckett's drama, here and elsewhere. The poetic logic of Wagner's *gesamtkunstwerk* seems analogous to Beckett's drama, specifically in its emphasis on the whole performance ecology, on visceral effects, and on coordinated visual effects. As suggested in chapter one, Beckett's stage craft takes the whole ecology of performance into consideration, unfolding as John Calder maintains, "primarily through sensation, then emotion, then reason" (89). Thus, it is more akin to a musical composition, than to a dramatic text operating with the logic of ordinary language use. The analogy with Wagner therefore seems pertinent. Just like Wagner, Beckett seems to conceive of performance as a narrative context in which everything that appears is relevant, not merely the linguistic elements. Indeed, Beckett stage directions could be compared to musical scores. Moreover, Beckett's desire to create 'a poetry of the theatre' (Knowlson 1996, 230), could be seen to approximate Wagner's symbolic drama, although there are of course importance differences, not least apparent in Beckett's insistence on failure and Wagner's assertions of supremacy. Notwithstanding, and most pertinent for my discussion in this chapter, in both Wagner's and Beckett's visceral work, interaction happens in the moment of performance, in the here-and-now of the performance event, a fact that has important implications also for the issue of interpreting the work.

The processes of re-cognition or synthetization of temporal perspectives that characterize acts of watching and listening signal that the problem of interpretation is not a straightforward matter of determining linguistic meaning. Rather, it involves thinking *from* embodied experience, a process that entails *carrying* something *forward*, something merely latent in experiencing, something that could perhaps be described in terms of the coded effects of the differences that preceded it (Bateson), or something not thought of before, something new, paradoxically already implicit in experience, still inchoate (Gendlin). Importantly, Gendlin explains, "[m]eaning is not only about things and it is not only a certain logical structure, but it also involves felt experiencing" (1997, 1). "What matters is the way in which the next step *follows from (*continues, carries forward, makes sense from) what preceded it" (Gendlin 1997, xiii). "We can think with a "….." after every word or sentence. Or we can phrase it: to employ *how experiencing functions in our cognitive and social activity*" (1997, xi). At stake in the process of interpretation seems to be our future, which arguably depends on our ability to carry felt sense forward. Thus, while carrying the implied intricacy of felt sense forward in language may be difficult, perhaps at times impossible since ordinary language hides much of what is going on in experience, still the obligation to try remains. By analogy, Beckett's dictum that the "expression that there is nothing to express, nothing with which to express, nothing from which to express, no power to express, together with the obligation to express", could be read as an admonition to pay careful attention to one's felt sense and to carry it forward in order to stay alive and open to the future (1983, 103). Indeed, speaking from the implicit intricacy of felt sense is always to move on (without necessarily knowing where one is going,) much as Beckett's characters always do, and much as Beckett himself seems to have done.

Moving on

In this second chapter, then, I proceed towards a phenomenological analysis of mis-movements by addressing the tacit dimensions of mis-movements—a move that shall entail engaging with phenomenological analyses of 'interaction' (Gendlin 2004), with phenomenological reduction (Husserl 1999; Sokolowski 2008), with Drew Leder's phenomenological analysis of 'the absent body' (2009), with Bateson's philosophical perspectives on thinking ('syllogisms in grass') as well as with more psychological conceptualizations of meaning-making ('double bind'), and with Martin Buber's analysis of the 'manifold attitudes of men' (1996, 10). Yet, while these perspectives afford useful perspectives on how mis-movements arrive to be meaningfully grasped in performance, not even these theories can help me explain what mis-movements mean. As stated in chapter one, experiencing mis-movements is not necessarily an intellectual process, although it may hold the seeds of such an activity. You may experience experiencing something specific, feel its effects, be intrinsically involved in the process of carrying it forward, and yet be unable to share its specificity with someone else, or describe it with any degree of precision. Beckett's drama has sometimes had this effect on me. In the darkness of an auditorium, I have experienced experiencing something highly emotional and specific—intuitively felt something—yet my efforts to describe it have been feeble. Sometimes I have opted for words such as 'moving', 'sad', or 'funny', even as these adjectives have not been able to convey anything about the specificity of my experience—nor have I always responded in the same way, even if I have been watching a performance that I have seen many times before in various contexts. Yet, the fact that I can experience experiencing and arrive to describe it in words, even if those words are not precisely what I mean, means that I can deliberate with myself about the relevance of my responses. Remembering that there is always something *more*, something *different*, something of a different order etc., I may then arrive to trace the relations between what is implicit and explicit in my experiencing, without reducing one to the other.

Addressing mis-movements, I shall therefore not be disregarding either the implicitly experiential or the explicitly conceptual. Whether as *dys*-appearance (Leder) or as shifts in logical typing (Bateson), mis-movements are examples of occurrings (Gendlin), founded in interaction (Gendlin), and encountered (Buber) as experientially significant, and this is also how mis-movements allow us to think differently about experience; and so to do phenomenology, as it were, on a level of communication that is arguably more precise than words. Importantly, "language is implicit … in our muscular movements and in every organ. It is implicit in what rouses or spoils our appetites, and in what disturbs our sleep. Language is part of culture and history, but the body is always freshly here again, and can say 'no,' even when culture and reason say 'yes' (Gendlin 2004, 133). However, when we use words to speak of "more than conceptual distinctions" (Gendlin 2004, 130), we use them in new ways. Therefore, rather than suggesting that mis-movements stand in for specific ideas, I shall move on to address them as 'patterns that connect' (Bateson), *abductions* (Charles S. Pierce), and 'syllogisms in grass' (Bateson). My argument is, in part, that mis-movements inspire us to think from experience, carrying felt sense forward, but I shall also discuss our own complicity in producing the meanings we perceive. Ultimately, I shall maintain that we need not arrive at any conclusions about the meanings of mis-movements to feel their effects.

With reference to these stated aims, addressing Beckett's innovative stage craft through the lens of Gendlin's analysis of interaction seems specifically apt. In Gendlin's account, human beings *are* embodied interaction, a mode of being that, according to Donata Schoeller and Neil Dunaetz, could be more fruitfully understood in terms of "Kung Fu" or dance, than in terms of "object theories" (2018, 124). In Kung Fu, they explain, one learns to absorb the energy or the other as part of striking back or shifting direction. The point is that human beings are not entities that somehow interact, they *are* interaction, and notions of subjectivity or identity therefore emerge from interaction. And as a former dancer, I confess to be particularly attuned to this description. In my experience, to dance is to interact (with the corners in a room, the floor, other dancers). Dance *is* interaction. To dance is to absorb and produce weight, orientations, rhythms, shapes. It is to be entangled in various ways.[50] By analogy, in Beckett's drama, mis-movements *are* interaction, and so they are open-ended invitations to participate in the construction of meaning. Located somewhere in-between the descriptive and the hermeneutic, mis-movements afford a mode of experiencing that partly calls language into question, specifically by inviting spectators to attune to the performance context as a context for aesthetic experience, but which also prompts careful attention to the processes by means of which such experience arrives to be meaningful. However, Beckett's drama is not didactic. It does not explain what mis-movements mean or tell us what to do with them. It merely offers up a range of embodied experiences to be imaginatively inhabited by spectators in the context of performance, and in this chapter I shall procced to discuss some of the ways in which this happens. The discussions in this chapter thus build of Gendlin's notion of interaction, although this notion will here be expanded sideways to address various modes in which mis-movements emerge to be experienced in the ecology of performance that is Becket's drama.

The phenomenology of performance

A theatrical performance is a mediated presentation of reality in which an aesthetic object (*viz.* the play) appears to be perceived by a spectator. In the foreword to Mikel Dufrenne's book, *The Phenomenology of Aesthetic Experience*, Edward S. Casey likens the

---

[50] Perhaps dancing could be described in terms of the kind of 'timespacemattering' that Barad associates with "performatively materializing entanglements" (2011, 147). Cf. musicians who perform a piece cannot play 'along-side' each other but need to attune to each other and the music emerges precisely from their musical entanglements.

performance situation to an unprompted phenomenological reduction, when he writes: "in experiencing works of art, particularly those of a dramatic character, the spectator spontaneously withholds credence in the content of this experience as actually present or taking place" (xvii–xviii).[51] Phenomenologically speaking, *what* is perceived is conditioned by *how* and *to whom* it appears, and in the context of Beckett's drama, these aspects are firmly under consideration. Borrowing a term from Stanley Cavell, I have previously suggested that mis-movements serve as 'touchstones of experience'—designed to persuade the spectator to step back from what phenomenology terms the natural attitude, where things are always already meaningful, and to reflect on how things appear in the act of being so perceived (Einarsson 2017, 138). Perceiving meaning is necessarily contingent on a multitude of factors, which the phenomenological reduction seeks to momentarily bracket, and theatre of affect, I have suggested, draws its momentum from such withdrawal.

Yet, even if a performance could be described as a phenomenological reduction in the making, spectators will habitually take it within the natural attitude. Indeed, how could they not? It is the work of art that performs reduction, not necessarily its audiences, although arguably, Beckett's drama could be seen to stage spectator perception with the aim to have them precisely do this. And, within the natural attitude, Merleau-Ponty explains, we frequently fall prey to "the experience error", that is "what we know to be in things themselves we immediately take as being in our consciousness of them

---

[51] In a footnote, Casey also comments that "Sartre and Merleau-Ponty disagree with Husserl as to the nature of phenomenological reduction […] for both consider reduction to be a spontaneous affair and not the result of laborious mental exertion" (xviii). Accordingly, and "contrary to first impressions", Casey continues, this situation offers, in fact, "only further confirmation of the parallelism in question", since the Husserlian phenomenological reduction is attuned to appearances, and so is essentially a passive attitude in a manner like the theatregoer's (xviii). Although not a phenomenologist and although his dramas are not dramatizations of the phenomenological method, Beckett's use of mis-movements could thus be seen to set the stage for a different encounter between audience and work.

[thus we make] perceptions out of things perceived" (2005, 5). The natural attitude corresponds to what Bourdieu calls *habitus,* and only if in some way prompted, will spectators arrive to adopt a phenomenological attitude. Thus, as Coleridge famously suggested, a 'willing suspension of disbelief'" (qtd in Dufrenne 1973, xviii) is a decision to bracket the work, akin to Husserl's later conception of reduction, put forward in *Cartesian Meditations, § 11.*[52]

Derived from the ancient Sceptics' recommendation to "practice abstention from judgement" (Sokolowski 2008, 49), this definition draws on the Latin *reducere* which means 'to draw back'. The phenomenological attitude entails that "we suspend all the intentionalities that we are examining" (Sokolowski 2008, 48). Such a shift of attitude "does not mean ... that we begin to doubt these intentionalities or the objects they have; we do not change from ... doxic assurance to doubt'" (Sokolowski 2008, 48). Rather, we "contemplate the involvements we have with the world and with things in it" (Ibid.). The process of reduction constitutes a series of stages leading back to "the domain of the transcendental ego which must be kept distinct from the psychological domain of the empirical self" (Moran 2000, 148). Yet, importantly, as Sokolowski explains, in the phenomenological reduction, the "skeptical overtone of the term is not kept. The *epoché* in phenomenology is simply the neutralizing of natural intentions that must occur when we contemplate those intentions" (Sokolowski 2008, 49). What the phenomenological reduction seeks to bracket is merely such common-sense meanings or

---

[52] According to Moran there are however no clear boundaries between Husserl's different definitions of reduction as Husserl is not consistent in the way he defines his concept: in *Crisis,* as many as "eight different forms of reductions have been catalogued" (Moran 2000, 147). Nevertheless, Husserl always considered "the formulations of the reductions as the real discovery of his philosophy and as necessary in order to reveal non-psychologically the essence of intentional consciousness and of subjectivity as such" (Moran 2000, 147). Most of all, the reduction provides access to "the infinite subjective domain of inner experience" (Moran 2000, 147).

objectives that immediately proposes themselves to the perceiving subject. As Husserl explains:

> We are no longer doing psychology, a positive science that takes its objects to be transcendent. We are not making an investigation of psychological phenomena, of certain occurrences in the so-called reality (whose existence remains in question throughout), nor do we speak of them. Rather we are investigating what remains and remains valid whether anything like objective reality exists or not, whether the positing of such transcendence is justified or not.
>
> (Husserl, *The Idea of Phenomenology* 1999, 34).

Seeking to distinguish between the "quasi-givenness of transcendent objects and the absolute givenness of the phenomenon itself" is thus a means to uncover those structures of consciousness that allow the world to open to us. Or, as Dermot Moran explains, the world cannot be grasped as something "out there" any more than consciousness can be said to constitute the world, but consciousness allows the world to open as it provides the *"conditions for the possibility of knowledge"* (2000 144). Nonetheless, the aim of the phenomenological method is to allows us to unveil the structure of consciousness.

Phenomenology revisited

Yet, as Eugene Gendlin maintains, many "gave up on phenomenology long ago, because it was recognized that neutral description is impossible" (2004, 127). And although there was a return to phenomenology, especially in France in the 1980s (Tengelyi 2010, 17), and in the early twenty-first century, as noted by Gendlin (2004, 127), the tenets of the critique against phenomenology's claim to objectivity remain. Thus, in *Queer Phenomenology* (2006), Sarah Ahmed maintains that the idea that "one can perceive an object without mediations by presuppositions, or that one could simply put such presuppositions aside", is problematic (2006, 9, *fn 5*). Taking an object in the mode of experience always entails interpretation. Considering this—says Ahmed—we "may need to supplement phenomenology with an 'ethnography of things'", in order to capture how "they arrive to create an encounter" (2006, 39). That is, according to Ahmed, "giving up on the fantasy of the bracket turns phenomenology towards hermeneutics, with its emphasis on interpretation as a stance that shapes what is apprehended in the first place" (Ahmed 2006, 9, *fn5*).

I concur with both Gendlin and Ahmed. The idea that *epoché*, or bracketing, would allow us to disregard what we already know seems difficult to reconcile with the fact that perception is an unconscious process of selection. In perceiving, we select (or *abduct*) what interests us so that the process of drawing from experience is also always a process of enveloping the objects selected in a context that is largely ineffable, always somatically marked, and deeply contextual (Schusterman 2022, 351). Moreover, with reference to scientific discourse as pointed out by Michel Polanyi in *Personal Knowledge* (1974), any scientific endeavour is always guided by the scientist's subjective views. Indeed, intuition is key to discovery and the objective ideal, so pervasive in scientific discourse therefore is inherently misleading (18). Scientific thinking, like any thinking, necessarily relies on a form of 'tacit knowing', which conditions our thinking, although the natural sciences are mistakenly, frequently taken to be more objective than the humanities (Polanyi 2009, 17).[53] Given that we habitually see whatever meanings we *already* know about the world, there is seemingly no way to break out of this epistemological circle. Yet, if this were true, we would never arrive at seeing things differently, nor would we arrive to say anything new. The issue, then, is how to move on from realizing that neutral description is impossible or how to come to terms with the inherent subjectivity

---

[53] Polanyi refers to this book as "an afterthought to my career as a scientist" (qtd by Amartya Sen 2009, x). The book comprises a series of lectures (the Terry Lectures) at Yale 1962.

of thinking, to understanding the potential openings for thinking, knowing or saying something new, and here both Gendlin's process model of thinking and Polanyi's emphasis on tacit knowledge afford openings.

As Gendlin points out, among the reasons for why phenomenology lost momentum after Husserl, was the fact that "Sartre's dialectical categories differed from Merleau-Ponty's functional approach", and "their descriptions 'differed' from Husserl's" (2004, 127). There is no neutral description because any description will inevitably produce different categories, a situation that generated doubts about the usefulness of the phenomenological method. Indeed, Gendlin reports, "it was soon said that phenomenology finds no phenomena at all, only the same philosophical issues that have always been contested" (Gendlin 2004, 127). In response to such critique, Gendlin explains, philosophers "were tempted, like Heidegger in the years after *Being and Time*, to deal with categories apart from phenomenology, from the top down" (2004, 127). Yet, "working with categories alone is not at all helpful. None are ultimate and their use always involves 'an excess' "which fits neither within categories nor can it be had separately" (Gendlin 2004, 127). Moreover, the discovery of the 'excess' in categories "led to the dead-end aspect of post-modernism", as the logical conclusion of having shown the impasse of objective thinking.[54] However, according to Gendlin, the fact that descriptions are necessarily tainted by subjective perspectives need not preclude the relevance of doing phenomenology. Like Polanyi, who maintains that we "must always assume ... that some trace of hidden personal bias may systematically affect the result of a series of readings" (1974, 20), Gendlin maintains that we need to "think with the so-called 'excess'" (2004, 127). That

---

[54] Correspondingly, Bateson maintains that to describe relations between things, is merely to "describe parts of our descriptions" (2002, 57). Descriptions provide no explanation because "*every* descriptive proposition is to be characterized according to logical typing of subject, predicate and context" (Bateson 2002, 58). In short, descriptions are always relative to some "*ongoing truth of some descriptive* proposition" (Bateson 2002, 58).

is, "experience is not separable from concepts, but it plays crucial, directly demonstrable roles in ongoing thinking" (Gendlin 20004, 128). Phenomenology should therefore not "back away from the problem of the relativity to descriptive categories or approaches" (Gendlin 2004, 127). Rather, we need to recognize that "direct experiencing of whatever we study always responds very precisely, always just so and not otherwise, and always with more than what could follow just from our categories" (Gendlin 2004, 128).

The implications of looking at interaction first are far-reaching. For instance, according to Gendlin, his "new phenomenology" (2004, 127), affords a way out from the impasse of "the dead-end aspect of postmodernism", which according to Gendlin results from the tendency to categorize and describe phenomena rather than focusing on the ways in which experiencing and concepts function together, or interact (2004, 127–128).[55] Thus, it makes it possible to address mis-movements in Beckett's drama, not in terms of what they mean, but in terms of the interactions they imply. Viewed thus, responding to mis-movements is a matter of taking experience as "a responsive order ... unfinished in regard to further conceptual form, but always more finely organized than any conceptual forms" (Gendlin 2004, 128). Interaction affords a mode of thinking about mis-movements that "is not separable from concepts", but not limited to concepts, either given that the body knows the world as interaction, *viz.* experience. Embodied cognition *is* world awareness, and world awareness *is* embodied cognition, and experiencing, therefore, says Gendlin, generates neither "objectivism nor indeterminacy" (2004, 128). Rather, he continues, "[w]here others see indeterminacy, we find intricacy—an always unfinished order that cannot be represented but has to be taken along when we think" (2004, 128). Given that thinking *from* experience is to think from the 'excess of concepts', it is also to "speak with and from what is more than categories", and in so doing, "we employ the capacity of language in new sentences" (Gendlin 2004,

---

[55] Cf. Beckett's admonition that the "danger is in the neatness of identification" (1983, 19).

128). By analogy, Polanyi suggests, we must consider the possibility that if "tacit thought forms an indispensable part of all knowledge, then the ideal of eliminating all personal elements of knowledge would, in effect, aim at the destruction of all knowledge" (2009, 20). We cannot arrive to encounter the world as if we had never seen it before, but we can arrive to *re*-cognize something that we do not know explicitly, something that we only have a *felt sense* of, something that we have been carrying with us (Gendlin), approaches us from the past, or perhaps even from the future. In short, acknowledging the tacit dimension of knowledge is to take *epoché* to be intrinsically illusory.

Indeed, according to Polanyi, the paradox of knowing corresponds to the "contradiction" that Plato "pointed out in the *Meno*", namely that "to search for a problem is an absurdity; for either you already know what you are looking for, and then there is no problem; or you do not know what you are looking for, and then you cannot expect to find it" (2009, 22). Plato's solution to this problem is to maintain that "all discovery is a remembering of past lives" (2009, 22). Notably, Polanyi points out, while this "explanation has never been accepted", neither has any other explanation been offered to refute it (2009, 22). Even so, he explains, the solution to the paradox has always been lying in plain sight:

> For the *Meno* shows conclusively that if all knowledge is explicit, i.e., capable of being clearly stated, then we cannot know a problem or look for its solution. And the *Meno* also shows, therefore, that if problems exist, and discoveries can be made by solving them, then we can know things, and important things, that we cannot tell.
>
> (Polanyi 2009, 22)

As Polanyi explains, there is a hidden dimension to knowing, a tacit intricacy (to mix Polanyi and Gendlin's terminology), that we *carry forward* towards a point of *re*-discovery, or we would not be able to 'move on', as it were. Tacit intricacies arrive at the "edge" of thinking, where concepts merely imply *something*, a vague recollection, or a new idea, that seems to capture the whole (Gendlin 2004, 130–131). Thus, when we perceive, feel, or intuit, we rely on *tacit* knowledge, which guides us to *re*-cognize, rediscover, or remember something *more than* we consciously perceive. We may for instance have a hunch that something could be important, although we may not be able to explicitly state what or why (see Gendlin 2004, 130). Or we may have a sense that the words we use to explain something merely approaches that 'thing', and yet we may be utterly at loss to explain what we mean. In short, we "can have a tacit foreknowledge of yet discovered things" (Polanyi 2009, 23), and in everyday life, such tacit foreknowledge produces anticipation and hope, but also deep conviction. Yet, importantly, it is not merely in everyday life that we are guided by tacit knowledge. Rather, as Polanyi explains: "the paradigmatic case of scientific knowledge ... is the knowledge of an approaching discovery" (2009, 25).

Like Gendlin, then, Polanyi acknowledges a hidden dimension of knowledge and maintains that this dimension is an "indispensable element of all knowing" (Polanyi 2009, 24). And like Gendlin, Polanyi maintains that the arrival of words, meanings, insights, knowledge, etc. comes from the body (see Gendlin 2004, 148; Polanyi 2009, 15–16), as the background or experiential, self-reflexive source of all experience, including aesthetic experience, and so of knowledge. Given that we cannot stop producing meaning, we can never really arrive at seeing the world neutrally. This is why "[p]henomenology is parasitic on the natural attitude and all the achievements thereof." (Sokolowski 2008, 63) If there is something implicit going on in thinking and knowing, then it is the natural attitude that holds the seed to discovering or knowing what that something is. Yet, to acknowledge a tacit dimension of knowing is also to acknowledge the limitations of rational thought—a position that I find both methodologically convincing and highly relevant to understanding Beckett's aesthetics of gesture. The notion that ignorance holds the seed to knowledge allows for more moveable, shifting perspectives on the things known. By enfolding ignorance, then, we may arrive to rethink our preconceived ideas, not because we have neutralized them but because we acknowledge and retain the connection with ignorance, a connection that allows us to look at knowledge more closely.

By analogy, addressing mis-movements within the ecology of performance involves neither teleology, nor bracketing or mysticism.[56] It entails recognizing that what Gendlin calls 'excess', or what Polanyi calls 'tacit' or 'personal knowledge', "forms an indispensable part of all knowledge" (Polanyi 2009, 20). If, as Polanyi maintains, "true knowledge lies in our capacity to use it" (2009, 17)[57], then thinking *from* the felt sense of concepts that we know, but which seem to hold something *more than* we know, could greatly enhance our capacity to use them in the service of creating and carrying meanings forward. Viewed in this light, however, the crisis of interpretation in Beckett's drama does not do away with meaning: it underwrites our complicity and participation in creating it, our capacity to feel that we are spoken to,[58] as it were, and it does so by tapping into that edge of thinking where the felt sense emerges to be carried forward, namely into the natural attitude. Thus, I see Gendlin's process model of thinking, Polanyi's tacit knowing, and Ahmed's queer phenomenology as opening 'new' phenomenological paths to understanding mis-movements in Beckett's drama.[59]

---

[56] As Bateson explains, "lineal thinking will always generate either the teleological fallacy (that the end determines the process) or the myth of some supernatural controlling agency" (2002, 56).

[57] Even as Polanyi is referring to the mathematical problem, I would say that his line of reasoning holds for Beckett's drama as well, since what is at stake in the event of performance is our willingness to respond to what is essentially an ethical challenge.

[58] See Gert Biesta on subjectification in *The Rediscovery of Teaching*, 2017.

[59] See Gendlin, "The New Phenomenology of Carrying Forward", *Continental Philosophy Review*, Vol. 37, pp. 127–151, Kluwer Academic Publishers, 2004.

Interaction first

My phenomenological analysis of mis-movements therefore begins with interaction, not as phenomenological reduction but as constitutive of the natural attitude within which experience and sense making takes shape. As interaction mis-movements generate spatial and temporal relations that speak to the characters' different worlds, and these worlds cannot be reduced to either body or environment. Indeed, as Eugene Gendlin explains, "environment is inherently part of every event. There isn't really a body or a person and then something around it" (see the lecture, "Interaction First: A Process Model")[60]. Only, we are used to thinking about interaction as mode of relation where two things interact, for instance body *and* environment, or performance *and* context. And we are also used to thinking about context separate from body. Thus, in chapter one, when I discussed separate entities that interact in performance or when I approached the body *in* performance as an entity among other entities (props, lighting, historical context etc), I did to explain the poetic logic of the performance ecology, a claim which I shall proceed to develop by focusing more on the modes of attention in which such an ecology may be taken. Importantly, the body cannot be taken separately from context or environment. As human beings, we *are* interaction so that "body and environment are one, … one event, one process" (Gendlin 1997, 4). The body, then, *is* interaction, *is* a 'body-environment complex', and thinking *from* experience entails taking the whole body-environment complex into account. More to the point, "our bodies *are* interactings" (Gendlin 1997, xix), and interaction generates different worlds, ecologies, and systems.

According to Gendlin, there are four different modes in which environment participates in interaction, and while there is a difference in degree between these modes of interaction, they are all characterized by the fact that the "body is a nonrepresentational concretion of (with) its environment" (Gendlin 2018, 4). The first

---

[60] YouTube: https://www.youtube.com/watch?v=xaopap6K_JQ , (1.26–1.30).

example, en#1, "is the spectator's environment, what spectators define in *their* environment which may affect an organism. For example, it is en#1 when scientists or hunters define the environment of an animal" (Gendlin 2018, 4). Yet, the body may also be 'reflexively identical environment" and en#2 therefore denotes interaction of a kind where the body "is identical with the organism's living process. Body and en are one event, one process. For example, it is air-coming-into-lungs-and-blood-cells. … [but also] walking" (Gendlin 2018, 4). En#1, then, "is a model of sheer sensory inputs mistakenly taken as real objects" (Parker, foreword to Gendlin 2018, xii), whereas en#2 is the world "generated by body-environment interactions" (Parker, foreword to Gendlin 2018, xii). Furthermore, en#3 denotes:

> environment that has been arranged by the body-en#2 process. The body accumulates (is) a resulting environment. The molusk's cell, the spider's web, or the beaver's tree when it falls, these are their main environment, but they are the results of the animal's body-en#2 process. En#3 is wider than En#2.
>
> (Gendlin 2018, 5–6)

Last, there is en#0, which is a fourth type. This category suggests that something:

> may someday affect the life process and be en#2, but is not now. This has never happened, and is not now any creature's en, not even the spectators. In the seemingly infinite richness of the unborn, something may happen which has not yet, and will then be definable in terms of the process in which it participates.
>
> (Gendlin 2018, 6–7)

Unlike with en#1, 2 (and 3), in en#0, the "space relation is yet undefined" (Gendlin 2018, 8). Still, what is implied in en#0 "is right here *in* what is participating" (Gendlin 2018, 8). Importantly, Gendlin explains, "this use of 'imply' stems from the fact that the whole event is already referred to, when we think only of the body, or only of the en" (Gendlin 2018, 8). In Gendlin's process model of thinking the different body-world complexes define us, even though this fact frequently eludes us, by being implied in the interaction.

Body-en#2 interaction

The body-world complex that is most conspicuous in Beckett's drama, however, is body-en#2, which is to say body-world complexes where the body is reflexively identical with its environment, and my discussion of body-en# here mainly concerns this category. To illustrate how interaction of the body-en#2 type works, Gendlin refers to the movement of walking:

> the same pressure which is the foot's on the ground is also the ground's pressure on the foot. We can separate ground from foot, but not the ground's resistance from the foot's pressure. The en#2 is not the ground, but the ground-participating-in-walking, its resistance.
>
> (Gendlin 2018, 4)

On the terms provided by Gendlin's 'body-en#2', walking is not a process in which two entities interact, because it is the combination of these two entities that produces the walking: the foot's pushing down and the ground's resistance, occur 'only together' as process. Unless the ground participates in walking, walking stops and something else begins. Indeed, anyone who has walked in mud or water would have experienced that lack of pressure from the ground transforms walking into something else entirely. That is:

> the behaviour cannot be separate from this ground-participating. If the body is hanging in air and attempts to walk, its swing will be much wider and it will not move

forward; it won't be walking.[61] In deep water 'walking' will immediately be thrashing; the motions will be different.

(Gendlin 2018, 4)

In interaction, therefore, "[a]ny occurring *is* also an implying of a further occurring" (Gendlin 2018, 10). Moreover, interaction as experience, imply relations that always carry forward something implicit, entailing *both /and,* never *either /or*.[62] And "any way of attending to *an* experience or experiences *is* already a carrying forward from the implicit intricacy" (Gendlin 2004, 143). Absence, for instance, is merely one mode in which the implicit is brought forward, although this does not mean that the implicit is made explicit. Only that "[t]he implicit is never just equal to what will occur" (Gendlin 2018, 12). Importantly, too, "occurring is also an implying of further occurring (and of change in implying)" (Gendlin 2018, 14). Thus, walking in water will be different from walking on firmer ground. If the ground we walk changes, then our 'body-en#2' interaction changes and even though change is intrinsically an implying, this does not mean that we can predict what this implying is or how something will change. And yet, certain modes of resistance (or difference) are latent in certain grounds and so imply occurring and further occurring (and of change in occurring,) even though both such occurring (and change of occurring) remain implicit. Thus, "if an aspect of en#2 is missing, we can speak of 'a' stopped process that is separated and stopped" (Gendlin 2018, 14). (This could be compared to when a mismovement emerges as incongruous or conspicuous, and it does so on account of failing to achieve some kind of purpose that otherwise would not even have been identified, for instance in *Footfalls*, when

---

[61] With reference to walking, Gendlin therefore maintains that "no single foot-pressure ever simply *is*. If there were suddenly such a single is, the animal would fall. Its weight *is* already on the way to … (Momentum cannot be expressed as mere change of location.)" (2018, 10)

[62] I am grateful to Ishrat Lindblad for always emphasising this idea, even as it took me years to understand its implications.

May's walking fails to take her here anywhere, it could be perceived as a change in the occurring of walking.) Yet stopping affords new body-en#2 interactions, which could be spoken of in specific ways as different from that which stopped, *viz.* as change.

Notably, Gendlin's analysis of body-en#2 interaction could fruitfully be compared to Drew Leder's concept of '*dys*-appearance' (2009). In his phenomenological study of human experience, Leder explains both the structure of embodiment and the significance of bodily absence in cultural, philosophical, and social contexts, specifically through explaining "why the body, as a ground for experience, yet tends to recede from direct experience" (1990, 1). According to Leder, the experience of bodily absence supports Cartesian dualism, but only in the sense that it explains how and why the tendency of the body to disappear from perception has generated this conceptual confusion about the relation between body and mind (2012, 3).[63] Leder's project is to give "a phenomenological account of why Cartesian-style dualism would be so pervasive" (Ibid.); and, according to Leder, it is "the phenomenological absence of the body that will provide a tool for understanding previous concepts of self" (2012, 4). The philosophical consequences of his phenomenological investigation of absence are considerable. The body is a complex of absences and presences, yet its participation in experience is rarely acknowledged, other than as pain, illness, or discomfort (Leder 1990, 103). Thus, "[w]hile in one sense the body is the most abiding and inescapable presence in our lives, it is also essentially characterized by absence" (1990, 1). We do not see our eyes in seeing, the ears in hearing or the legs in walking, unless, of course, something about our legs is missing in walking. And, in such moments, what is missing *dys*-appears for perception. Leder emphasizes the relation between occurring and implying, which he ascribes to the way in which our

---

[63] By analogy, Gregory Bateson maintains that it is generally easier to describe pathologies: "It's very difficult ... to talk about those living systems that are healthy and doing well; it's much easier to talk about living matters when they are sick, when they are disturbed, when things are going wrong" (2000, 265).

"being-in-the world depends upon [the] body's self-effacing transitivity" (1990, 15). Only, in Leder's analysis of the absent body, it is the fact of some aspect of the ongoing body-environment interaction that is missing, for instance impaired hearing or eyesight, which brings the body to the fore.[64]

Gendlin's description of interaction and Leder's concept of '*dys*-appearance' illuminate the significance of mis-movements, both as examples of interaction, as interruptions to interaction, and as *dys*-apperance. The prefix 'mis'- in mis-movements indicates that there is a difference between movements that serve clear purposes and movements that, for some reason or other, stand out for perception. Yet as interaction, mis-movements, for instance idiosyncratic walking, turning, falling, stooping, etc., also *imply* specific 'body-en#2', as well as interrupt generalized conceptions about such interaction. In Leder's terminology, mis-movements could be described to '*dys*-appear' on account of being incongruous, which is also why they are perceived to be relevant. If Beckett's characters would 'merely' walk to get

---

[64] In addition to Leder's theory of dys-appearance, Maurice Merleau-Ponty's distinction between *abstract* and *concrete* movements similarly also opens a perspective on the difference between healthy and pathological movements that could be used to illustrate the significance of mis-movements. According to Merleau-Ponty, "the background to concrete movements is the world as given, whereas the background to abstract movements is built up" (2005, 127). Merleau-Ponty's examples pertain to pathologies, which he discusses in terms of "morbid motility", and his examples derive from studies of patients whose body-image schemata are disturbed due to illness (2005, 117). Yet, even if Beckett's characters are fictional, Merleau-Ponty's phenomenological examination of pathological movements as well as Leder's "phenomenological account of why Cartesian-style dualism would be so pervasive" (2012, 3), hint at the misconceptions about the nature of perception. Notably, it is because "the body is a conglomerate of absences and presences, [that] participation in experience is rarely acknowledged, expect as pain, illness, or discomfort (1990, 103). And, notably too, it is because our perceptive acts always take place in a time-space from which we cannot free ourselves, that perception is so inherently selective. There is always more going on than we can possibly register, and so, while we believe we are objective or unbiased, most of the time we are oblivious to the extent at which we merely confirm what we already believe.

somewhere, merely fall on account of stumbling over something, or merely stoop to see something better, then such movements and gestures would be invisible on account of serving clear purposes. Yet because the characters mismove, their idiosyncratic movements become content for perception, and subsequently for processes of interpretation whereby 'old' or conventional concepts of walking, immobility or stasis, or spatial and temporal relations (for instance, prepositions or the order of events,) may be placed *next to* the experiencing of such concepts as they *dys*-appear. The prefix 'mis'- in mis-movements thus indicates that there is a difference between movements that serve clear purposes and movements that, for some reason or other, stand out for perception. Yet this is also how mis-movements produce difference, for example, the difference between interaction as it is conventionally perceived, namely as an exchange between two individual identities, and interaction as that which cannot be functionally reduced.

Correspondingly, according to Gendlin, "[t]he body (when a process stops) is what continues; because as soon as we have more than one process, the body is the other process, the one that is not stopped" (1997, 20). Mis-movements, then, *both* block interaction *and* imply new perspectives on interaction. Yet even as mis-movements arrive to stop interpretation, they also arrive to produce change, and so the process of interaction that conditions participation in the ecology of performance continues. That is, because interruption imply occurring, mis-movements imply further occurring, and so spectators are invited to reconceptualize the stopped interaction as a new whole, enfolding both old and new concepts, old and new experiences of interaction, whereby they become involved in attending to difference or change as aesthetically significant.

Interaction in *Krapp's Last Tape*

A telling example of how mis-movements stop interpretation yet continue to generate new modes of interaction (and so continue to imply further occurring,) emerges in *Krapp's Last Tape* (1962). The play was written "in the first two months of 1958 with a particular actor, Patrick Magee, in mind" (*TN III* xiii). Knowlson reports that "it was the distinctively cracked, world weary, 'ruined' quality of Magee's voice, as well as its Irish rhythms and intonations that appealed to Beckett" (*TN III* xiii). The play is about an old man who listens to a series of recordings he has made earlier in his life, recollecting those key moments that his younger selves have recorded. The stage-directions specify that Krapp is "*a wearish old man*" (*TN III*, 3:7), who walks in a "*laborious*" manner (*TN III*, 3:14). Krapp's movements and gestures seem to have been internalized to the point of being sedimented and so forgotten.[65] However, the revisions Beckett made to the play toned such aspects down (*TN III*). When spectators meet Krapp for the first time, he "[*sits with both hands on the table. He*] *remains a* [*good*] *moment motionless,* [*staring before him*]. { *He shudders,* } *looks at his watch,* [*grunts, puts it back in his pocket, and returns to his first attitude.*]" (*TN III*, 3:17–18). And as indicated by the pointed brackets, the shuddering gesture is a revision. The textual notes to Beckett's own production at the Schiller Theatre Werkstatt in Berlin, 1969, state that: "– '*He shudders*' replaced 'heaves a great sigh'" (*TN III* 15). According to Beckett, "[t]he shudder is, … a gesture of self-containment: 'more inner than outer chill'" (ibid.) By contrast, heaving a great sigh would have been more explicitly expressive and so symbolic of various emotions (regret, nostalgia, sorrow?). Notably, all Krapp's postures, movements, and gestures, are clearly visible to spectators who may deduct various significances from the tension in shoulders or the stiffness in his gait.

Only, viewed thus, Krapp's idiosyncratic manner of walking would not be disruptive at all. Also, viewed thus, the stage directions would merely serve to accentuate Krapp's belonging to a group or category of individuals for whom walking is expected to be associated with effort. Indeed, his idiosyncratic walking or difference would

---

[65] On the idea of internalised, sedimented movements, see *fn*60; see also Merleau-Ponty on abstract movements (2005, 127), and Purves (2019, 14–15).

merely be an aspect of the habit of old age, a feature by means of which Krapp may arrive to represent others of his kind, indistinguishable from other members of the same class of bodies, namely old decrepit men. In *Krapp's Last Tape,* by contrast, a new concept of the body in performance emerges through interaction between non-discursive and discursive experience, and it does so through mis-movements.

The stage directions to the 1969 version of the play reveal Beckett's preoccupation with walking, not a means to generalize about old men, not as symbolic of ideas, but as interaction. As director, Beckett's insisted that the sound of Krapp's feet should be "right" (*TN III,* 13). Indeed, Beckett reportedly even brought his own slippers to a rehearsal of the play (ibid.). Consequently, in a subsequent production at San Quentin where Rick Cluchey performed, "Krapp wore dark slippers" (*TH III* 13).[66] Yet, the sound of Krapp's feet, the length of pauses etc. were also "carefully varied and timed so as to avoid [the] pitfalls ... that an excess of stylisation would produce". Such insistence on the coordination of visual and auditive patterns signal Beckett's attention to interaction. The emphasis on patterning diminishes the possibility of pigeonholing Krapp or pinning him to a category of solitary, pathetic men, whose "best years are gone. When there was a chance of happiness" (*TN III* 10: 275). Although this is undeniably a feasible interpretation, it does not sufficiently account for the 'co-incidence' of visual and auditive patterns that emerge in performance where "the repetitions of postures, actions, looks and ways of saying certain phrases in *Krapp's Last Tape* function in terms of balanced opposites" (*TN III* xix). [67]

---

[66] The instruction that Krapp should wear a *[s]urprising pair of dirty white boots*" (*TN III* 3: 9), has however been retained in the stage-directions.
[67] The textual notes to the production of *Krapp's Last Tape* documents that "Schiller was the first production in which the bunch of keys was omitted in the interest of simplicity and in which the envelope was not taken from his pocket at the beginning of the play" (*TN III,* 15). As the textual notes accompanying the theatrical notebooks observes, it is for the sake of "simplicity" that this sequence of gestures was omitted by Beckett and

Moreover, in a play "divided fairly equally between listening and non-listening" (Beckett qtd in *TN III* xix), Krapp's shuffling proposes itself differently to different audiences. Taking Krapp's walking merely as incongruous is therefore to miss out on its potential significances. The changes Beckett affected to the play as he returned to direct it in 1969, illustrate why interaction cannot be reduced to either body or environment. As interaction, walking is part of a balanced structuring of opposites (rhythms, patterns etc.), which combine to produce a whole. And, importantly, Krapp is not an individual who walks in different shoes, but different footwears imply different wholes, which is to say different Krapps. Approached as an instance of his belonging to a certain class of individuals, Krapp merely confirms preconceived ideas, or prejudices about old men. But, approached as patterns, rhythms, and sounds, which is to say as unifying nameless qualities that imply tacit intricacies, Krapp is an occurrence capable of interrupting habitual interpretation. Any change to Krapp's walking transforms the whole performance since, in any given performance, Krapp's walking *is* interaction, *is* ongoing process. Within the performance ecology, it therefore matters whether Krapp walks in shoes, slippers, or on his bare feet because walking will sound differently with each mode of interaction that *is* Krapp. The issue of how Krapp arrives to be meaningfully apprehended in the context of *Krapp's Last Tape* therefore depends on different modes of interaction.

A new syntax

Beckett's attention to the connections between body and mind could thus be seen to produce a new syntax, one in which interaction affords perspectives on various modes of being in the world, which cannot be reduced to their components. Thus, there is no Krapp other than the Krapp that emerges through interaction between floor and footwear. Whatever environment (ground, space,

---

subsequently from any other production "with which the author has been associated" (*TN III*, 15).

darkness,) it is implied in the different en#2 that appear, and which signal Beckett's attention and attunement to human situatedness. As body–en#2 relations, mis-movements are both heterogenous and deeply general. What seems to be at stake in such images is the carrying of such implicit intricacies that are entailed in interaction, forward. Notably, then, "to *think and speak with* what is more than categories (concepts, theories, assumption, distinctions …)" (Gendlin 2004, 127), offers a helpful taxonomy for distinguishing between different modes of interactions, *viz.* modes of being in Beckett's drama (but arguably also in his prose although this is not my focus here).

How spectators arrive at the point of attending to interaction, however, is a different matter. In examining mis-movements, my aim is not to identify their potential meanings, and nor do I claim that mis-movements inevitably must touch spectators beyond words. They might—but this is not a given. Even as mis-movements *are* interaction, they are not the spectators' personal problems. Addressing mis-movements as interaction is not about what specific mis-movements mean, but about *how* they imply beyond the words used to describe them, and this arguably depends on whether anyone shows up to carry their implicit intricacies forward. The question of how mis-movements arrive to be experienced in the context of performance, and as shall be discussed below, it cuts through the basic words used to describe them.

Moreover, communication in the context of performance is the product of *timing*.[68] No single sound, posture, look, way of saying certain things etc, merely *is*, but within the space time of performance, sound relates to sound, posture to posture, ways of saying things to ways of saying things, and all these interactions contribute to shape the whole of performance, which is also the result of interaction. As, Gendlin explains, "a whole string of en#2 is implied by the (any this) body-en#2" (2018, 9). Beckett's meticulous attention to interaction,

---

[68] Both *Kairos* and *Chronos* determine experience, yet whereas both are needed, it is the synchronised interaction *between* subjective (*Kairos*) and objective (*Chronos*) time that conditions perception.

as indicated by the stage directions, reveals why *Krapp's Last Tape* must be carefully coordinated to *be* performance. That is, a performance is an intrinsically dynamic, organic, and fluent event in which dramatic action, intensity, and characterization predicates on sustained communication within the whole performance context. This is why performance without audience is not performance, and why performance always changes. Performance is never the same from one moment to the next. Performance is not predictable even as it is performed to the same script. Performance *is* rhythm (for instance the rhythm of Krapp walking,) but performance also *moves* to a steady beat or pulse, and for as long as this underlying beat remains, actors may improvise *around* it. Actors may have to adjust the tempo of their interactions to maintain the rhythm of performance. This can be done, for instance, by modifying the tempo in which they deliver their lines. But actors may also maintain the rhythm of performance by knowing each other's lines and fill in for the one who forgets their lines, thereby maintaining the flow of performance.[69] Performance must go on to be performance, and performance *is* timed collaboration. Flow and interruption comprise sequencing, which builds tension, suspense, anticipation, and prediction. After all, if an interruption is too long, for instance if actors pause too long between their lines (or if the next tone in a musical piece comes too long after the former etc,) then audiences may not notice the arrival of the next sequence. Moreover, as the twelve *Warstellen* in *Godot* reveal, to take another example, the rhythm of performance may be modified, but only so far. The twelve *Warstellen* are staged for audiences to feel the "pressing reality of the silence", which according to Beckett, "is pouring into the play like water into a sinking ship" (*TN 1*, xxiv), yet unless carefully timed these *Warstellen* risk destabilize the performance, and actors must sense when to break the interruption and pick up the rhythm. In short, for

---

[69] By analogy, music and dance need not be metrically performed. If the underlying beat of the music and the dance is steady, then the musician and the dancer are free to move *around* that beat, linger and catch up as part of maintaining the music or dance, meeting and separating from each other yet held together by the underlying beat.

performance (any performance) to be performance, all elements within the performing ecology must consistently adjust the rhythm of performance. Indeed, performance *is* interaction, and a new syntax may be needed to account for this situation, one that takes *more than* words into consideration but also one that does not mistake what are merely parts for wholes.

Experiencing *vs* encountering

Now, so far, I have been talking about experiencing interchangeably with encountering, but there are important distinctions to be made between these two concepts that have implications also for my discussion of mis-movements in Beckett's drama. Notably, Martin Buber's 'twofold' attitude of man affords another route to further understanding the implications what Gendlin terms en#2 interaction, and since Gendlin's discussion is much more nuanced and complex than my discussion here is capable of rendering, I find Buber's distinctions to be a useful addition. My use of Gendlin's term 'experience' has centred on the mode of interaction that characterises body–en#2, although all Gendlin's modes of interaction depict ways in which to perceive body *and* environment. What Buber's perspective adds, however, is a perspective on interaction that helps me nuance my discussion of experience, specifically with reference to perception. Ultimately, Buber's assessment of the body's modes of interaction therefore allows me to qualify my claim that mis-movements necessitate a new syntax, one capable of capturing the bifocal nature of interaction.

According to Buber, the "attitude of man is twofold in accordance with the two basic words he can speak", yet the

> basic words are not single words but word pairs. One basic word is the word pair I–You. The other basic word is the word pair I-It; but this basic word is not changed when He or She take the place of It. Thus, the I of man is also twofold. For the basic word I–You is different from the basic word I–It"

(Buber 1996, 53)[70]

Notably, Buber's distinctions between 'I–it' and 'I–Thou' correspond well to Gendlin' notion of interaction: the basic word pair 'I–It' denotes a mode of experiencing analogous to Gendlin's notion of interaction type one (en#1), and the basic word pair 'I–You' corresponds to a mode of encountering analogous to Gendlin's notion of interaction type two (en#2). Each word pair denotes different modes of approaching the Other that seem analogous to the different modes of being in the world revealed by interaction type one and two. That is, both Gendlin's en#1 and Buber's word pair 'I–it' denote a spectator's view on interaction; and both Buber's word pair 'I–Thou' and Gendlin's en#2 denote a mode of interaction where body and other are entangled (cf. Gendlin 2018, 4).

On Buber's terms, then, both experiencing and encountering denote interactions, but the former denotes the type of interaction that 'I' has with its own 'I' (or with something that the I experiences,) and the latter the type of interaction that 'I' has with 'You' (or with something other than 'I' that approaches the I). Importantly, however, according to Buber, "Those who experience do not participate in the world. For the experience is 'in them' and not between them and the world" (1996, 56). Moreover, Buber maintains, experiencing the world of objects as already meaningful, is to be oriented towards the past (1996, 64).[71] By contrast, encountering 'You' entails interacting with

---

[70] Buber frequently refers to 'man', 'he', and 'it' and more rarely to 'she', never to transgender, non-binary, or something else. Given the nature of the topic discussed, however, I understand Buber's understanding of relations to be intrinsically inclusive and I have therefore chosen to retain the original wording throughout.

[71] This is how Buber phrases it: "Man goes over the surfaces of things and experiences them. He brings back from them some knowledge of their condition–an experience. He experiences what there is to things. But it is not experiences alone that bring the world to man. For what they bring to him is only a world that consists of It and It and It, of He and He and She and She and It."
(Buber 1996, 55).

the other, a mode of interaction takes place in the present since there are no words or concepts that could express what have not yet taken place. This is not to say that experiencing on Buber's account does not involve interpretation, or that spectators could not create meanings based on experiencing, as explained by Gendlin, nor is it to say that such meanings could not be true or valid in the sense of being deductively or inductively relevant. Only, to take the world as *already* meaningful in specific ways is to dwell in the natural attitude, and even if, as already discussed, most of life is lived in this mode, according to Buber the difference is that in such a mode, "one must pull and tear to turn a unity into a multiplicity" (Buber 1996, 59). By contrast, encountering proposes the other such that saying 'You' is to stand in relation to something or someone such that the immediacy of one coincides with the immediacy of the other. Experiencing, as opposed to encountering, then, is a mode of interaction that could be associated with the effort to interpret mis-movements in terms of linguistic or symbolic meanings, such that could be dug out by an inquiring mind. To those who encounter, however, "[e]very means is an obstacle" (Buber 1996, 63). Encountering entails participation, a mode of being directed at wholes rather than at parts. Encountering is also future-oriented since the future is an intrinsic dimension of the present, whereas the mode of experiencing takes the world as already given meaningfully in perception and so corresponds to the past. Indeed, says Buber, "[p]resence is not what is evanescent and passes but what confronts us, waiting, and enduring" (1996, 64). There are thus important nuances that distinguish Buber's modes of approaching the world from Gendlin's, yet their combined lenses provide fruitful perspectives on the role and function of mis-movements in Beckett's drama to solicit acts of meaning-making that predicate on interaction.

Notably, Ada, a female character in *Embers* (1959), understands the difference between experiencing and encountering well and talks about it with some degree of precision:

> ADA: Yes, you know what I mean, there are attitudes remain in one's mind for reasons that are clear, the carriage of a

head, for example, bowed when one would have thought it should be lifted, and vice versa, or a hand suspended in mid-air, as if unowned. That kind of thing.

(Beckett 2006, 263)

According to Ada, certain attitudes stand out for reasons that are clear, which is to say they stand on account of being ostensive, that is on account of deviating from what would be expected based on one's tacit knowledge of social and cultural meanings: A head tilted the wrong way or the gesture of a hand seemingly unowned fall short of embodied physical regimes of control, and this alone is reason enough to notice them. What Ada describes is therefore strikingly like approaching mis-movements as experiences in Buber's sense, or as interaction type en#1 in Gendlin's terminology.

However, as Ada explains, there are also attitudes that emerge to be noted for reasons that are not clear, and Henry's father sitting on a rock is a case in point (Beckett 2006, 262):

ADA: But with you father sitting on a rock that day nothing of the kind, no detail you could put your finger on and say, 'How very peculiar!' No, I could never make it out. Perhaps, as I said, just the great stillness of the whole body, as if the breath had left it.

(Beckett 2006, 263)

For reasons that are not clear, then, the father's posture is striking. Qualifying her claim, Ada explains that his posture "was a common one. You [Henry] used to have it sometimes. Perhaps just the stillness, as if he had been turned to stone. I could never make it out" (*CDW* 262). More than the shape of his body, however, it seems that it is the quality of stillness that speaks to her, a quality that pulls Ada into its centre, perhaps on account of a felt sense of belonging. In *Embers*, the father's stillness *dys*-appears and confronts Ada, awaits her, proposes her, in the sense described by Buber (1996, 64), but it also generates an en#2 (Gendlin) that forecloses preconceived ideas about meaning. What Ada describes is thus an encounter that involves a bodily knowing or felt sense, a perception that in Gendlin's words, constitutes a "going-on-in the en that is being perceived" (1997, 92). Ada senses the father's stillness in a manner that implies something *more than* merely watching the father sitting still, and notably Tolle's explanation of stillness seems to capture the mode of stillness she encounters:

> See that in the moment of noticing the silence around you, you are not thinking. You are aware but you are not thinking. / When you become aware of stillness, immediately there is that state of inner still alertness. You are present. You have stepped out of thousands of years of collective human conditioning.
>
> (Tolle 2003, 4-5)

Such stillness "dissolves the barriers created by conceptual thought" (cf. Tolle 2003, 19). It is a stillness that can only be encountered beyond the realm of thought. Indeed, such stillness prompts us to stop being "completely identified with thought, possessed by thought" (Tolle 2003, 25), and brings us back to the implied intricacy of felt sense as a source for meaning-making. Indeed, as Eckhart Tolle maintains, the "innermost sense of self ... is tied to stillness" (2003, 3).

The difference between experiencing and encountering thus implies that there are certain wholes, certain modes of interaction, certain paths or openings that speak to us, that sets up a structure of perception, which cannot be reduced to its parts. Arguably stillness is a quality that may be difficult to describe even if its power may be overwhelming. Yet, in encountering the father's stillness, Ada takes it as a whole, without particulars. Thus, she observes, there is "no detail you could put your finger on and say, 'How very peculiar!'" (Beckett 2006, 263). Encountering such stillness is to enter a relation with the basic word 'You', which is "more than It knows ... does more, and more happens to it, than It knows. No deception reaches this far: here is the cradle of actual life" (Buber 1996, 60). In contrast to the relation 'I–It', which characterizes the mode of experience, the reciprocity of encountering entails *re*-cognizing something—a tacit intricacy to be carried forward—but it also entails participating in something. If we try to categorize it as a concept, using words already known to us, then we shall encounter nothing because it exists "only insofar as presentness, encounter and relation exist" (Buber 1996, 63). The father's stillness is therefore not an object. It cannot be spoken about in terms of conventional knowledge because concepts are all 'the past', and encountering stillness is an act of recognition that takes place in 'the present', and "[b]efore the immediacy of the relationship everything mediate becomes negligible" (Buber 1996, 63). Ada's description of encountering stillness therefore illustrates the difference between modes of interaction that takes the world as already meaningful in and modes of interaction that attunes to the implicit intricacy of felt sense, which is characterised by something *more than* what we know.

Thus, stillness prompts reflection. Stillness implies a mode of interaction through which a body–en#2 complex may appear. To be still is to mismove, and so to momentarily stop or block the natural attitude. Yet even such blockages generate new occurrings, new implicit intricacies to be carried forward. As Ada observes, the father's stillness is an interruption, a stop in the communication which enfolds her. Indeed, the father's stillness cuts through the fabric of interaction like a knife.[72] Yet, the cut is an occurring into the future, which opens

---

[72] In a sense it corresponds to what Gaston Bachelard terms "a poetic instant", which is an instance of ordered time that cuts vertically through the layers of time, connecting layers of perspectives (2013, 58). Bachelard labels such "poetic time" *vertical* and contrasts it to "prosodic time", which he maintains is *horizontal* (2013, 58). The notions of vertical and horizontal are firmly temporal but the "poetic instant is ... complex: it moves, it

towards the unknown. While stillness seemingly prompts reduction in the phenomenological sense of bracketing Ada's habitual attitude, therefore, it does so only to the extent that it prompts, for instance, processes of abduction and interpretation, which is tantamount to generating the necessary conditions of possibility for perceiving past, present and future meanings. As the analysis of stillness in *Embers* reveals, mis-movements *always* imply *something more*. With reference to Henry's stillness, Ada says she cannot make it out, yet her descriptions of the differences between attitudes that 'remain in one's mind for reasons that are clear' and the father's stillness, illustrate the notion of felt sense. There is always something more to be felt and carried forward. In *Embers,* that something occurs *into* the implying of stillness and derives from stopped en#2-body interaction. By analogy, mis-movements in Beckett's drama are blockages or interruptions to interaction that imply *something more,* and in trying to carry that something forward, we may arrive to embrace the invitation to intellectual freedom that opens out in the context of Beckett's drama.[73]

Timing

As the analysis of mis-movements reveals, then, the 'zone of being'[74] that Beckett creatively explores is permeated by the invisible structures that make up interaction, for instance body–en#2, occurring, implying, and encountering., and the rich and nuanced

---

proves—it invites, it consoles—it is astonishing and familiar. It is essentially a harmonic relation between two opposites", ambivalence and passion, "knit together in time" (Bachelard 2013, 59).

[73] Indeed, as Lois Oppenheim observes about Beckett's work, "the visual work of art comes to be revealed not as an object or thing, but agent of both artist's and spectator's seeing" (2003, 100). The ambiguous contour of Beckett's artistic project therefore evolves precisely around the notion that artistic expression makes claims on the spectator's attention without explaining what it means to perceive and experience it.

[74] Beckett qtd by Israel Schenker from an interview in *The New York Times,* May 5, 1956

understanding of time consciousness provided by phenomenology affords a perspective on *how* mis-movements arrive to enfold both interaction, blocking, and carrying forward of various levels of temporality. Phenomenologically speaking, objective time "can be experienced as enduring, only because we experience a succession of mental activities in our subjective life" (Sokolowski 2008, 132). The "domain of internal time consciousness underlies both the subjective flow of internal time and the objective flow of world time, transcendent time" (Sokolowski 2008, 140):

> the fact that things and experiences unfold and persist in time is not a just a mechanical or psychological fact; it originates from a deeper level. This level is the spring for all formal structures, such as those found in logic, mathematics, syntax and the various modes of presentation.

(Sokolowski 2008, 144).

Time is thus the dimension within which "the living present succeeds itself" (Sokolowski 2008, 141); and so "the issues of internal time consciousness underlie the issues of truth and disclosure" (Sokolowski 2008, 145), a situation that seems mirrored in Buber's understanding of encountering as a mode of being future oriented. Indeed, as Sokolowski explains, "[t]ime pervades all things, both noematic and noetic" (2008, 130). If experiencing is mode of taking the world of objects for perception as *already meaningful* and so is towards the past (equivalent to en#1), therefore, then encountering is a mode of inviting the future (equivalent to en#2) in which, as Gendlin explains, the "carrying-forward sequence gives us a new concept of time", a concept that is nonlinear, which is to say a "time of internal relations, rather than the usual time which consists of perfectly present positions that are not related to each other unless an observer externally relates them" (Gendlin 2004, 137).

Unless we manage to synchronize objective clock time with our internal subjective time, however, we shall not arrive anywhere, and nothing will arrive at us. As Ahmed points out, "At least two entities must arrive to create an encounter" (2006, 39). Things must "co-incide"—the dash here seemingly carries the implied intricacy of multiplicity forwards—for the arrival to be "a happening that brings things near to other things, whereby the nearness shapes the shape of each thing" (Ahmed 2006, 38). Notably, as has been discussed above, mis-movements generate temporal layers for perception. This is not to say that mis-movements prompt an introspective gaze. On the contrary, mis-movements call us to be with the aesthetic object, to stay with it, and—in so doing—to abandon our subjectivity, *viz.* our preconceived notions about meaning.[75] Phenomenologically speaking, however, *both* temporal *and* spatial relations structure perception. Both qualitative time (*Kairos*) and quantitative time (*Chronos*), respectively, provide a useful explanation of different levels of temporality. For instance, to meet up with another person, it is not enough to show up *in* the right place (*Chronos*), but you must also show up *at* that precise moment in time (*Kairos*), as Vladimir and Estragon painfully discover. Many have probably experienced a situation like that of Vladimir and Estragon's in *Godot*. The two characters show up for their appointment with Godot, but— since they not to do so at the time when the appointment was scheduled, and since they also have a somewhat imprecise idea of where they agreed to meet ("You're sure it was here?" *TN I* 13: 154; "You're sure it was this evening?" *TN I* 14:194)—they end up in limbo. Didi and Gogo's situation may be unusually precarious, yet the feeling of being in limbo, of being consistently in the wrong place at the wrong time, seems to haunt contemporary life. The two characters could thus be seen to epitomize a very human predicament, namely that of timing. The potential arrival

---

[75] In Eugene Gendlin's theory of subjectivity, there is no subject and no object separate from interaction, but shades of subjectivity emerge in and through interaction with other subjects and objects. The split between object and subject is therefore no longer valid as both the subject and the object will be different in different contexts.

of Godot shapes Didi and Gogo's waiting. Even though Godot never comes, the perhaps of his arrival, together with the characters' need to be saved, 'co-incides' or interacts. Waiting is therefore *more than* an interruption in the characters' lives. Waiting proposes Godot's coming, and Godot's coming proposes waiting; indeed, it is this double bind (see Bateson 2000, 276) that conditions the characters' waiting, even if Didi and Gogo seemingly preoccupy themselves with whatever they can think of, "blathering about nothing in particular" (*TN I* 59: 1902), perhaps to foreclose this insight. Yet perhaps, too, this is all we can do unless we arrive to synchronize objective and internal time, in which case we may arrive to discover something new. Arriving somewhere is a matter of being directed at something (a place, an object, and idea), but it is also a matter of how that something "approaches" us, which is to say it is a matter of *timing* (Ahmed 2006, 2). Thus, for instance, a novel that did not speak to us at all may open up a whole new perspective as we return to read it ten years later. We now find that we are perfectly aligned with its message, in sync with the text in a way we could not be before and so we experience it differently. Likewise, our interactions with people, animals, food, houses, paintings, books, etc. will never be the same from one moment to the next. Indeed, being in sync with the world is key to how we feel about ourselves and others.

Abduction

To expand the interpretative frame for addressing mis-movements and to reconfigure mis-movements as interaction that proposes encountering implied intricacies, is therefore not to discard meaning. It is merely to acknowledge that the process of carrying forward always entails discovering something *more*. Gendlin even suggests that we "can think with a '…..' after every word or sentence" (1997, xi). There is around every "experience, something that gives the experience meaning", says Gendlin, and his use of experience here seems to comprise both experiencing and encountering. The effort to prompt audiences to abandon their foothold in linguistic meanings is therefore not to foreclose meaning, but a way to create openings from which thinking may proceed, a way of 'paying it forward', as it were.

Arguably, however, attention is too simplistically understood along the lines of perception (Gendlin 2004, 128). Because to carry something forward, which is self-reflexively to carry one's attention forward, is also a discovery of how the past "happens into" the present:

> As a concept, "carrying forward" does also have the usual kind of pattern, a structure, a kind of diagram in empty space. It contains the spatial pattern of forward (and backward), and also the pattern of "carrying," i.e., something taken and moved by something else. But this alone says very little. The concept means our use of it at this juncture, where words (it could be actions) let a precise implying no longer hang there, but take it along.
>
> (Gendlin 2004, 138).

As Gendlin maintains, "'[m]ere attention' is not 'mere' … What attending lifts up is a product" (2004, 144). We are not neutral subjects directing neutral beams towards objects, but we "live in situational bodies which always sense themselves in sensing anything else" (2004, 128). Thus, attending to for example mis-movements is always to *imply* a next step, to generate a product (experience, encounter, perspective insights, association etc.,) to reckoned with, *as well as* acknowledging such responses. This is no different from attending to the meaning of words, only we rarely acknowledge our own complicity in manufacturing the ideas that we cherish or disregard.

The mode in which such occurring may be taken to imply seems analogous to what Pierce terms 'abduction' or 'snatching'. According to Pierce, "[a]bduction is the process of forming an explanatory hypothesis. It is the only logical operation which introduces any new idea; for induction does nothing but determine a value, and deduction merely evolves the necessary consequences of a pure hypothesis" (Pierce 2014, 5.171.[76] Importantly, abduction differs from deduction and induction in that "Deduction proves that something must be; Induction shows that something actually is operative; Abduction merely suggests that something may be." (Peirce 2014, 5.171). That something may be abducted or snatched sideways, however, does not suggest relativism. Rather, according to Daniel J. McKaughan, "Pierce takes abductive reasoning to lead to judgements about the relative *pursuitworthiness* of theories" (McKaughan 2008, 447). Thus, for instance, with reference to mis-movements, the patterns they produce may arguably be *pursuitworthy* occurrences in this respect, or they may not, depending on our inclinations. Yet, if mis-movements are 'differences that make a difference', which is to say information (see Bateson 2002, 92), then the question is: what is the nature of the information produced by mis-movements in the context of performance and what do spectators do with it? And abduction seemingly opens a fruitful perspective on such questions. Abduction proposes an epistemology that not only takes the connections between pre-linguistic and linguistic meanings into account, but also the kind of double description where one characteristic component, for instance social relation, is mirrored in another realm, for instance physical comportment. If the natural attitude makes it difficult for people to see through the veil, then double description, or abduction, entails 'seeing the world in a grain of sand' (William Blake, "Auguries of Innocence"). Indeed, abduction is poetic in that it connects phenomena on different scales (in Blake's poem a grain of sand plus world), but it also proposes a new syntax within which such experiencing or encountering may take linguistic shape.

---

[76] Peirce: CP 5.171 Cross-Ref: †† (*The Collected Papers of Charles Sanders Peirce*. URL:

Syllogisms in grass

Notably, according to Bateson, one could also fruitfully compare abduction to a "syllogism in grass" (1988, 26).[77] In fact, Bateson maintains, "all preverbal and nonverbal communication depends on metaphor and syllogisms in grass" (1988, 28), a kind of seeing that connects things across domains. This is not to say that verbal communication is not also metaphoric (Bateson 1988, 28–29). But the syllogisms in grass, according to Bateson are primordial, in fact there would be no syllogisms in Barbara without syllogisms in grass.

The difference between a 'syllogism in Barbara' and a 'syllogism in grass' is in Bateson expressed in the following:

> Men die;
>
> Socrates is a man;
>
> Socrates will die.
>
> The basic structure of this little monster—its skeleton—is built upon classification. ... The syllogisms of metaphor are quite different, and go like this:
>
> Grass dies;
>
> Men die;
>
> Men are grass.
>
> (G. Bateson and M.C. Bateson, 1987, 26)

A 'syllogism in grass', in contrast to a 'syllogism in Barbara' (AAA), "connects biological data" (Bateson 1987, 27), such as, for instance, "the whole of animal behaviour, the whole of repetitive anatomy, and the whole of biological evolution—each of these vast realms is within itself linked together by syllogisms in grass whether the logicians like it or not" (*Ibid.*). Thus, the syllogism in grass works like abduction in

---

[77] "A 'syllogism in grass' "is considered an example of how an abductive reasoning process can offer an alternative way of reasoning to deductive (and inductive) reasoning" (Lockton 2022,4).

that it suggests potential relations between components without saying anything valid about the components themselves, a fact that does not rule out the possibility of saying something true. Yet according to Dan Lockton, "the point is that 'people are grass' offers something unusual, unexpected, yet still, perhaps, profound, and so affords an opening to re-construct our understanding of the world. In short, it gives us a way of seeing" (Lockton 2018); a lens "for seeing the systems we are in differently" (2022, 6). A syllogism in grass, however, is a way of linking ideas, of connecting patterns, that does not pertain to validity or veracity, but to association. It is "a provocation [that] can prompt seeing larger patterns —patterns that (might) help us see relationships and connect ideas across scales and seemingly unconnected parts of the living world" (Lockton 2022, 5). And if the process of abduction proposes "conclusions that could be thoroughly disconnected from assessments of truth-value (McKaughan 2008, 447), then the syllogism in grass could be seen to do the same.

Bateson's discussion of 'syllogisms in grass' affords a fruitful conduit to understand the processes by means of which mis-movements arrive to be meaningful in Beckett's drama. Phenomenologically speaking, the phrase 'people are grass' suggests an eidetic perspective on both people and grass that require comparing seemingly unrelated things and, perhaps, experiencing them as connected, without necessarily having to drive home a specific point. Even if you accept the first premise of a syllogism in grass you may struggle to accept its illogical conclusion. And this is also mis-movements work. Mis-movements solicit processes of abduction on account of linking seemingly unrelated realms of the lifeworld together in thought provoking images that connect biological data of various kinds, and so they afford a route to see the system differently. Many characters in Beckett's drama interact with their environment in unusual ways. For example, Winnie is buried in a mound (*Happy Days*); May verifies her existence by listening to the sound of her feet falling (*Footfalls*); and Krapp's recorded voice simultaneously dislocates Krapp in the present and connects him to the past *(Krapp's Last Tape)*. Moreover, Beckett's drama connects bodies with objects, for instance urns (*Play*) and bins (*Endgame*). Moreover, with reference to Beckett's prose, Amanda Dennis observes that "embodiment in Beckett … often involves a human body literally inserted into language, packed earth, mud, jars, urns, bins and so forth" (2023, 210). Notably, the syllogism in grass structure of such presentations evokes notions of human situatedness and embodied experience, framed by various modes of interaction, that open new perspectives on the world.

To give this idea a bit of context, I propose that the syllogism in grass-structure of Winnie's situatedness in *Happy Days* emerges as an interruption to the audiences' habitual strategies of sense-making, simultaneously part of the narrative discourse that *is* performance, and of the interpretative context for interpretation that *is* human situatedness in the world. Winnie's body is not separate from its environment, but Winnie and the mound *are* one 'body-en#2', a situation which implies something *more than* merely a woman stuck in the ground. In act one, Winnie is "[e]mbedded up to above her waist in exact centre of mound" (Beckett 2006, 138), and in act two "embedded up to neck, hat on head, eyes closed. Her head, which she can no longer turn, nor bow, nor raise, faces front motionless throughout act" (Beckett 2006, 160). The syllogism in grass structure of Winnie's situation inevitably draws attention to her immobility, not as a signpost for philosophical mobility bias, nor as an instance of Beckett's creative fictionalisation of her reality, but *as* body–en#2 interaction, a mode of being which disrupts habitual modes of interpretation.

Yet Winnie is also occurring that implies *more than* what she says or does. Interaction defines her being and implies a human situatedness which is paradoxically universal. In a sense, we are all Winnie, intrinsically earthbound: we are all part of the environment, defined by interaction, only we may not realize it. Even more to the point, Winnie's existential fit, *viz.* 'body-en#2' makes it impossible for spectators to disregard her situation. Winnie's situation affords an encounter *with* and thinking *from,* the specific context presented in *Happy Days*, a context conditioned by the interaction between body–en#2, between Winnie and the mound. Winnie in the mound is also an interruption to interpretation, much like Ada describes the father's stillness in *Embers*, Winnie interrupts habitual strategies of meaning-making, just like pauses interrupt the flow of her speech, or like the way in which her speech interrupts her silence, or like the bell interrupts her sleep. In the context of *Happy Days*, interruption is conditioned by interaction, which paradoxically partakes *both* in the fictive context of performance *and* in the real world of the stage as the prefigurative general context within which the performance must be taken. What spectators arrive to abduct from encountering Winnie in the mound, or what they arrive to make of such an interruption to interpretation, however, is similarly a matter of interaction, between spectator and performance; and spectators are invited to carry such implicit intricacies forward even as their felt sense of the implicit intricacy of encountering Winnie may never reach the level of conscious experiencing.

Importantly, therefore, the image of Winnie buried up to her waist and neck in a mound implies modes of interaction that are difficult to capture. Given that we tend to think about body and environment, self and Other, You and I etc. as separate entities that may or may not interact, we may say that our conceptualisation of interaction (as intrinsic to our situatedness) is hampered by a language use (or syntax) that implies separation, division, fragmentation, and individuation. Interaction on this account is that which happens between discrete units, be that people or entities and things. Yet, it could also be something entirely different. Something that implies our intrinsic belonging to the ground, as well as blocks or disrupts habitual strategies of interpretation. Interaction resembles a kind of double description (abduction). As such it affords a kind of seeing where one characteristic component (social relation etc.), is mirrored in another realm (physical comportment), a syllogism in grass that prompt abduction.

'Binocular vision'

To capture the meaning of Beckett's stage images we may therefore need what Bateson calls "a binocular vision", that is a kind of phenomenological eidetic seeing that synthesizes things named within a mode of experiencing an encounter. Mary Catherine Bateson links it to "the same kind of looking that recognizes the spirals of growth in shells as the frozen form of cyclones and galaxies" (qtd in Lockton 2022, 5). Arguably, mis-movements have the potential to provoke binocular vision. Mis-movements seem to provide what Lockton describes as a "creative method of provocation and reframing" (2022, 5), a kind of binocular vision or double perspective on the patterns that connect. And it is the 'syllogism of grass'-structure of mis-movements that affords such mode of attention. Mis-movements become conduits for thinking about interaction (although obviously not all spectators will arrive to connect the different realms that open up through mis-movements or follow such lines of flight), because the structure of mis-movements, the fact of their being ostensive, suggests a direction for thinking about something *more than* words could perhaps convey. Just as a name is not the thing named, or the description of mis-movements is not the mismoving, so the syllogism in grass-structure of mis-movements may give rise to a myriad of things, potentially to be named, or merely carried forward as tacit intricacies that may imply new occurings. Experience always takes place in a context, is always 'experience of *something*', an encountering with feelings, situations, for instance in a drama that predicates on interaction. Yet, even as the mind thinks in images, and even if we give all sorts of names to such thinking, there is always something *more than* the name, something merely implied in the experience that the name cannot capture, but which is key to our felt sense of the experience, the encounter, or the perception.

This is not to say that all mis-movements provoke binocular vision. The question of responsiveness to binocular vision is another matter entirely, even as the syllogism in grass structure of mis-movements imply connections beyond the words used to describe them. Gendlin writes implying in terms of '(…..)', to indicate that what appears need not be known to us in such a way that we can categorize it in order to be known *as something*. What Lockton says about syllogisms in grass therefore seems relevant also for mis-movements:

> there is *something* here—a glimpse of what could be a kernel of a creative process which links concepts across domains and scales, particularly those involving living systems (which give [*Sic.*] humans' presence in everything, means that most technological and societal systems also come within scope). It is not about logic: as Bateson (1980/1991: 240) put it, "it seemed that perhaps, while not always logically sound, [the syllogism in grass] might be a very useful contribution to the principles of life. Life, perhaps, doesn't ask what is logically sound, I'd be very surprised if it did."
>
> (Lockton 2022, 3)

The *something there* is the information implied by the syllogism in grass. And I would argue that that is also how mis-movements imply *something* in this sense.

'A sacred unity'

Mis-movements, then, invite following new paths of thinking, invite us to co-create meaning in the context of performance. In any given context, we are actively, but also passively, involved in creating meaning through a process interconnecting non-discursive experience to self-reflective thinking. Bateson conceptualizes this process as a "sacred unity" between creator and created—"a creative filter between us and the world, [which] is always inevitably there" (1991, 264), and so we are always both "creature and creator" (1991, 264.). To create inevitably entails self-reflexive thinking, which is to say learning something more about oneself (Bateson 1991, 263). And, according to Bateson, it is the something more implied in experience that prompts self-reflexive re-cognition. Quoting a stanza from Wallace Stevens' "The Man with the Blue Guitar",[78] he comments that "the poet sees himself divided from 'Things as they are.' Indeed, there is matter about which the organism (the poet, in this case) can say nothing" (1991, 264). Things that are "ineffable", but which will still be part of the poem, and therefore also of its criticism. This, Bateson maintains, "is the circumstance for all organisms" (1991, 264). Everything we read, see, hear, or engage with, has always been "doctored" (Bateson 1991, 264). And perception is therefore always guided by what we already know about the world or believe that we know. As already discussed, in phenomenological terms this is called the natural attitude, and it is the process by means of which we make sense of the world: "'We', like the general of a modern army, read only intelligent reports already doctored by agents who partly know what we want to read. And our outputs are similarly doctored—the outputs must, forsooth, be harmonious" (Bateson 1991, 264). By analogy, aesthetic experience is similarly never merely a matter of seeing an object as aesthetic. Rather, it entails a process of "selecting, shaping, and combining 'data chosen' from the lower levels", which is to say from the deeper levels of pre-logic perception (James qtd in Schusterman 2011, 350). Thus, the:

> world we perceive or experience is not a fixed, independent, mutable given but rather a product of human selection in which the selective process involves different levels and can be likened to artistic creation, especially because the criteria for selection are in large part aesthetic.
>
> (Schusterman 2011, 350)

In short, according to William James, whose account is strikingly like Bateson's, the "mind works on the data it receives very much as a sculptor works on his block of stone" (qtd in Schusterman 2011, 350).

---

[78] "Poetry is the subject the poem, /From this the poem issues and .../ To this returns ..." (Stevens, 1937).

At the "core of aesthetic experience"—but arguably any experience—is "a unifying, nameless quality that resists conceptual description or explicitly foregrounded reference" (Schusterman 2011, 358). And those backgrounds that we are at loss to explain have shaped our understanding of the whole and envelop our snatchings (abductions) with "a halo of felt relations" (see Schusterman 2011, 359). The issue of how to move beyond the natural attitude, without discarding it, is therefore central to artistic creation.

Notably, mis-movements provide a useful artistic means to this effect. Mis-movements afford a mode of apprehending the sideways relations that enfold objects of perception in Beckett's drama. Mis-movements open processes of emergence and solicit a mode of attending to such sideways relations. To experience mis-movements is to trace their points, lines, alignments, directions, orientations etc.—in other words, their spatial and temporal qualities. Importantly, therefore, the significance of mis-movement is not related to the actual mis-movement—indeed causes are not effects—but to their effects. By means of mis-movements, Beckett is not merely able to jolt audiences out of habitual linguistic appropriation of meaning, but he is also able to refocus the spectators' attention on the dynamics of aesthetic experience.

Slanting perspectives

In this chapter, I have extended my analyses sideways, trying to capture what it means to experience mis-movements in Beckett's drama rather than explain what mis-movements mean. In so doing, I have followed up on Beckett's scepticism towards language by tracing mis-movements back to their embodied roots, specifically to address how mis-movements arrive to *imply* in the sense described by Gendlin's phenomenology, which emphasize focusing as a route to understand experience as determine by interaction (1978). Admittedly, Gendlin's process model of thinking is a psychotherapeutic methodology, and its aim is to open a path to "personal change", specifically by means on the "inner act" of focusing (Gendlin 1978,

11). Yet my aim has not been to suggest that focusing on mis-movements in the context of Beckett's drama would solicit personal change (although I would not rule out such a possibility). Nor have I sought to expand on the psychological implications of Beckett's drama. Rather, my aim is to suggest that mis-movements open paths to embodied cognition and that Gendlin's process model of thinking is useful for explaining how this happens. My use of Gendlin's terminology has thus aimed to clarify why tracing mis-movements in performance could entail tapping into the felt sense. Even so, I have not attempted to address what such experiencing would be like for individual spectators. In other words, I have not been suggesting that Beckett's drama is therapeutical, although, again, I am not denying this possibility. But I have suggested that Gendlin's model of interaction is helpful to understand how mis-movements draw spectators into the event of performance, how mis-movements block habitual strategies of interpretation, how mis-movements solicit carrying forward of implicit intricacies, and so why encountering mis-movements may be a highly specific experience even as it may be difficult to state in words and to share.

Mis-movements afford encounters. They invite spectators to become involved, to see new connections and to cultivate a different mode of attention to the stage presentation, one that does not rehearse conventional ideas but rather stays attentive to that "gleam of light", which, according to Emerson announces personal, genuine thinking (2009, 59).[79] The process of undermining habitual modes of thinking, however, is as much matter of reframing the context for interpretation as it is about finding a strategy to capture the audiences' attention; and mis-movements are instrumental to this effect. That is, the play's creation *as* performance seems contingent on the spectators' responsivity to mis-movements. Thus, I have suggested that Beckett's drama affords routes to re-connect with personal experience,

---

[79] Indeed, Emerson maintains, "in every work of genius we recognize our own rejected thoughts; they come back to us with a certain alienated majesty" (2009, 59).

specifically, by letting aesthetic experience pave the ground for intellectual freedom. That is, because mis-movements appear as forms without content that nonetheless have the power to capture the audiences' attention, they open a feedback loop whereby spectators may tap into their embodied responses to such presentations, and embodied responses are always more precise than words. In short, words and meanings always come after the fact. And the intrinsic interconnections between experiencing and thinking act as conduits to interpretation that prompt spectators to engage with their own responses to the patterns that appear in the context of performance. To ask about the status of mis-movements as tools for artistic expression in Beckett's drama is therefore to ask about the potential implications of a drama that has reconfigured the context for communication from an aesthetic object to a performing ecology within which aesthetic experiencing is defined as interaction. Notably, however, it is not to abandon interpretation or analysis. It is to tap into the implicit intricacy of felt sense, a dimension of experience underneath or beyond the reality we conceptualize in language, inherently shaping the meanings we create.

Indeed, there is "a deep relationship between artistic possibility exploration and possibility exploration in phenomenology which reveals the kinship between phenomenology and art" (Idhe 1986, 148). This relationship, Don Idhe asserts, is specifically noticeable at the level of imagination, as the human faculty which makes both art and phenomenology possible, and it is therefore "no accident that almost every phenomenologist … has made some comment on the arts or a more systematic foray into examining them" (ibid.). By analogy, in the foreword to *Phenomenology, Modernism, and Beyond,* Kevin Hart suggests that all artists could be seen to do phenomenology (2010, xi). Referencing a letter from Edmund Husserl to Hugo von Hofmannsthal, he maintains:

> The artist was doing phenomenology before the term was coined. The artist sees into the heart of things, sees eidetically. More, the artist sees how meaning is made: it is his or her craft that

prompts reduction, and his or her experience of writing or painting or composing that teaches us that reduction is never complete.

(Hart 2010, xi)

Hart's comment is thought-provoking as it emphasizes the power of art to show us something more about the natural attitude, something that phenomenology perhaps otherwise would be at a loss to express. A work of art "it is a place where many regions of being overlap and commune" (Hart 2010, xiii). Like phenomenology art invites us to rethink and question what we already know, and "[i]t is out of possibility that the undiscovered is found and created" (Idhe 1986, 148). Indeed, phenomenology and art both function as explorations of the possible and "the freedom of essential research in phenomenology re-quires necessarily 'operating in fantasy'" (Elliott 2005, 60). If to create is to take away (for example objects, substances, meanings, and values,) then this is in order clear a path for seeing things more clearly in the contexts where they appear. It is also to clear a path for attending to that which dwells underneath, behind, inside, or beyond the ideals, standards, or materials that propose themselves to the natural attitude. Thus, "it possible to see the practice of the artist as latently phenomenological from the outset" (Idhe 1986, 148).

Phenomenology, then, seems to provide a useful mode of apprehending the relations that enfold objects of perception in Beckett's drama, on the one hand because it emphasizes processes of arrival, but on the other hand because its understanding of intentionality as a mode of perception within which the world emerges, proposes a route for attending to "the flow of perception itself" (Ahmed 2006, 37). Indeed, much like kōans, Beckett's drama affords a specific frame for interpretation, one that takes off from embodied cognition and interaction as the basis for evaluation. Kōans are riddles "said to be intentionally designed to illustrate the illogicality—or at least the alogicality—of existence" (Sansonese 1994, 12). As riddles, kōans could potentially be solved and so they would seem distinctly different from Beckett's drama. Yet as J. Nigro Sansonese explains: "It's not necessary to plead the universe guilty of felonious illogic when a confession of *petite doubl'entendre* would do" (1994, 13). Solving a kōan is less about rational thinking and more about embodied cognition: in short, a kōan "is the same riddle as the sound your ears make, of one hand clapping, of snow falling" (Sansonese 1994, 14). Kōans invite us to encounter the immediacy of the body's participation in experience, which always enfolds the body *and* something else: I, You, the Other, touching, falling, remembering etc. The answer to the question of 'what is the sound of one hand clapping?', is basically *"the sound of your own ears"* (Sansonese 1994, 13). To solve a kōan, one must pay attention to the relationship *between* the body *and* the world, and this is also how Beckett's drama resembles kōans. Kōans produce the necessary conditions of possibility for finding heuristic solutions to conceptual problems. By analogy, Beckett's creative solution to the predicament of expression entails letting mis-movements serve a similar function.[80] Mis-movements invite audiences to encounter the sound of feet falling (*Footfalls, Krapp's Last Tape*) or the image of a woman stuck in the ground (*Happy* Days), to name but a few examples. Such images invite spectators to pay attention to the patterns that connect (Bateson) and to think *from* such experiencing (Gendlin). To pay attention to mis-movements is to pay attention to one's own experiencing, and to the modes of encountering such experiencing in the context of performance. It is also to re-connect with embodied cognition as a path to insight, which

---

[80] Admittedly, many twentieth century artists seem to have been interested in capturing this insight, such as, for instance, Marcel Duchamp's *In Advance of the Broken Arm* or John *Cage's 4.33*. Notably, Duchamp was not interested in art that was visual but believed that the idea always came before the visual 'representation' of the same. John Cage's most famous work is the 'silent' composition, *4.33*, first performed by the German pianist David Tudor. The piece consists of the pianist sitting by the piano without playing a single note for four minutes and thirty-three seconds.

is why mis-movements could be seen to afford a route to *do* phenomenology as it were.[81]

Unsurprisingly, Beckett has been frequently lauded for his capacity to challenge convention and for his integrity as a creator of works that defy simple categorization. In a 1954 interview, Harold Pinter stated the following:

> The farther he goes the more good it does me. I don't want philosophies, tracts, dogmas, creeds, ways out, truths, answers, nothing from the bargain basement. He is the most courageous, remorseless writer going and the more he grinds my nose in the shit the more I am grateful to him. He's not fucking me about, he's not leading me up any garden path, he's not slipping me a wink, he's not flogging me a remedy or a path or a revelation or a basinful of breadcrumbs, he's not selling me anything I don't want to buy — he doesn't give a bollock whether I buy or not — he hasn't got his hand over his heart. Well, I'll buy his goods, hook, line and sinker, because he leaves no stone unturned and no maggot lonely. He brings forth a body of beauty. His work is beautiful.
>
> (Pinter qtd in Graver & Federman, 1979, 12)

Without commenting on the body in performance, Pinter's appreciation of Beckett's work still captures the quality of Beckett's drama that I associate with mis-movements. According to Pinter, Beckett does him good precisely because he is not trying to do him anything at all. There are no concealed messages, no clues, no appeal to the rational faculty of the mind or the empathic faculty of the heart:

---

[81] In this sense Beckett's drama is also reminiscent of Butho, the "dance of utter darkness ... *ankotu butho* ... attributed to the legacy of Hiroshima (Au 1997, 199). In Butho, "time is frequently slowed down" to create images that, by means of "the precision and economy of movement [,] heighten the anonymity and impersonality of much of human existence" (Au 1997, 199). And, as Susan Au explains, "Butho's primary aim is the expression of man's inner life" (1997, 199).

no 'creed' or 'dogma', as it were. And yet, Pinter seems to be affected, perhaps even transformed, by Beckett's work, even as he vouches that Beckett has no intention to change him; and it is seemingly the experience of being taken along or carried forward, at certain precise junctures in Beckett's work that thrills him. Of course, what Pinter welcomes in Beckett's work is unrelated to aestheticism, and my drawing out links between Pinter's response to Beckett's work and the process of responding to mis-movements may thus seem unwarranted. But my aim is not to challenge Pinter's statement about the lack of intention in Beckett's work. It is merely to suggest that Beckett's work, seemingly, is an experience that transports you somewhere, and that this was also what Pinter's statement signals.

Indeed, what Pinter's statement reveals is that Beckett's work is an invitation to experience something merely implicit, beyond language. By analogy, my argument in this chapter has been that mis-movements are intrinsic to producing implied intricacies, and that mis-movements therefore are more important to the formation of meaning in Beckett's plays than has previously been acknowledged. Mis-movements open paths to ineffable or tacit dimensions of experience. But mis-movements also present a challenge Cartesian dualism in that they accommodate interconnections between sense and sense-making, embodied experience and language. If the flow of experience is a tidal wave enfolding *both* sense *and* non-sense, *both* body *and* mind, *both* absence *and* presence, *both* sound *and* silence, *both* parts *and* wholes, *both* identity *and* difference etc., then making sense of mis-movements in the context of performance entails *both* experiencing something (a felt sense,) *and* carrying this experience forward into new contexts. Mis-movements make spectators agents of meaning-making such that the binary structure of presentation/representation dissolves. The implicit demand of experiencing *something* is to carry it forward in language, not necessarily to explain it (this may even be impossible) but to merge it *both* with previous experience *and* project new modulations of implicit intricacies, ambiguities, that may or may not become insights or that may or may not, arrive to be captured in language as meaningful statements, whether about Beckett's drama or about the experience of Beckett's drama. In short, even a holistic ecological perspective on Beckett's drama must recognize that the lacunas, gaps, and inconsistencies that condition experience in this context seem inherently meaningful, and that the process of carrying such implicit intricacies forward is not the same thing as rendering its shape in language. Comparing Beckett's solution to the predicament of expression to Bateson's ecological theory of mind, but also to Gendlin's phenomenological analysis of carrying forward and to Buber 's analysis of the difference between experiencing and encountering, I have therefore suggested that neither explicit nor implicit aspects of mis-movements should be discarded. More than interpretative dilemmas mis-movements are conduits for spectators to re-connect with the implied intricacy of felt sense. By setting the stage for a participatory engagement with the stage presentation, Beckett's drama projects an intricate, messy, collective, open background for perception that enfolds *more than* the mis-movements perceived, *more than* the flow of shifting typologies, and *more than* the effects of such transformations.

Clearly, then, Beckett's drama demands attention beyond recognizing its obscurity or lack of signification. After all, Beckett's writing was transformed by the recognition of 'his own stupidity', *viz.* his failure to recognize the significance of feeling: "*Molloy* and the others came to me the day I became aware of my own folly. Only then did I begin to write the things I feel" (*DF* 319), a statement that merits attention, not because feelings are personal responses but because feelings are firmly embodied and Beckett's acknowledgement of feeling as a resource for writing hints at his recognition of the significance of embodied meaning for intellectual growth. In short, Beckett's drama solicits feelings rather than analyses, and as E. M. Forster suggests in the epigraph to *Howards End*, feelings always mean: "Only connect ..." (2002).

Chapter 3   Down

On August 18, 1955, Beckett comments in a letter to Pamela Mitchell that *Waiting for Godot* is really a "skeleton simple" play, and that he is puzzled by the "endless misunderstandings it seems to provoke everywhere" (Beckett qtd in Craig et al. 2011, 540). The claim is difficult to reconcile with the enormous response the play has generated. It is also difficult to reconcile with the enormous response generated by Beckett's creative work more broadly, *Godot* being a case in point. Beckett's creative productions span drama and poetry, as well as works for radio, television, and film, and he also wrote a substantial number of critical essays and reviews on art and literature. In addition, Beckett has won the Nobel Prize in Literature (1969), several Obie Awards, and prizes have also been instigated in his name.[82] In fact, he is generally acknowledged to be one of the twentieth century's most important literary artists (Oppenheim 2004, 1). Notably, too, Beckett's reputation precedes him. Epigrammatic notions of the complexity and the relevance of his work and of its themes have seeped into popular culture, influencing a range of dramatist, poets, and novelists (McDonald 2006, 1). Indeed, as Rónán McDonald points out, "[t]he word 'Beckettian' resonates even amongst those who know little Beckett", evoking notions of "sparseness and minimalism and, with them, a forensic, pitiless urge to strip away, to expose, to deal with piths and essences", (McDonald 2006, 1). Finally, Beckett's work has lent itself to a variety of readings, as reflected by the multitude of critical orientations in Beckett studies. It is therefore difficult to accept Beckett's own claim about simplicity. In fact, given the massive response generated by his creative work, including *Godot*, how could it be described as 'skeleton simple'?

With reference to the issue of audience response, however, Beckett's complaint that *Godot* is 'skeleton simple' takes on a different meaning. Typically, complexity is considered a quality marker of

---

[82] For example, The Oxford Samuel Beckett Theatre Trust Award (2003).

literary works. Complex works are evidence of artistic aptitude and audiences tend to valorize complex works over simplistic ones. To say that a work is complex is therefore to suggest that it possesses a level of intricacy deserving of interpretation. By contrast, to say that a work is simple is to indicate that it is lacking in this respect. Simple in this context thus suggests deficiency, as simplicity is conventionally seen to be a feature of naïve or crude works that generally appear to be lacking in sophistication, refinement, or finesse. Admittedly, Beckett does not suggest that his work is simplistic. He uses the phrase 'skeleton simple', seemingly to indicate that *Godot* is a play that is open about its aims and meanings, albeit audiences and critics are unprepared to appreciate this aspect of the play. The letter mentions a few papers that have been given the play "a lot of space and serious criticism" (Craig et al. 2008, 539), although for the most part, Beckett maintains, the play has been "[v]iolently attacked by the daily rags" (qtd in Craig et al. 2008, 540). Later in the letter, Beckett also concludes that: "[p]eople are never happy unless they are digging" (qtd in Craig et al. 2008, 540). It would therefore seem that Beckett distinguishes between those who understand the play and those who do not, and that a line is drawn between those who overestimate interpretation, those who want to dig into the play's deeper layers of meaning, over and against those who merely arrive to experience the play, seemingly without trying to penetrate its rippling surface.

A couple of years later, in 1957, Beckett comments in another letter to Alan Schneider, who had directed a production of *Godot* at the Coconut Grove Playhouse in Miami 1956: "[m]y work is a matter of fundamental sounds (no joke intended), made as fully as possible, and I accept responsibility for nothing else. If people want to have headaches among the overtones, let them. And provide their own aspirin." (Harmon 1998, 24). The analogy with music here signals that Beckett envisions a different interpretative paradigm for his play than the study of linguistic meaning, one in which aesthetic experience could be seen to take precedence over intellectual analysis. Acknowledging Beckett's claim, Knowlson, in the introduction to *The Theatrical Notebooks Samuel Beckett, Volume I: Waiting for Godot,* also establishes that "the directions that are set out in the Schiller notebook resemble a choreography performed to the 'music' of the text" (xii). Notably, such concerns tend to fall under the remit of the aesthetic. The foregrounding of visual and auditive patterns in Beckett's work therefore projects a new context for interpretation, one that takes aesthetic experience as its foundation. However, the significance of aesthetic experience has tended to be devaluated or displaced by the linguistic turn (Johnson 2009, 209). In fact, aesthetics, as Elisabeth Schellekens points out, "is often considered to be either irrelevant or misleading ... charged with dealing merely with 'soft' issues" (Schellekens 2007, 1). Even so, as shall be discussed below, and as Beckett seems to have realized, the nature of aesthetic experience is neither irrelevant nor misleading, and nor is it merely a theory of the arts. In fact, "aesthetics ... is the study of how humans make and experience meaning ... [and] the processes of embodied meaning in the arts are the very same ones that make linguistic meaning possible" (Johnson 2009, 209). Aesthetic experience, then, is intrinsically part of linguistic meaning. And, if, as shall be discussed below, the deepest reservoirs of linguistic meaning are embodied, then Beckett's emphasis on aesthetic experience paves the way for new modes of making sense of his dramatic work.

The notion that the 'skeleton simple' in Beckett's work implies an emphasis on aesthetic experience has already been picked up by scholars seeking to reframe Beckett's *oeuvre* within aesthetic, affective and ethic perspectives, most notably of these S. E. Gontarski (affect), Derek Attridge (aesthetics), Alain Badiou (ethics).[83] And their efforts to draw attention to Beckett's examination of human situatedness have not gone unnoticed. Embodied perspectives on Beckett's work are increasingly coming into focus and include

---

[83] Nina Power and Alberto Toscano point out in the preface to *Alain Badiou: On Beckett* (2003) that Badiou's readings of Beckett are inherently different from "the interpretations of most, if not all, his contemporaries when it comes to the writings of Beckett", specifically with reference to their focus on method and on the "unequivocal character of Beckett's thought" (xvii).

perspectives on performance as a specific context for human interaction, as well as considerations of the effect of Beckett's work on its readers and spectators. A recent example is the film *Echo's Bone* by the artist Sarah Browne, who, in collaboration with young people in the Fingal County in Ireland, places Beckett's short story, "Echo's Bones" (1933), in relation to neurodiverse styles of language and gesture, specifically to examine their aesthetic aspects (2022)[84]. And in "*Not I:* Touretteshero, 2017–2020", Hannah Simpson reports on the actress Jess Thom's work on "autistic individuals as a key group of target spectators" (2018, 229).[85] Both Simpson and Browne could be seen to follow Gontarski, Attridge and Badiou in paying attention to affective, aesthetic and ethic aspects of Beckett's work, but they also seem to answer to McMullan and Maude's call for more experience-centred perspectives on Beckett, as suggested in the introduction to this book. More to the point, however, their work opens productive new perspectives on the body in Beckett's drama, perspectives that are key also to my present examination of mis-movements.

In this third and final chapter, then, I delve into the poetic logic of mis-movements, specifically to tease out the aesthetics of gesture resulting from it. Derived from Beckett's artistic solution to the predicament of expression, the aesthetics of gesture is concerned with framing perception, specifically to produce the necessary conditions of possibility for perceiving afresh. Thus, it also has an ethical dimension. As discussed in chapter two, the strategic use of

---

[84] A report of the project has subsequently been published as *Echo's Bones: A Parallel Play*, published by the Fingal County Council, 2023.

[85] Simpson writes about the Relaxed Performance Project both in chapter 4 "*Not I:* Touretteshero 2107–2020" (2023), and in an earlier article, "Tics in the Theatre: The Quiet Audience, the Relaxed Performance, and the Neurodivergent Spectator" (2018). Thom's performance with Beckett's *Not I* came out of her involvement with the "Relaxed Performance Project", a project which according to Simpson "takes a relaxed approach to sound and movement coming from the audience", most specifically since it "understands that focus and attention can look different to different types of bodies, and doesn't make assumptions about how an audience might 'be' or watch a piece" (Simpson 2022, 129).

mis-movements produces a situation where audiences cannot rely on conventional interpretative strategies but are prompted to carry their felt sense of whatever implicit intricacy produced by mis-movements forward. Thus, audiences are prompted to enfold ignorance as the bedrock of knowledge, a process that also links the capacity for perceiving afresh to the capacity for using language thinkingly. However, I also suggested that the strategic use of mis-movements in performance speaks to an experienced-based practice aimed at disrupting both conventional assumptions about the performance context as well as conventional assumptions about the processes of meaning-making in such a context. In this chapter, I build on these discussions to suggest that attending to mis-movements in Beckett's drama entails taking seriously a form of knowing that is not primarily based upon formal or public knowledge, *viz.* linguistic meaning. It also entails taking aesthetic experience seriously, as the "goal of art" (Schusterman 2002, 28). In short, mis-movements safeguard aesthetic experience. By means of mis-movements, Beckett is able to reframe the context of performance so that aesthetic experience takes precedence over linguistic interpretation, although as spectators we may not acknowledge this 'skeleton simple' design on perception in Beckett's drama. Thus, what is at stake in Beckett's complaint to Pamela Mitchell is less the question of whether *Godot* is simple or complex, and more the question of whether we, as spectators, may experience a performance without jumping to conclusions, or whether bias and habit hold us captive in the public realm of linguistic meanings, seemingly confirmed in acts of judgements about intellectual complexity rather than perceptual clarity and simplicity.

Beckett's aesthetic of gesture is intrinsically ethical. Yet, contrary to how it may appear, it offers a mode of apprehension that is epistemologically coherent with scepticism, only scepticism here is not about the object or concept: it is an aspect of perception. While it is not surprising that Beckett's drama has been addressed as a forerunner of post-modernism, nor that it has spawned a multitude of critical orientations that probe Beckett's texts in search of evidence in support of formalist, existential and nihilist interpretations (Birkett &

Ince 2000, 1–2), like Nietzsche, Beckett seems to have been aware of the need to safeguard human thinking against the potential scepticism lurking in the notion that meaning—and, by extension, value—is unattainable. Thus, even though Beckett work is permeated with ambiguity, vagueness, existential doubt, and philosophical conundrums, this is not to deflate meaning: it is to prompt a more affirmative mode than what the so-called 'hermeneutics of suspicion' would typically allow. In fact, the naïve position of the lay-reader, commonly perceived to have no real interpretative value in comparison with the piercing analyses of the expert-reader (See Rita Felski, *The Uses of Literature* 2008; *The Limits of Critique* 2015), is seemingly one that Beckett cultivates in his audiences. Such a naïve position may be more apt at taking a holistic stance *vis-à-vis* the experience of performance, which is arguably what Beckett's skeleton simple work invites us to do although preconceived ideas about the performance context as a context for linguistic interpretation may have prevented us from acknowledging this dimension of Beckett's drama.

Beckett as director

In a sense, Beckett shifts focus from telling to showing. He shifts from stating that we are all ignorant of the structures that uphold our ignorance, to trying to expose those very structures. As Beckett seems to understand the situation in 1955, the problem is mainly that audiences' fail to appreciate his 'skeleton simple' drama (see letter to Pamela Mitchell). That is, the problem is more related to audiences' and critics' desire for complexity than to his own capacity as a playwright. Yet, in 1975, when he returns to direct *Waiting for Godot* at the Schiller Theatre in Berlin, Beckett's appreciation of the situation has changed, possibly due to his involvement with the staging of his own work. James Knowlson comments that "Beckett often remarked that when he wrote *Waiting for Godot*, he was extremely inexperienced in writing for the stage" (*TN I*, xi). A conversion, however, occurred as he "explored the implications of performance fully in the mid

1950s, [and] began to understand its necessity to his theatrical creative process" (Gontarski 2004, 199).[86] This transformation was long in the making and included acting as an advisory, for instance, to Roger Blin in Paris (1961) and to Anthony Page in London (1964), but it also included assisting Deryk Mendel in Berlin, and corresponding with directors Alan Simpson and Alan Schneider about productions of *Godot* in Ireland and North America, respectively (*TN I*, xi). The decision to take full responsibility for directing *Godot* at the Schiller Theatre, however, allowed Beckett to express his transformed understanding of performance, and so to highlight the rhetorical, poetical, aesthetical, and ethical implications of his skeleton simple drama.

Notably, as Knowlson observes, "by far the greatest number of changes made by Beckett were additions to and revisions of the stage directions" (*TN I*, xvii). That is, the bulk of the changes Beckett makes in the process of staging *Godot*, concern the characters' modes of comportment, and various mis-movements are made even more conspicuous through Beckett's revisions. For instance, in the opening scene in Act I, "Beckett… deliberately chose to have both figures on stage together at the beginning of the play" (*TN I*, xiii). Yet, says Knowlson, Beckett also decided to "plunge the spectator immediately into the atmosphere of 'waiting'" by means of letting the "opening moments of the play consist of a still, waiting tableau, identified as W1 in the notebooks" (*TN* I, xiii). All in all, twelve such waiting tableaux, or *Warstellen*, were also carefully timed to make the spectators feel the effect of such moments (*TN I*, xiii–xiv). Thus, immobility and stillness

---

[86] The Schiller Theatre production of *Endgame* in 1967 was the first production for which Beckett kept and wrote a production notebook (*TN II*, xv). Staging *Endgame* allowed Beckett fully to engage in working with other parameters of expression than words, and so to get it "right" for the first time (*TN II*, xiii–xxii). The notebook revealed Beckett's strong concern with textual simplicity and with the nature of physical movement, but it also revealed Beckett's expanded notion of text. Indeed, Beckett's involvement in the staging of his work transformed his conceptualisation of the text to the point where, "in the theatre, performance is the final text" (Gontarski 2002, 91).

were highlighted in ways that implicated audiences in the event of waiting for Godot. Other examples of changes that would qualify as mis-movements include the structuring of the "balletic elements" (Knowlson *TN I*, xii), and the consistent harmonizing of the characters' orientations towards the ground or the sky (Knowlson *TN*, xiii). What specifically guides Beckett in the process of revising the Schiller Theatre production, is the question of whether the change would "function theatrically", or not (*TN I*, xvi). To work theatrically a change must contribute to the overall atmosphere in the play, but also to the rhythm of performance (*TN I*, xvi). And mis-movements seem especially useful in this regard.[87]

Yet the many changes to the stage directions that Beckett makes also signal his transformation as a playwright. Indeed, if initially mis-movements merely afforded Beckett with a means to challenge language (Beckett 1983, 171)[88], then the changes to *Godot* in the 1975 production testify to a development in Beckett's understanding of the dramatic context that goes beyond merely seeking an opportunity to undermine language. The many changes listed in *The Theatrical Notebooks Vol. I–IV* indicate Beckett's awareness of the processes by means of which human subjects arrive to create meaning. They also signal his awareness of the processes of valorisation underlying such creative acts, as well as his awareness of the subtle workings of language as the mediating structure whereby cultural values are

---

[87] Indeed, mis-movements could be described as the physical equivalents of the characters' "music-hall or circus" routines, which, according to Knowlson, include repeating names and "echoing Laurel and Hardy films" (*TN I*, xvi–xvii). Importantly, however, many of the mis-movements lack such cultural references, although not all. For instance, "the 'balletic' element" (*TN I*, xii) in *Godot* could be fruitfully approached as an allusion to Laurel and Hardy, as could the hat routine (*TN I*, 65:2118–2137), but the twelve *Warstellen* do not suggest such connotations.

[88] This seems to have been the poetic logic of mis-movements in his early drama, which I have previously labelled the "material phase" (1952–1962). In this context, mis-movements mainly appear as anomalies, seemingly designed to break the spell of habitual appropriation of meaning in language (Einarsson 2017, 84).

produced and disseminated. Indeed, in any given culture, the 'affects of power' (Roderick 1991) consistently work to shape our consciousness so that normative values are tacitly internalized and assimilated through social and linguistic practices. Thus, values emerge subtly, and, for the most part, remain merely implicit in the spectators' attitude, internalized in epistemology and hermeneutics. However, in Beckett's innovative drama, the performance context affords an opening to perceiving meaning beyond the realm of language, and so beyond the realms of those 'affects of power' that hold spectator's captive. And it does so, specifically on account of a strategic use of mis-movements in performance.

In Beckett's drama, and especially his late drama, then, spectators are invited to pay attention to holistic visual and auditive images, *viz.* interactions made up by 'body-en complexes' (as discussed in chapter two), and they are also invited to engage in processes of reflection on whether and how such images are relevant. As McMullan observes, "in the drama after *Play* (1962), Beckett experiments even more radically with the nature and limits of theatre" (1993, 2). From this phase and onwards, however, it is not the actual mis-movements that matter, but their effects. The changes Beckett makes to the play draw spectators into the event of experiencing the performance, but importantly they also reveal Beckett's concern with the audience's response, as well as his awareness that this response can be modified. In fact, Beckett's reinvention of the dramatic genre hinges on the recognition that interaction conditions human communication and takes place beyond the confines of words.[89] As formal aesthetic aspects of the presentation come to the fore, then, such aspects of performance seem to have the capacity to produce in audiences a concern with meaning and knowing beyond the limits of language. There is therefore a poetic logic to be traced in Beckett's

---

[89] Notably, the body is an important—albeit frequently overlooked—aspect of communication. The nature of aesthetic experience in Beckett's drama therefore opens a new field of investigation, one that has arguably gained momentum in recent years.

reconfiguration of performance, one that pivots on mis-movements as interfaces, openings, interruptions, or interactions, setting the mood of performance, one that recognizes that while conditioned by interaction, the body is frequently absent from perception. According to this poetic logic, mis-movements *are* interaction (that is an ongoing process), yet mis-movements are also interruptions that blocks interaction, and this is how they arrive to be occurrences that imply something beyond words. The strategic use of mis-movements is thus both rhetorical and aesthetical—rhetorical because it robs spectators of their habitual strategies of interpretation, and aesthetical because it hones the spectators' attention to the event of performance as aesthetic experience. Indeed, if, as Joseph Früchtl suggests, "[a] work of art 'appeals' to us in both senses of the word, passive and active" (2016, 74), then Beckett's drama is a beautifully crafted 'thing' that also has something to say (albeit not explicitly). [90]

Systemic perspectives

Notably, the modes in which spectators arrive to negotiate or make sense of experiencing involve embodied perspectives that may be addressed within the phenomenological perspective afforded by Eugene Gendlin's process theory, the pragmatist aesthetic theory of

---

[90] Among the consequences of realizing that works of art have "something to say to us" (Früchtl 2016, 74), is that the "body politic appear in an idealised fashion as a work of art, but also [that] art appears as a surveillance body analogous to the state" (Früchtl 2016, 76). Viewed thus, art may be "embraced politically in a secular form of its panoptic competence" (2016, 76.). Früchtl also refers to Peter Sloterdijk as presenting a similar notion in *Du must dein Leben ändern. Über Anthropotechnik.* [*You Must Change Your life*]. (Frankfurt/M.: Suhrkamp, 2011, 38). Moreover, says Früchtl, "mythological, theological, and state-social semantics overlap in the area of aesthetics preferred since the emergence of Modernity some 200 years ago – that is, art" (2016, 75). However, he maintains, there is reason to challenge this analogy between the body politic and art: the work of art "is not, as Rilke purports, merely the thing which has something to say". Rather, its capacity to appeal to us also depends on our own willingness to accept its authority to do so (Früchtl 2016, 87, *fn* 3).

Richard Shusterman, as derived from William James, the 'aesthetics of human understanding' theorized by Mark Johnson, the 'aesthetics of appearing', explained by Martin Seel, or the ecological perspective on the mind proposed by Gregory Bateson. Put differently, the modes in which spectators may arrive to make sense of Beckett's drama may be more fruitfully approached within perspectives that suggest occasion, relation, and correspondence than within perspectives that confine us to the stage image alone (cf. Gontarski 2015, 154–155). To approach Beckett's drama within the frameworks afforded by such perspectives necessarily excludes approaching it as complete or determined. Notably, both embodied and systemic perspectives allow for different conceptualizations of experience, for instance in communication, interaction, and interpretation. Yet even such perspectives acknowledge the relevance of context. Thus, for instance, in chapter one, in connecting Bateson's ecological perspective on mind and matter to Beckett's performing ecology, I could arrive to suggest that a performance is a self-regulating system within which change appears as a result of mis-movements being repeated. Mis-movements are both parameters that affect change, and 'leverage points'[91] that can be identified and possibly intervened with to produce such slight changes from which bigger shifts in perception may issue. Yet, if attention shapes and modifies the experience of the whole performance context, then paying attention to mis-movements inevitably entails lifting them out of this context as phenomena worthy of attention, before merging them once again with the whole performance experience. Embodied perspectives therefore do not abolish context. Rather, they predicate on context as the frame within which things appear to be perceived *as* relevant, *by* someone, who may arrive to create highly specific meanings based on such experiencing.

---

[91] Leverage points are "places within a complex system (a corporation, an economy, a living body, aa city, an ecosystem) where a small shift on the one thing may produce big changes in everything" (see Donella Meadows, "Leverage Points: Places to Intervene in a System" ("Donella Meadows Archives", URL: https://donellameadows.org/archives/leverage-points-places-to-intervene-in-a-system/ .)

Notably, however, and most pertinent to the discussions in this chapter, Beckett's drama prompts attention to whole stage images, before inviting spectators to trace the different patterns that connect. More specifically, the skeleton simple images that characterize Beckett's drama—a body stuck in a mound (*Happy Days*) or a woman walking a strip of floor (*Footfalls*)— invite audiences to see whole body-environment complexes first, and only subsequently arrive to trace the smaller patterns contained within such larger wholes. The poetic logic of such 'reverse engineering' produces more holistic and more artistic perspectives on the fullness of lived experience than inductive or deductive reasoning would allow for.[92] That is, a holistic stance invites consideration of the interaction between various parts in the system.

Beckett's drama, then, comprises *more than* the stage directions and *more than* the words on the page. Indeed, it may not be possible to account for all the factors that contribute to shape a spectator's holistic perception of a Beckett play. Just as a musical piece will only emerge as an orchestra performs the score, and just as *that* specific instantiation of the piece will be unique to *that* specific performance context (even as it will resonate against the backdrop of many potential past and future instantiations of that same score), so a Beckett drama is one whole system emerging to be perceived as *that* play, a unique instantiation of the dramatic script, in *that* specific performance context. The process of making sense of such a whole, however, is necessarily forward oriented. It entails making sense of *that* play, a totality greater than the sum of its parts, which necessarily unfolds in the here and now of performance. That is, it entails carrying the implicit intricacies of those whole stage images forward, and even the process of tracing the patters that connect should in this sense be seen to project onwards.

---

[92] I am indebted to my fried Marina Ludwigs for drawing my attention to the processes of thinking that could be seen to characterize artistic vision.

Asking different questions

Now, in *Creative Involution: Bergson, Beckett and Deleuze* (2015), Gontarski suggests that as "readers and spectators of Beckett's oeuvre ... we might ask ourselves ... whether or not we have been mis-asking questions about Beckett's art" (154). He continues, "[e]specially suspect are questions that suggest occasion, relation, or correspondence, questions that take us outside the text, or in the theatre outside performance, that this outside the image, finally" (Gontarski 2015, 154–155). Ultimately, Gontarski asks, what can we hope to learn about life from works of art, or specifically from the works of Samuel Beckett (2015, 155)? Such questions are relevant. Indeed, the questions we ask will determine the nature of the answers we receive. The admonition to reflect on what we seek to learn from Beckett's work thus has theoretical, critical, and political implications, which Simpson and Browne's work illustrate, respectively.[93] Importantly, however, the tendency to overestimate archival, theoretical, discursive or historical perspectives, risks working in the

---

[93] For instance, Simpson's study into relaxed performances reveals that audiences generally conceive of interaction in the context of performance as limited to passively absorbing the presentation, and that audiences also largely assume that their silence is mandatory. Individual members of an audience who fail to exhibit proper deference—for example, by keeping still or being silent—are generally thought of as a nuisance (Simpson 2018, 227). Yet such preconceived notions become a mechanism of exclusion for individuals with neurodiversity, such as, for instance, autism or Tourettes (Simpson 2018, 229). Thus, Simpson explains, "ableist intolerance", or the "assumed right to a silent auditorium often works in direct opposition to the right to simply be able to access the theatre space" (2018, 229). And, not infrequently, members of the audience with neurodiversity feel judged or even avoid going to the theatre altogether, on account of this bias (Simpson 2018, 230). The concept of relaxed performances is thus politically charged. Indeed, Simpson maintains, it is possible to read "a closer more immediate politics in the disruption of the quiet audience: not only increased accessibility for neurodivergent spectators, but a renewed training ground for the acceptance of others' existence within one's own phenomenological sphere, and of the possibility of being affected by this interaction" (2018, 232).

opposite direction from attention to human situatedness, thereby excluding aesthetic and embodied perspectives. I therefore disagree with Gontarski on his claim that Beckett's "virtual worlds" (2015, 163) include everything we can imagine, "past, present, material figures, imagination, and memory" (Gontarski 2015, 163). Gontarski warns that the effort to recontextualize what Beckett has so carefully decontextualized risks "under-appreciating" the intrinsic newness of his drama (Gontarski 2015, 154). Yet, even as Beckett operates with non-discursive aesthetic experience, seemingly to reframe the interpretative context of performance, the process of absorbing, sensing, assimilating, or even interpreting aesthetic experience, remains inevitably and indelibly related to interaction as the background that shapes experiencing and encountering in the context of Beckett's drama. Experience always takes place in a context that enfolds *more than* the object experienced. That is, experience enfolds *both* the perceiver *and* the perceived, *both* the subject *and* the object, *both* the audience *and* the performance etc., and so on. Hence, it cannot be reduced to an object that comprises all that a subject (or an audience) needs to be able to make sense of or perceive it. Importantly, audience and performance interact. They co-depend. In short, audiences create performances and performances creates audiences and so there is no performance without audience and no audience without performance. Gontarski reports that, on May 11, 1959, Beckett "referred to the staging of *Krapp's Last Tape* as its 'creation'" (Gontarski 2004, 200), and that on several occasions he also halted the publication of his dramatic texts to work on the texts in rehearsals before they could be completed and published (Gontarski 2002, 91). Given that Beckett saw the performance as the final text (Gontarski 2004, 200), he must therefore have been keenly aware of the ways in which the process of staging it would change the material, and of the effects such changes presumably would have on audiences.

Indeed, as Sara Ahmed reminds us, "[i]t matters how we arrive at the places we do" (2006, 2), and while Gontarski's admonition that we need to reflect on the contexts within which we approach Beckett's work is pertinent—"we have learned [says

Gontarski,] that the context of Beckett's art, its intellectual milieu, or the generation and production of the published work is invaluable" (Gontarski 2015, 155),—Beckett's work also solicits other perspectives. Thus, about Beckett's prose, Derek Attridge maintains that "we must not forget that it is enjoyable read" (2017, 16), even as the experience of reading Beckett's work over searching it "for hidden meanings" (Attridge 2017, 10). Notably, however, such perspectives have tended to be slightly overlooked in Beckett's studies, perhaps in favour of "the superb array of new possibilities ... presented by the increasing availability of manuscripts, notebooks, memoirs, letters, and other archival materials (Attridge 2017, 12). Attridge's example is Beckett's novel *The Unnamable* (1953), yet his observations are relevant also with reference to Beckett's drama. Further to the significance of mis-movements, I therefore maintain that if Beckett's prose modulates and shapes more than the story told—specifically because the words on the page also emerge to be experienced by readers "beyond [their] closed world of habitual thought and feeling, [which is to say that they] emerge only from the event of reading, and from the reader's painful, pleasurable experience of that event" (Attridge, 2017, 21),—then this could be said about the experience of Beckett's drama, which similarly predicates on aesthetic experience and which is always re-contextualized (socially, historically, culturally etc.).[94] Taking a more pragmatist, aesthetic perspective on embodied responses to Beckett's drama, however, need not exclude political or historical perspectives. In fact, it may afford harmonizing perspectives that may deepen analysis, all the while making room for the kind of self-criticism that Beckett's drama invites. If the event of reading Beckett's prose entails experiencing various textual features that

---

[94] Ultimately, "much of Beckett's late drama, like 'A Piece of Monologue,' became nearly indistinguishable from the late prose fiction, which is why so many theatre professionals were eager to stage the haunting, late, monologic short prose" (Gontarski 2002, 90).

increasingly gain momentum,[95] thereby intensifying the reader's expectations, and even as those expectations may be "either satisfied, postponed, or disappointed" (Attridge 2017, 17), then this does not exclude the possibility that such experiencing may be contextualized on historical or even political terms. Given that "[p]oetics is the grounds on which texts make sense" (Brooks 1994, 510), a new poetics would not exclude this possibility, only, it would produce new ways of making sense. Clearly, then, Beckett's poetics afford aesthetic experience, but clearly too, given the significance of how we arrive to meet Beckett's work, different poetics will take on different meanings in different historical, social, and cultural contexts.

While mis-movements are key to Beckett's poetics—for instance by dint of producing patterns that connect, or by connecting seemingly unrelated realms of experience—experiencing or encountering such presentations will inevitably propose different connections to different audiences. In short, the fact that "the work of literature ... is not an object but an event" (Attridge 2017, 10), does not exclude the fact that this event takes place in a context or that this context will influence the event. Yet, as Gendlin reminds us, attention is both creative and productive (2004, 144). In attending, we select from a vast array of possibilities, and whatever we select becomes "a product", the response to which may "surprise us and force us to change our categories" (Gendlin 2004, 144). As I proposed in chapter two, therefore, a new syntax is required to describe the interconnections between embodied, non-discursive experience, which characterizes the event of experiencing mis-movements in Beckett's drama, and the meanings that such experiencing generate. That is, the processes of making sense of experiencing are firmly embodied. And if Beckett's writing "tends towards affirmation" (see Badiou 2003, 40), and if "our enjoyment emerges from what happens to [its] content, how it fades in and out of view, how it is asserted and

---

[95] For example, diction (Attridge 2017, 19) or rhythm (Attridge 2017, 17), are examples of prosodic features that accumulate in the experience of reading, listening, or watching Beckett's work.

undermined" (Attridge 2017, 20), then an aesthetic and experiential approach to Beckett's work seems to provide a relevant basis for discussing Beckett's drama. Put differently, "the wrong questions" will inevitably produce the 'wrong' answers. Or perhaps it is merely that we repeatedly produce the same answers? Regardless, I concur with Gontarski that we should be wary of reducing thematic concerns in Beckett's work to specific moments in time when Beckett hypothetically may have been thinking or reading about specific problems in specific texts.[96] I merely disagree with his claim that Beckett's drama is complete, in the sense that it already comprises all that we need to understand it.

Beckett's drama invites audiences to be co-creators of meaning and the connections that propose themselves through mapping reality onto fiction. Yet while suggestive of many meanings, it cannot help us understand our own responses to the work. Perhaps, therefore, the main reason we should be wary of reducing virtual infinitude to actual finitude (Gontarski 2015, 163) is not that it risks re-contextualising what Beckett has gone to lengths to de-contextualize, but, rather, that such a process risks foreclosing self-reflection. Indeed, decontextualising always implies recontextualising, whether we realize it or not. There is therefore much to be said for taking the approach suggested by Gontarski and Attridge. Asking different questions of Beckett's drama will inevitably entail finding different answers, and the dimension of experience seems to afford a fruitful perspective on interpretation. Only, as stated above, Gontarski's claim that Beckett's drama comprises all that we can imagine (2015, 163,) is difficult to reconcile with the nature of aesthetic experience. Beckett's drama, seemingly, takes us beyond the realm of the text. Even though it predicates on sparseness of situational context, especially historical context, our responses are not

---

[96] According to Gontarski, the publication of *The Letters of Samuel Beckett, Vol. 1–4* (Cambridge University Press, 2008–2016) merely provides limited access to those conditions under which Beckett produced his work. In fact, "only 2.500 of an estimated 17.000 known letters [are] in possession of the editors" (Gontarski 2015, 154).

limited to what appears in this context, but the ambiguity that characterizes Beckett's stage images is intriguingly suggestive. Still, Gontarski is correct in maintaining that not all questions can be asked in all contexts. Clearly, "[t]here are conditions for the possibility of certain questions being asked" (Roderick "101 Socrates and the Life of Inquiry (1990)", transcription). And the context of Beckett's drama invites questions about aesthetic experience, especially on account of its emphasis on non-propositional elements of performance.

All of this is not to say that any interpretation is as good as any other. Not all interpretation is discerning. In fact, interpretation is only discerning if it involves a responsive attitude, otherwise it merely amounts to confirming what we already know. What is more, when interpretation is merely confirmation of preconceived ideas, then it becomes an antidote to the kind of confusion that Beckett's drama asks spectators to experience. The question of what we can expect from Beckett's drama thus pivots on how we approach it. Or rather, it pivots on what we already believe that we know about it. And, if the issue of how we approach Beckett's drama relates to the issue of how aesthetic experience could be seen to frame perception, thereby conditioning the ways in which audiences arrive to process information in the context of performance, then the issue of responsivity in the context of Beckett's drama could be addressed as a function of the effects produce by mis-movements.

Mis-movements guide spectators to experience the stage images in Beckett's drama aesthetically. In the context of performance, they demand careful attention to the formal and structural aspects of the stage presentation and as I have argued above, the staging of the spectator's attention assumes that there is more to language than abstract concepts. That said, what constitutes the *more than* linguistic meaning is the main topic of this third and final chapter. Notably, and even though they seem limited with reference to analytical reason (cf. Roland Barthes 'third meanings'), mis-movements prompt spectators to attend to processes of appearing *as* mis-movements, and to take such processes of appearing, on higher and higher levels of abstraction, as in some sense noteworthy. Even so, attending to mis-movements is basically to attend to nothing and to perceive nothing *as* something, even as this something is nothing, and even as meaning cannot be reduced to either. Mis-movements such as, for instance walking, stooping, rocking, or stillness, would not stand out for perception or *dys*-appear, had they not been carefully choreographed to do so, yet what they mean, beyond being conspicuous, is not easy to explain. I therefore take Gontarski's appreciation of the virtual in Beckett's drama, but also Attridge's emphasis on experience is an important point of entry for continuing a discussion of what is at stake in experiencing mis-movements as aesthetically significant elements of performance. More specifically, I take the question about what we stand to gain from Beckett's drama to open considerations of two things: (1) the nature of aesthetic experience solicited in Beckett's drama, and (2) the question of how such experiencing becomes meaningful.

Perceiving aesthetically

Paying attention to mis-movements entails perceiving aesthetically, a mode of approaching phenomena that Martin Seel describes as being attentive to the phenomenal presence and individuality of phenomena in their momentariness (Seel 2005, 25–26). By means of mis-movements, Beckett can foreground "the shape of ideas over the ideas themselves" (Beckett qtd in Dearlove 1982, 1). Yet, mis-movements also extend the purview of attention far beyond the realm of the linguistic, and so far beyond the realm of the disengaged spectator guided by habit.

Simply put, writes Seel there are "three dimensions of perception" (2005, 25): "Every living being who can perceive possesses the capacity for the *perceiving of* something" (2005, 25). Yet, "only beings who can know conceptually have the capacity for *perceiving that*, which is present only in connection with the capacity for *perceiving as*" (Seel 2005, 25). According to Seel, aesthetic perception is characterized precisely by our human capacity to "disengage" ourselves "from any theoretically or practically determined directive as to what [our] perception is a perception of" (Seel 2005, 25). This essentially Kantian account argues that works of art are different from mere presentations or aesthetic presentations because they are "constellational presentations", whose "meaning is tied to a nonsubstitutable rendering of their material—nonsubstitutable in the sense of not being replaceable by any other combination of elements" (Seel 2005, 95). Basically, "works of art are objects that need to be understood in their performative *intent*" (Seel 2005, 96, *my emphasis*). The definition of the aesthetic is thus that it "generally unfolds in the context of an interpretative, an imaginative, and occasionally a reflective disclosure of artistic objects" (Seel 2005, 96). Of course, we may aesthetically contemplate the sunset or deem the measured, highly technical skills of an athlete's performance aesthetic. Seel does not exclude the possibility that such modes of perception happen in a certain atmospheric 'sense-catching', so that they may appear to be intuited in their "existential significance to the perceivers" (Seel 2005, 92). However, works of art "produce a special presence and present a special presence", because they are aesthetic constellations, and it is only "through attentiveness to the constellations of this presentation that we can participate in the constellations presented by the artistic work" (Seel 2005, 97). Or as Seel explains, "[i]n the encounter with works of art, we *encounter* presences of human life" (2005, 97).[97] Notably, Seel's explication of the appearing *as*—a correlate to perceiving *that*—is useful for understanding the poetic logic of mismovements, specifically because it broaches the issue of the mode within which works of art are approached. Aesthetic perception in

---

[97] According to Jonathan Loesberg, "the Romantic aesthetic concept of symbolic embodiment" has been increasingly attacked for "enabling totalitarian ideology" (2005, 1). But there is no contradicting the fact that the "particular kind of experience afforded by art" may not also serve "ideological ends" (Loesberg 2005, 2). Scholars who defend "notions of beauty or aesthetic experience" by explicitly posit the value of "a special experience created by the art object" on account of psychological grounds, therefore do not "adequately respond to the political critiques of aesthetics" (Loesberg 2005,2).

Seel's account acknowledges "a feature diversity of objects that cannot be exhausted conceptually" (Seel 27), in part because the intention of the perceiver is "to disengage themselves from any theoretically or practically determined directive as to what their perception if a perception of" (Seel 2005, 25). In so doing, it establishes mood to be an intrinsic aspect of perception.

With reference to the issue of the nature of aesthetic experience in Beckett's drama, however, I take this to be underpinned by a different poetic logic. That is, I follow Seel's lead in emphasising the significance of the mood of perception within which spectators approach them, but I part with Seel's emphasis on the disengaged spectator. Mis-movements proliferate 'becomings' (whether of something or nothing) that afford a variety of potentialities or criteria of experiential, or even Barthesian 'third' meanings.[98] Just like Barthes's obtuse images, mis-movements open towards the infinity of potential meanings. Designed to be aesthetically perceived, mis-movements slip out of the linguistic grid by proposing *more than* the words used to describe them. Yet the nature of aesthetic experience prompted by mis-movements is not disconnected either from language, concepts, context, or meaning. Rather, mis-movements prompt spectators to approach them as significant in some way, and in a mood that takes the qualitative differences that appear in performance *both* as relevant *and* irrelevant. Yet, whether we conclude that mis-movements are relevant or irrelevant, we shall arrive to carry the experience of mis-movements forward. And it is precisely the

---

[98] Roland Barthes's coins the term "obtuse" to indicate or describe a level of meaning beyond the levels of communication (semiotic) or signification (symbolic) (1978, 52). The semiotic and symbolic levels of meanings are "obvious" (1978, 54). The "obtuse meaning", by contrast, is "the supplement that ... intellection cannot succeed in absorbing" (Ibid.) Outlining the concept, Barthes explains that "[o]btusus means that which is blunted, rounded in form", and so it seems a suitable terms to describe that which seems to "to extend outside culture, knowledge, information ... has something derisory about it ... [is] opening out into the infinity of language ... [and] belongs to the family of pun, buffoonery, useless expenditure" (*ibid.*).

interplay between conceptually inaccessible qualities of mis-movements appearing *as* mis-movements, in the here and now of performance—for example, in this light, from this perspective or from this change of perspective, —as well as the qualities opening *from* mis-movements, which give them the potential for becoming something, even they appear as nothing.

'Carnal hermeneutics'

Implicit in Beckett's reconfiguration of the performance contexts is a shift from interpretation to experience. It is a shift from 'hermeneutics proper' to a form of 'carnal hermeneutics' (see Kearney 2015). It is also a shift that corresponds to an essentially phenomenological understanding of attention as "an active symbolizing", which is never arbitrary" since "experiencing is always symbolized at least by the events that led up to this moment, and it almost always implies, demands, and pre-figures a next step" (Gendlin 2004, 144). Seemingly a reaction against the linguistic turn in modernism, phenomenology implicates the body in the process of meaning-making and signals a commitment to finding a new syntax capable of showing our inherent belonging to the world, as well as our inherent capacity for making sense of the world, and so for moving on, as it were. Among the effects of the so-called linguistic turn (Rorty 1967), was that the value of aesthetic experience as the premise for critical reflection began to dwindle. The linguistic turn held that the frames that condition and shape perception operate entirely within *logos*. Consequently, seeking to take stock of aesthetic experience beyond the realm of language makes no sense; indeed, it could be deemed naïve, or even unacademic. As Felski maintains, a "hermeneutics of suspicion … that prides itself on its uncompromising wariness and hypervigilance" against the ideological or emotional allures of a text, seemingly confirms that intellectual detachment safeguards objectivity in observation and interpretation (Felski 2009, 29). Consequently, for example, New Historicism, Poststructuralism, and Deconstruction, each for purposes of their own, have been "against aesthetics" (Loesberg 2005, 1).[99] In fact, with the advent of the linguistic turn, the very idea that there may be experiences outside language could be seen to have been refuted, once and for all.

Yet, as both phenomenological studies and studies into embodied cognition have revealed, the mind does not work in 'splendid isolation' from the body, and in-the-flesh-human-beings are anything but detached observers. Rather, lived experience is shot through with aesthetic sensations, derived from the environment, and equally appealing to body and mind. Indeed, the event of experiencing the world as aesthetically meaningful seems to precede our capacity to perceive it as meaningful in the sense associated with linguistic meaning (see James 1890; Dewey 1934; Johnson 2009; Gendlin 1997). Already in the late nineteenth century, the American philosopher William James's pragmatist definition of aesthetic experience thus highlights the continuity between aesthetic experience, memory and thinking, and suggests that "aesthetic experience has also been identified as key to embodied cognition" (James *Principles of Psychology*, 1890; Schusterman 2012, 349). As Richard Schusterman explains,

> One of James's central arguments in epistemology, ontology, and philosophy of mind is that the world we perceive or experience is not a fixed, independent, immutable given but rather a product of human selection in which the selective process involves different levels and can be likened to artistic creation, especially because the criteria for selection are in large part aesthetic.

(2011, 350).

---

[99] According to Jonathan Loesberg, there has even been a tendency to label "believing in a concept of literary value ... a cardinal theoretical sin", although he goes on playfully to assert that "many of us indulged on the sly" (2005, 1).

The mental process of thinking and judging involve more than the shared concepts used for rational deliberation of facts to be stated in language: it involves paying attention to unformed sensation as the stuff that produces knowledge. Viewed thus, knowledge becomes something personal and deeply subjective, founded on a process of selection of which we are relatively unaware.

And yet, an experience, Dewey maintains, still "has a unity that gives it its name, *that* meal, that storm, that rupture of friendship" (2005, 38). The reality of such a unity, moreover, "is constituted by a single *quality* that pervades the entire experience in spite of the variation of its constituent parts" (2005, 38). Notably, "this unity is neither emotional, practical, nor intellectual, for these terms name distinctions that reflection can make within it" (Dewey 2005, 38). Seeking to recover "the continuity of esthetic [*sic*] experience with normal processes of living", Dewey therefore suggests that we go "back to experience of the common or mill run of things to discover the esthetic quality such experience possesses" (2005, 9).[100] Indeed, Dewey explains,

> thinking goes on in trains of ideas, but the ideas form trains only because they are much more than what analytic psychology calls ideas. They are phases, emotionally and practically distinguishable, of a developing underlying quality; they are its moving variations, not separate and independent, like Locke's and Hume's so-called ideas and impressions, but are subtle shadings of a pervading and developing hue.

---

[100] According to Dewey, the continuity between somatic, non-discursive experience and intellectual experience, *viz.* culture and ritual, was broken with the advent of "art for art's sake" in the 19th century (2005, 6). Dewey links this rupture in the fabric of artistic experience to the advent of modernity, and the rise of nationalism and capitalism (2005, 7). However, "to isolate art and its appreciation by placing them in a realm of their own, disconnected from other modes of experiencing, are not inherent in the subject matter but arise because of specifiable extraneous conditions" (2005, 7). Hence, Dewey's effort to frame art as experience.

(Dewey 2005, 39)

In reflecting on embodied experience, however, we often resort to habitual concepts and to words that we already know are part of such concepts. Depending on what language we speak, we also end up mapping such experience to the structure within which we are more accustomed to shaping our thoughts, namely our language of preference, although different languages may in fact establish different connections between experiencing and conceptualising.[101]

In habitually using the words that we already know, however, we risk losing track of our sensations. Merely mapping sensations to sense does not capture the intrinsic relationship between a "felt dimension ... that is prelogical" and "the logical and objective orders" (Gendlin 1997, 1). Indeed, the process of thinking is itself experience, in so far as it projects a context for an enveloping unifying quality, and in so far as it is "rounded out with this quality" (Dewey 2005, 40). Reaching for concepts that could be seen to capture the meaning of experience in words we risk falling prey to epistemological biases, lodged in preconceived notions, derived from historical, cultural, and social contexts, and oriented towards the past as that context within which these words have been seen to make sense. With reference to mis-movements this means that to see a movement precisely *as* a *mis-movement*—that is to pay attention to a movement *as* nothing *or* something, even as you do not arrive to specifically categorize it as such—is already to recognize in that movement, something *other than* what you would expect, and so to take it in its discursive *and* non-discursive mode, *both* meaningful and meaningless. It is also to contextualise it in terms of measuring it against its conventional use or purpose. The carnal hermeneutics invited by mis-movements, by

---

[101] Notably, "[l]anguage is central to our experience of being human, and the languages we speak profoundly shape the way we think, the way we see the world, the way we live our lives" (Mykhailyuk and Pohlod 2015, 37).

contrast, entails straddling the divide between sensation and sense.[102] To speak with and from what is *more than* the categories we employ in language—that is, to speak from embodied experience—is on the one hand to embark on a 'return to language' (see Kearney 2015, 100), which is why the emphasis on mis-movements in Beckett's drama does not jettison language; yet it is also to produce a new, future oriented syntax, one that is *both* capable of creating new sentences to speak about experience, *and* of unearthing the deeply rooted meanings of the human body as reflexively sensed from inside.

The consistent foregrounding of mis-movements as non-conceptual presentations therefore indicates that they are prompts for spectator attention that target deeper structures of perception. According to McMullan, Beckett's experiential dramaturgy is a 'site' in which "audience are not detached observers, but rather are positioned as an inherent part of the performance, though individual spectators may resist or redefine that role in particular productions" (McMullan 2010, 13). And, within this context, the body is arguably also a site for experience for characters and audiences alike, regardless of the fictionality of the former, and even as this site is not a location but an event. Crippled and frequently condemned to stasis, Beckett's characters comment on their situation, and their narratives can be seen to yield metaphysical explanations for the event of embodiment. Expelled from the world of the past and framed within the limits of

---

[102] According to Kearney a divide opened with the linguistic turn in the 1960s and led to the expulsion of the body from phenomenological examination (2015, 100). And, he maintains, "when the explicit 'hermeneutic turn' occurred ... the journey from flesh to text all too often lacked a return ticket" (2015, 100). Also, Mark Johnson, in "Mind Incarnate: from Dewey to Damasio" (2006), comments on the change in philosophy and cognitive science towards recognizing the embodied nature of human beings, which entailed giving "up the notion of a transcendent soul and disembodied mind". If we give up on this idea, "then we must give up as well some of our most commonly cherished assumptions about what it means to be human" (2006, 46)—a change that he calls problematic, since it "excludes (or at least hides) most of what goes into the ways we make sense of our experience" (2008, 9).

the present, the characters seem to have lost their freedom of choice. Estragon and Vladimir cannot leave because they are waiting for Godot. Hamm and Clov cannot end but only wish for the end to come: "CLOV: Finished, it's finished, nearly finished, it must be nearly finished" (*CDW* 93). Their situation parallels that of the performance. Yet, the site is not a place: it is an experience, a reconfiguration of the aesthetic object that has considerable implications for our processes of making sense of it.

In other words, not only are mis-movements foregrounded to be noticed, but even the perceptive act itself is staged. Given that mis-movements are non-propositional elements of performance, there are no connections between, for example, the shape and form of a movement and specific meanings, since mis-movements do not represent concepts in the sense that words do. Yet, the repetition of movement patterns will inevitably begin to acquire meaning, in part because spectators are goaded to perceive and remember mis-movements, and in part because the meaningfulness of mis-movements is drawn from spectator attention.

Embodied cognition

The new syntax produced by mis-movements is therefore bifocal in that it takes *both* the perceiver *and* the perceived into consideration—*both* subject *and* object, *both* performance *and* audience etc. Thus, it has implications also for the project of conceptualizing subjective acts of interpretation. Put differently, the project of shifting theoretical ground entails reconfiguring the perceiving subject, yet what counts as a body is not a given (Johnson 2008). The biological body's affective, cognitive, or behavioural attitudes, the ecological body's contexts, the phenomenological body's experience of qualities, such as—for instance—softness, fixation, intensity etc., the social body's intersubjective relations, and the dimensions of the cultural body, for example gender, race, class etc., are all examples of overlapping—yet different—dimensions of the body (Johnson 2008,

164–165).[103] By analogy, Ariane Mildenberg points out that "[b]y reflecting upon and imposing meaning upon the world, we separate ourselves from it, and yet we are always already an integral part of the same world: both encroaching upon the world and, simultaneously, being encroached upon" (2017, 114). We must therefore be careful to "assume a simplistic or monolithic reductionist conception of the body" (Johnson 2008, 166). Rather than unified, autonomous subjects, "we *are* interaction" (Gendlin),[104] consistently modified by the contexts into which we blend. There is thus "no mind entity to serve as the locus of reason." What "we call 'reason' is neither a concrete nor abstract *thing*, but only embodied *process*," by which our experience is "explored, criticized, and transformed in inquiry" (Johnson 2008, 13). Consequently, the "idea that meaning and understanding is based solely on propositional structures is problematic as it hides most of what goes into the ways we make sense of our experience" (Johnson 2008, 9). If somatic experience determines human sense-making, then what Kant terms judgments are perhaps "merely the more conscious, selective dimension" of the vast field of experience which afford such meanings (Johnson 2008, 10). In fact, Johnson explains, repudiating Kant, "meaning is not just a matter of concepts or propositions, but also reaches down to into the images, sensorimotor schemas, feelings, qualities and emotions that constitute our meaningful encounter with our world" (2008, 9). Somatic experience is deeply qualitative, which is to say it enfolds "aspects of experience traditionally regarded as the purview of aesthetics" (Johnson 2008, x), and the meaning of such experiencing is both cumulative and relational Johnson 2008, 10). In this sense, the "meaning of a thing, is its consequences for experience––how it 'cashes out' by way of experience, either actual or possible experience" (Johnson 2008, 10). By analogy, judgment cannot arise *ex*

---

[103] Indeed, a human body "has [at least] five dimensions", and it cannot be reduced to "any one (or two or three) of them" (Johnson 2008, 165). Rather, we must be careful to "assume a simplistic or monolithic reductionist conception of the body" (Johnson 2008, 166).

[104] YouTube: https://www.youtube.com/watch?v=xaopap6K_JQ , (2.18–2.22).

nihilo but must be based on something, must be judgement *of* something. Notably, then, the relation between audience and performance is therefore not a bloodless relation but a communicative relationship built on interaction and honed by sensation, feeling and emotion, taking place on different levels of affective responses (*viz.* precognitive, personal, and social).[105]

If the issue of making "sense of sense" relates to "how we make sense of our lives in the flesh" (Kearney 2015, 99),[106] therefore, then understanding is necessarily fluid and vacillating. Indeed, "hermeneutics begins ... in the flesh" (2015, 100), and because discernment is carnal "hermeneutics goes all the way down" (Kearney 2015, 101). That is, sense and sense making are intrinsically connected so that meaning travels in sensation *before* it reaches the level of linguistic understanding (Johnson 2008, 9). In short, thinking begins in sensation, and "propositions are *not* the basic units of human meaning and thought", but "meaning is shaped by the nature of our bodies, especially our sensorimotor capacities and our ability to experience feelings and emotions" (Johnson 2008, 9). Both Kearney and Johnson, then, acknowledge the body's participation in sense making, and maintain that interpretation and discernment begins in sensation.[107] Indeed, Kearney maintains, what Husserl's phenomenological investigation into the lived body revealed is that "[a]esthesiology grounds gnoseology" (2015, 111). Notably, this

---

[105] See Brian Massumi, "The Autonomy of Affect". *Cultural Critique*, No. 31, "The Politics of Systems and Environments", Part II, Autumn, 1995, pp. 83–109.

[106] Specifying three different ways in which this happens, namely by "i) sensation, ii) meaning, iii) orientation" (2015, 99), Richard Kearney maintains that the body participates in experience both at the precognitive level of sensation and at the level of language or intellectual understanding, and that our modes of orienting ourselves in the world result from such mediation.

[107] Yet, importantly, they also acknowledge that the body's tendency to recede from perception has rendered its significance for interpretation, evaluation, and judgement less conspicuous (Kearney 2015, 104; Johnson 2009, 4).

means that attending to mis-movements within the framework of embodied meaning, *viz.* interpreting mis-movements, necessarily entails getting in touch with a deeper level of experience. On this level, the body always extends its material limits, whether we are talking of a spectator's body or about bodies perceived by a spectator. The challenge more broadly is merely to "stop thinking about a human body as merely a thing" (Johnson 2008, 163), in favour of recognizing its intrinsic participation in the world of meanings.

Thinking from experience with language

This is not to say that non-discursive experience should be confused with immediacy. Remembering Bateson's warning against the "muddling of logical typing" (2002, 58), I merely propose that meaning-making is founded on our visceral connections to the world and best understood on a continuum of aesthetic experience, *both* discursive *and* non-discursive, *both* immediate *and* mediated. My emphasis on embodied cognition is thereby complemented by a more pragmatic aesthetic approach to counter my reliance on Dewey's emphasis on non-discursive experience as less foundational. Indeed, according to Richard Shusterman, embodied experience necessitates a variety of mediating perspectives to be fully grasped (2002, 33). The interconnections between somatic, non-discursive experience generated by mis-movements, and those modes of mediation—be they linguistic, visual or auditive—serve to imply the relevance of mis-movements. Thus, I maintain that there is a poetic logic to Beckett's 'carnal hermeneutics' that indicates the interconnection between body and mind.

Clearly, making sense of mis-movements entails more than merely tapping into non-discursive, immediate experiencing. As Shusterman explains, one should be careful not to conflate "immediate experience with non-discursive experience … [or] all somatic experience with immediate experience (2002, 32). Somatic experience need not be non-discursive, but could be immediately recognized as, for instance, pain or noise. That is, somatic experience may of course be interpreted. In somatic methods—such as, for instance Alexander Technique,™ or the method of Moshe Feldenkrais™ (the latter a method that Shusterman himself practices (Dolezal 2014, 2)—the "means of verbal mediation and conscious reflection [may] be used to improve the functioning of non-discursive experience" (Shusterman 2002, 33).[108] Just like Gendlin, Shusterman therefore emphasizes the importance of thinking *from* somatic, embodied experience *with* language, whereas Dewey's emphasizes the body as primary. My discussion is thus more aligned with Kearney's and Shusterman's poetics than with Johnson's and Dewey's aesthetics, despite my obvious affinity with their perspectives. If, as Richard Kearney suggests, "dilemmas of authority betray anxieties of value" (1999, xi), then the application of mis-movements in performance could be seen to betray an anxiety about the value of language. But it could also be seen to betray an anxiety of freedom of mind and clarity of vision. Mis-movements testify to Beckett's awareness of audience's expectations and so, the aesthetics of gesture is rhetorical. That is, mis-movements activate a feedback loop whereby spectators are prompted to recognize that those (re-)sources needed to understand the text are

---

[108] As a practitioner of the Feldenkrais method, Shusterman complies with its aims to "improve our immediate, non-discursive bodily habits and experience by bringing them into greater consciousness so that they can be better appreciated and modified" (2014, 33). The objective of such a method is thus to regulate the individual's mode of interacting with 'body-en#2' (see Gendlin 2018, 4), partly to achieve more ergonomic movements patters but partly, also, to modify the conditions of possibility for such interaction on the level of attention (Shusterman 2014, 33). As a former dancer and dance pedagogue, I have often used a combination of verbal (specialist terms and explanations), visual (showing by doing the movement), and tactile (for instance using my hands and feet to guide a pupil's moving) as mediators to facilitate or help a pupil experience and conceptualize a movement. Verbal and sensory mediation are useful methods for modifying a dance student's non-discursive experience of moving in dance teaching, even if few dance teachers would claim that their means of instruction seek to replace a mind-centred perspective on life with a more somatic outlook. Still, I believe that this is a side-effect of dancing that is by no means negligible.

not in the text, or to paraphrase James Phelan, they're not *only* in the text (2017, *ix*)—they are also in the spectator's felt sense of embodied experience. Mis-movements disrupt the idea of interpretation as detached, objective, and rational. The frustration or sympathy we feel because of our involvement with the drama bleeds into us on account of our vicarious involvement in the performance ecology. Thus, Beckett's drama problematizes the notion of freedom associated with action and movement as the prerequisite for moral judgment, through problematizing the notion of art as practice, and the notion that audiences as the recipients of artistic practice. The relation between aesthetic experience and interpretation is therefore key to understanding the significance of mis-movements in Beckett's drama. Partly, because of the ways in which mis-movements disrupt language but partly, also, because of the way mis-movements could be seen to intersect with the issue of responsivity. Indeed, mis-movements disrupt the linguistic realm of communication and the effects of such disruption include the reconfiguration of the aesthetic object, *viz.* art as experience, as well as the reconceptualization of the performance context. Notably, such disruption is not comfortable, yet it is *as* interruptions that block interpretation mis-movements solicit thinking from the edge of interruption—that is, from the edge of ignorance, which is where new modes of interaction may be carried forward into new wholes.

The poetic logic of mis-movements

As discussed above, the carefully choreographed mis-movements that appear in Beckett's drama are of equal purport and significance as the linguistic material presented. The aesthetic aspects of mis-movements ostensibly comprise the material for whatever propositions spectators arrive at, based on their felt sense of these experiences. Yet, mis-movements are also meaningful on account of offering a conduit for spectators to connect with embodied cognition. In fact, the compelling allure of Beckett's aesthetics of gesture rests on the capacity of mis-movements to meaningfully sustain our sense of belonging to the world, whether we recognize this call to experience or not.

Over time, however, Beckett seems to have realized that "to cast aside one veil it was necessary to assume another veil, or veil an otherness, that a language not his own could supply" (Leslie Hill qtd in Lawrence 2018, 81, *fn5*). Like Vico, his exploration into the limits of language seems to have been propelled by a desire to understand the processes by which we make sense of the world, and specifically by a desire to understand the role of language in such efforts. The issue that most preoccupies Vico is the question of what kind of knowledge is possible to attain under various conditions and the role of language under the conditions that apply (see McMullin and Pompa 1976, 458). That is, specifically given that the production of knowledge seems contingent on language as a medium for thinking[109]— a notion that resonates with the poetic logic of mis-movements in Beckett's drama where mis-movements arrive to challenge language as the primary medium for thinking, although not abolish language since language still remains an important vehicle for thinking.[110] Moreover, linking language to stages in the socio-cultural development of nations Vico suggests that the poetic logic of language takes the form of "the mode or manner in which they arise" (Vico 2013, 81). According to Vico, the earliest poets' language expressed an enchanted view of the

---

[109] As a "professor of rhetoric, a learned philologist, [and] a historian of jurisprudence" (McMullin and Pompa 1976, 450), Vico's understanding of the poetic as a function of language, but also his "grasp of explanation through origins, [and] his conviction that human culture and human knowledge grow through transformation", leads him to reformulate science in a manner more aligned with contemporary definitions, "one where metaphor (or model) would play a central role, where scientific concepts themselves would be seen to be developing, where theory would be regarded as never definitive but always open to reformulation in the light of new challenge" (McMullin and Pompa 1976, 460).

[110] According to David Price, "Vico observes that, 'For the Latins, *verum* (the true) and *factum* (what is made) are interchangeable [and] [t]his leads Vico to declare that the ancient sages had attained an important insight to which we are blind, namely, that 'The true is precisely what is made' (1994, 120).

world: "pointing mutely, they ... imagined ... the substances of the sky, earth and sea ... to be deities; and, trusting the truth of their senses they believed they were gods" (Vico 2013, 158). As Donald Phillip Verene explains, "Vico derives logic itself from the form of the poetic (2015, 129), such that "poetic logic is propaedeutic to the active sciences of poetic morals, economy, and politics, as well as the speculative poetic sciences of nature" (Verene 2015, 128). Or, as Beckett succinctly summarizes Vico's thesis in "Dante ... Bruno .. Vico . Joyce" (1929): "In the beginning was the thunder: the thunder set free Religion, in its most objective and unphilosophical form — idolatrous animism" (1983, 20), thus, "[t]he first men had to create matter by the force of their imagination, and poet means 'creator'" (Beckett 1983, 24).

The aspect in Vico's poetics that interests me most with reference to Beckett's aesthetics of gesture is thus the fact that Vico's poetic logic a) assumes an embodied foundation for meaning-making and understanding, and b) assumes that to imagine is to create. In Vico's poetics, the embodied roots of language are intrinsic to its use, which is to say that the "faculties belonging to the mind ... are rooted in the body and derive their power from it" (2013, 369). The first speech, says Vico, is pre-linguistic, born of awe and rooted in the senses, only as these meanings became more and more abstract, a figurative sense was seen to stand-in for sensation, their embodied roots fell into neglect (2013, 158).[111] To Vico, however, "[p]oetic speech ... [is] a product of poetic logic" (Vico 2013, 163). By analogy, Beckett's assault on language could be seen as an effort to unveil the deeper layers of sense making, layers that have been overwritten or replaced by abstract linguistic structures, and to grant this dimension

---

[111] According to Vico, "[m]etaphysics contemplates things in all the categories of their being, but it becomes logic when it considers them in the categories by which they are signified" (2013, 157). This can be deducted from the etymology of words: "[t]he word logic comes from Greek *logos*, which first properly mean fable, or *fabula* in Latin, which later changed into Italian *favella*, speech. In Greek, a fable was also called *mythos*, myth, from which is derived Latin, *mutus*, mute" (Vico 2013, 157).

creative power by producing such conditions as would afford moving beyond language, delving into its embodied dimension, but also thinking from this dimension to re-examine concepts. Indeed, as Beckett writes to Axel Kaun: "to bore one hole after another in it, until what lurks behind it—be it something or nothing—begins to seep through.": "I cannot imagine a higher goal for a writer today" (1983, 172). Both Vico and Beckett, then recognize the significance of context for language use.[112] And both arrive at examinations of the continuity between sensation and sense-making, albeit in different contexts.

'Thickening' the narrative web of performance

Considering the above, my aim is not to map affinities between Vico and Beckett, beyond pointing out the emphasis on creativity for the process of understanding. That said, I do not maintain that it is taxonomical issues that seem to have propelled Beckett's creative exploration of the dramatic genre. Rather, the aesthetics of gesture in Beckett's drama seems driven by a persistent exploration of being—centred on the question of knowledge, what it is and how it can be gained. Perhaps the best way to conceptualize mis-movements is to borrow the metaphor of "thickening" (Caraccioli and Kukkonen 2021, 15), which implies that the narrative web has been enriched and complicated by elements of communication that usually are not considered in literary analyses. Marco Caracciolo and Karin Kukkonen point out that what the metaphor seeks to capture, namely the "the wide gamut of experiential effects that are probabilistically correlated with literary stories" remains hypothetical, albeit based on empirical evidence (2021, 15). By analogy, the corpus of Beckett's stage directions that serve the foundation for this present

---

[112] Vico's concern with the historical periods of human history leads him to conclude that each age has its own language, appropriate to its understanding of common sense, which he defines as "an unreflecting judgement shared by an entire social order, people, nation, or even all mankind" (Vico 2013, 80).

study only hypothetically substantiates my claim that the changes Beckett made to his dramas in the processes of staging them, were based on an insight into how the context of performance would profoundly change a text. Considering this, mis-movements could be fruitfully approached as gateways to embodied cognition. Mis-movements challenge the radical scepticism intrinsic to language, for instance by producing doubt about interpretation, and they do so partly on account of their capacity to draw spectators into the event of performance—an event within which the tacit intricacy of embodied cognition figures as source for meaning-making—but also on account of their capacity to prompt a concern for embodied life, which is an important aspect of the aesthetics of gesture. Beckett's drama, then, is appealing in many different senses of the word: it appeals to our embodied sense of what it means to be a human being who feels and (often) suffers, but it also appeals to our powers of deduction, to our aptitudes and tendencies for interpretating and evaluating everything we encounter, through processes of abduction, snatching, best explanation, felt meanings etc. While mis-movements may be understood as metaphors for specific experiences, I do not propose mapping experiences to mis-movements to discuss semantic or propositional meanings. Rather, what I suggest is that mis-movements are an intrinsic part of the narrative context.

As part of discussing the significance of mis-movements in the context of performance, both their status as fictional and their function within the narrative structure of performance must be considered. Indeed, as Caracciolo and Kukkonen explain, storytelling (and performance is arguably a form of storytelling) profoundly "plays on the reader's embodiment" (2021, 3), and literary research more broadly has increasingly sought to create "awareness of how the body plays a significant role in the interpretation of individual narratives" (Caracciolo and Kukkonen 2021, 3). Yet, they continue, "even though the embodied mind ... springs from interactions between our biological makeup and the experienced physical and sociocultural contexts in which we are immersed ... research on embodiment in literature has concentrated almost exclusively on the social and cultural dimensions of the body" (Caracciolo and Kukkonen 2021, 5). In other words, the biological body, its movements, and interactions, are nominally in the background in the context of literary analysis even as "all narratives—including stories as trivial as an account of an ordinary day at work—are deeply embodied in that they tap into a repertoire of embodied interactions with the world (through situation models, motor resonance, and so on)" (Caracciolo and Kukkonen 2021, 15).[113] Whatever is foregrounded in the literary context will be deemed relevant so that on a general note we tend to find what we are looking for, and the fact that literary scholars rarely look for the body in texts might therefore explain why so relatively few have found it. Thus, as Gendlin reminds us, it is important to realize that "[l]anguage is never alone, it is implied by the body in situations" (Gendlin 1986, 269).

Notably, then, the strategic use of mis-movements in Beckett's drama speaks to the wider implications of reconfiguring the communicative context. In fact, it could be argued that all plays documented in *The Theatrical Notebooks, Vol. I-IV*, correspond to Beckett's late, or atmospheric, phase and that the stage directions to *Godot*, but also to the other plays documented in the *Theatrical Notebooks* series, are more a testament to Beckett's transformed understanding of the context of performance than a set of rules indicating how each performance should be staged. The discussions in this book rest on the assumption that the stage directions are not meant to be slavishly followed. Indeed, neither prescriptive nor authoritarian, they are exemplary of the poetic logic of mis-movements, which takes interaction to be foundational. This is especially evident in Beckett's late drama, which seem to present 'onto-ethico-epistemological' statements (see Barad 2007). This rather complex notion is taken from Karen Barad's book *Meeting the Universe Halfway* (2007), in which she convincingly explains that "[t]o be is not simply to be intertwined with another, but to lack an independent self-

---

[113] Cf Gendlin's descriptions of various body-environment modes of interaction (2018, 6–7).

contained existence" (2007, ix). From Barad's standpoint, "[e]xistence is not an individual affair [but] individuals emerge through and as part of their entangled intra-relating" (*ibid*), a perspective that opens a completely different understanding of what it means to be human, but also on what it means to be a sign, or a text. Viewed thus, mis-movements—but also, for example, memory, subjectivity, anxiety, *apatheia* or suffering (all of which are central topics in Beckett's dramas)—are not individual achievements but deeply entangled, intra-active rather than interactive experiences, that generate our conceptualizations of individuality. It is not as individual agents that we move about, constitute, or produce recollections, biases, troubles, or values etc., but our imaginative and creative involvement with the world is conditioned on our entanglements with other entities (animate as well as inanimate). Notably, we cannot escape being inherently part of the world of objects as well as part of each other's lives. Viewed thus, attending to mis-movements is not merely a matter of evaluating ideas, but of participating in creating them, and so it becomes a matter of ethics, namely the ethics of selecting and the ethics of understanding our intrinsic interdependence, which conditions our ability to think and to feel. Interestingly, therefore, and considering the above, mis-movements do not have to be meaningful before being perceived as such. That is, the status of mis-movements as significant phenomena hinges on the recognition that interaction conditions human communication and takes place beyond the confines of words. Notably, the body is an important albeit a frequently overlooked aspect of communication and it is this complex relationship between *being* nothing and *becoming* something that is at the core of Beckett's aesthetics of gesture.

The value of aesthetic experience

If Beckett's drama is an outlet for a life-long enquiry into what it means to become a human being through interacting with other human beings, then it seems propelled by a sense that this is a worthwhile project to pursue. Indeed, Beckett's creative effort is seemingly founded on a belief that the truth of human situatedness can be told even as it is difficult, if not impossible, to capture it in language. Comprising a radical questioning of what it means to be a thinking and, above all, a feeling being, the hallmark of Beckett's drama is that it is frames the issue of interpretation as an embodied practice. Yet it also invites reflection on whether we are capable of authentic judgements or whether "our personal decision-making process merely reflect social and political control" (Gendlin 1986, 265).[114] And according to Gendlin, "[e]thics is best cared for as distinctions between kinds of processes. After all, it is the process which determines the contents" (Gendlin, 1986, 265).[115] The fact that the process of discernment carries implicit intricacy *forward* is what safeguards its authenticity. Admittedly, the notion of authenticity fell in disrepute on account of Sartre's and most notably Heidegger's negative definitions, but also on account of their relativism (Gendlin 1986, 265). By contrast, an ethical process on Gendlin's account is specific and proceeds through "(1) steps; (2) in which what is found can also change; (3) and in which new facts can appear ... [that is step three] involve more coming out of the process than went in (1986,

---

[114] And Gendlin's caim that Heidegger's account of authenticity borders on relativism is corroborated by Rick Roderick, who maintains that on Heidegger's account you can be authentically anything. Indeed, Heidegger's "project is one to get away from empty conformity and to live authentically. Now here is its tremendous drawback ... The trouble with leaving the account of being human this abstract, you know 'We come from a culture, we flee from conformity, we try to get authentic' the trouble with leaving it that abstract is that you could be an authentic anything, you follow me? I mean, it turns out that you could be authentically a member of the Third Reich, authentically a member of Reagan administration... I'll just leave those two together for a while in your minds... authentically a friend of Richard Nixon... no wait a minute, that's logically absurd... no it isn't, I think that's possible." (URL: http://rickroderick.org/302-heidegger-and-the-rejection-of-humanism-1993/).

[115] Correspondingly, Rick Roderick explains that "[n]ot all kinds of inquiry can appear in just any setting. There are conditions for the possibility of certain questions being asked" (Roderick "101 Socrates and the Life of Inquiry (1990)", transcription).

266).[116] What the process of carrying the implicit intricacy forward shows is that "[i]mposed form is not the only order" (Gendlin 1986, 275), although "[a]nything human is also social" (Gendlin 1986, 268). Even though subjectivity is *also* a social order, this is not to say that it is merely an imposed form. Theories and concepts enable a step process, whereby we may arrive to challenge the concepts and theories we operate with, and as Gendlin explains, "a finer cognition feeds back from the body's implicit order in process steps" (1986, 275). What Gendlin terms "authentic decision-making process" (1986, 268) therefore entails a set of descriptions that help us understand why it is not the case that anything goes. Clearly, there is more to ethical discernment than merely reflecting on social norms. Social norms and concepts are therefore still important content for ethical discernment. The issue is merely whether the process of distinguishing between different kinds of processes can "change or exceed social norms and in what respects it perhaps cannot" (Gendlin 1986, 268). Indeed, "[w]e are not blank slates. The *tabula rasa* hypothesis has been disproved" (Gendlin 1986, 270). Yet, "[t]houghts, feelings, desires, and other experiences are not just given things. They are generated by processes. A certain kind of process creates the ancient virtues. It is not the case that just anything at all can be the content of any process. Far from it" (1986, 265). Only, there is an important distinction to be made between the process of being invited to think and the process of being taught what to think—the former is ethical, the latter is a process of socialization (Gendlin 1986, 272–273).[117] Arguably, Beckett's drama is

---

[116] There is also "a fourth and fifth characteristics of the authentic decision-making process" (Gendlin 1986, 268), namely that "[t]here is often a 'sense' of something not known but needed, required", and there may also "be many steps, each further forming what the previous 'really' was" (Gendlin 1986, 268).

[117] Also, says Gendlin, the "social patterns are not imported on a mere chaotic drive energy. They are imposed on a more intricate texture, a greater order – but this shows itself only in process. ... All order is not from society. Animals are already very complex. Society develops that further, but the body also develops these forms still further. It is not just a copy of society." 1986, 270).

affiliated with the former. It is an invitation to think, in steps, on the process of making sense of embodied experience. Self-scrutiny or introspection in Beckett's drama is thus an inevitable result of being invited to think about meaning rather than being told what things mean. Yet, attending to mis-movements also reminds us of our ignorance *vis-á-vis* self and other. We basically have no idea about the lives of others, human or non-human, and nor do we necessarily understand what we perceive. The moment we give ourselves precedence of interpretation in the context of Beckett's drama, mis-movements call on us to reckon with our mistake.

Intellectual freedom

Whether it should be understood in terms of "willed creative mismaking", "logoclasm" (Durantaye 2016, 2; 14), or a "word-storming in the name of beauty," (Banville March 22, 2012), Beckett's creative project thus initially entails a carefully coordinated attack on language "All his life", writes John Calder, "Beckett struggled with language, dissatisfied with its inability to express exactly the meaning that always just eluded him" (2001, 94). In his critical writings, Beckett also frequently returns to the predicament of expression, often evaluating the strategies taken up by various artists in response to this dilemma, which is to say he is concerned with the impossibility of giving shape to the 'mess' that is life (see Dearlove 1982, 12–13). Over time, however, Beckett reconfigured his understanding of communication. Importantly, therefore, Beckett's assault on words does not stop interpretation; it paves the ground for perceiving things more clearly. If the ecology of the mind is a heterogenous web of significances, then this web comprises networks of significations that more resemble "the sort of complicated, living, struggling, cooperating, tangle like what you'll find on mountain slopes" (Bateson 2000, 265). This is not to suggest that some significances cannot be self-reflexively perceived. Indeed, my argument rests, at least in part, on the assumption that Beckett's drama affords opportunities for spectators to reflect on creative minds at work—their own and

Beckett's. Only, it would be impossible to account for all perceptions generated through such processes. We are automatically geared towards that which stands out for perception on account of being different, strange, or pathological. The nature of perception is fleeting, and it would be impossible to capture all images that mis-movements produce. Yet the interpretative gaps that open with mis-movements reveal interpretation to be a much more fluid process than the experience/content division could capture. As Beckett shifts focus from telling to showing, therefore, he also shifts from stating that 'people are bloody ignorant apes' to showing the very structures that uphold such ignorance.

Quoting from an interview with Beckett, James Knowlson describes how Beckett came to realize the need for reduction in his work, possibly in order to show this situation more clearly, in all its simplicity:

> I realized that Joyce had gone as far as one could in the direction of knowing more, [being] in control of one's material. He was always adding to it; you only have to look at his proofs to see that. I realized that my own way was in impoverishment, in lack of knowledge and in taking away.
>
> (1996, 319)[118]

No information is given about publication in the footnotes although there is a reference to another interview with Beckett by Israel Shenker, in which Beckett states:

> "The more Joyce knew the more he could. He's tending towards omniscience and omnipotence as an artist. I'm working with impotence, ignorance. There seems to be a kind of esthetic axiom that expression is achievement – must be an achievement.

---

[118] Knowlson is here quoting from an interview he himself had with Samuel Beckett on October 27, 1989.

My little exploration is that whole zone of being that has always been set aside by artists as something unusable– as something by definition incompatible with art.

(Beckett qtd by Israel Schenker, from an interview in *The New York Times*, May 5, 1956 ; also qtd in Knowlson 1996, 686)

The 'zone of being' that Beckett explores, however, is permeated by invisible structures that could be seen to make up the phenomenological natural attitude, whether defined in terms of ideology, *habitus*, or described as a form of 'epistemic injustice', which is to say in terms of the epistemic limitations that frame habitual sense-making.[119] Beckett subsequently rejected the "Joycean principle that knowing more was a way of creatively understanding the world and controlling it" (Knowlson 1996, 319). He also abandoned the writing techniques founded on the principle of adequate expressions and proceeded to focus on man as a "non-knower" and "non-can-er" (Knowlson 1996, 320). As discussed above, however, the process of reduction was gradual, beginning with a frustration with language that eventually led to a questioning of the notion of reality. Subsequently, as Beckett came to direct his own plays in the 1960s, the process started to involve more and more elements of performance—not least, the body and physical movements.

Clearly, then, spectators cannot stop producing meaning and mis-movements, by analogy, do not eliminate the relevance of linguistic meanings—they merely underwrite our complicity and participation in producing them. The desire to "world-storm" or "logoclasm" (Durantaye 2016, 14), is in this sense a call for justice. As spectators, we are always "the datives of disclosure" for the

---

[119] By analogy, Simon Critchley explains, the theatre was once a *theatron*, a theorization of practice that presented audiences with the opportunity to engage in 'adversary reasoning' (2017, *npage*). In a context dominated by war, ancient Greek dramas played out opposing views to help spectators see the other's perspective— the perhaps that lingers in-between self and other, us and them.

intelligibility of any presentation (see Sokolowski 2008, 4). In other words, we are always already invited to respond and "exercise responsibility and truthfulness if we are to be human" (*Ibid.*). It is perhaps not by coincidence that all Beckett's characters face the threat of having nowhere to hide from the voices of accusation (see Llewellyn Brown 2021). Yet, if characters suffer from having to realize that they have greatly overestimated their ability to think and act., then audiences are also invited to do the same. Beckett's dramas call audiences to witness presentations demanding attention and response.

However, to witness is not enough. The act of witnessing also entails a call to judge the significance of what is being witnessed, and this is also how the issue of responsivity becomes an ethical task. Indeed, if Sartre's notion of false consciousness suggests that the paradigm for ideology is faith, or perhaps blind conviction paired with commitment to a truth that cannot be doubted—indeed, how can you doubt what you cannot know?—then the rupture in the lines of communication in Beckett's drama reveals and underwrites the complications of such blind conviction or faith, specifically by means of mis-movements as phenomena that demand attention beyond 'old' meanings. Even those satisfied in a state of ignorance or unconcerned with the ideological underpinnings of conviction stand to be liberated by the 'skeleton simple' structure of presentations that demand involvement beyond stating the obvious. It is thus to the effect of challenging habitual strategies of meaning-making that mis-movements arrive to transport spectators beyond the level of linguistic meanings. Yet, in so doing, mis-movements also produce a context for aesthetic experience that also has ethical implications.

As Gendlin's and Murdoch's linking of ethics and morality to perception reveals, interpretation is a generative process of responsiveness enfolding processes of introspection, transformation, and change, rather than actions in accordance with certain norms that imply behaviourist or existentialist predicaments. Consequently, the work of Gendlin, but interestingly also the work of Iris Murdoch, provide useful perspectives on the aesthetics of gesture in Beckett's drama. Both Gendlin and Murdoch recast ethics as a perceptual, generative processes involving imagination, which also Beckett seems to have done; both Gendlin and Murdoch, respectively, connect ethics and morality with process and with change (see Gendlin 1986; see Murdoch 1970); both Gendlin and Murdoch maintain that ethical discernment is a process that produces change, a fact that distinguishes it from other processes that merely confirm the *status quo*; and both Gendlin and Murdoch maintain that our capacity for ethical discernment predicates on our capacity to take seriously "introspectabilia", which "are likely on examination to prove hazy or hard to describe" (Murdoch 1971, 19–20), *viz.* a "'sense of something not known but needed" (Gendlin 1986, 268). Indeed, as Murdoch points out in *The Sovereignty of Good* (1970), "[k]nowledge of a value concept is something to be understood, as it were, in depth" (Murdoch 1971, 28), a mode of understanding that only careful perception can produce. Intriguingly, such an account of morality reads like a programmatic description of Beckett's drama, which similarly connects knowledge to perception and invites audiences to use language thinkingly. Looking at the ethical implications of mis-movements through the combined lenses afforded by Gendlin and Murdoch, I therefore suggest that attending to mis-movements entails acknowledging that morality is not necessarily based on action (the existentialist argument), but on a process of perception that takes embodied experience seriously as resource for ethical judgement. By analogy, in Beckett's drama, the call to attention has an ethical dimension. Founded in perception, the process of meaning-making is not the result of detached operations of the mind, nor the result of choice, but derived from embodied perception, and logic is therefore a poor model to understand it—not least since embodied experience is non-reversible. Mis-movements invite non-discursive, embodied experiences, yet such experiencing cannot be traced back to mis-movements. Mis-movements afford connections between seemingly unrelated occurrences, yet the meanings that open from mis-movements are characterized by interaction, association, and imagination, and solicit processes of change.[120] Thus, mis-movements indicate a continuity between aesthetic experience and meaning that makes audiences' responsivity to mis-movements a tentative measure of the effect of Beckett's skeleton simple drama.

Beckett's drama, then, predicates on a reconfiguration of the performance context as a context for aesthetic experience that links ethics to perception and discernment, not as conclusion, but as process. The process of understanding Beckett's drama is different from what we conventionally imagine, but only to the extent that we try to 'subsume' it under 'old' categories or meanings (cf. Gendlin 1985). What Beckett's drama reveals is not that we cannot know, or even that what we know is "relative to our culture or tribe"—what Roderick in his lecture on "Socrates and the Life of Inquiry" calls "sophomoric relativism" ("101 Socrates and the Life of Inquiry, 15.10–15.12)—but that we cannot *not* know. We are perpetually engaged in creating knowledge based on our embodied situatedness, yet in this process we are often guided by meanings and values that hold us captive. Beckett's drama, however, invites us to move on. As Gendlin observes "I thought Beckett's man funny and odd—the one who talks to himself in the bathroom. But then it hit. I do that too. I am also that whole way he is." (1985, 384). Therefore, says Gendlin, "[d]o not subsume us under old categories, as if Beckett had merely found the category—found us formed that way ... Let 'found' or 'made' mean as they work ... as Beckett finds and makes us" Gendlin 1985, 384). Beckett's drama creates the "first instance of *that*, of which we are then the cases" (Gendlin 1985, 384). And it does this by letting words "mean as they work" (Gendlin 1985, 388). Indeed, Beckett's drama shows us how words work "by bringing their old situations into a new situation, thereby changing the whole cluster." (Gendlin 1985, 384) And mis-movements are exemplary vehicles to create the necessary conditions of possibility for letting words work in ways that supports thinking, knowing, and meaning in new ways.

---

[120] The 'syllogism in grass'-quality of the interactions presented in mis-movements and discussed in chapter two are cases in point.

Correspondingly, as Murdoch's argument shows, our embodied situatedness begs reflection on the techniques available for us as individuals to navigate morally or judiciously under the circumstances that frame thinking, knowing, and meaning. Freedom, says Murdoch, is "itself a moral concept and not just the prerequisite of knowledge" (1971, 37). That is, freedom cannot be "separated from knowledge" (Murdoch 2971, 37).[121] This is so, Murdoch maintains, because "[t]hat *of* which it is knowledge, that 'reality' which we are so naturally led to think of as revealed by just 'attention', can of course, given the variety of human personality and situation, only be thought of as 'one', as a single object ... in some remote and very ideal sense" (Murdoch 1971, 37). Thus, paradoxically, and contrary to the existentialist argument, what Murdoch defines as freedom is not the relativist notion connected with decision making—that is, with the "exercise of freedom" (Murdoch 1971, 34)—and nor is it "the sudden jumping of the isolated will in and out of an impersonal logical complex" (Murdoch 1971, 23). Quite the opposite. It is "essentially something progressive, something infinitely perfectible. So far from claiming for it a sort of infallibility ... [it] has built in the notion of a necessary fallibility" (Murdoch 1971, 23). With reference to a fictive example of a woman struggling to come to terms with her ambivalent feelings towards a dead daughter in law, Murdoch points out that freedom, "is a function of the progressive attempt to see a particular object clearly" (1971 23). The woman in Murdoch's example is confronted with her own hostility towards her daughter-in-law—her perceptions tainted with personal opinions, which moreover have changed over time so there is not one way of characterizing her feelings towards her daughter-in-law (1971, 16). Importantly, however, the daughter-in-law is dead in Murdoch's example, so there is no need for the woman to take any kind of action. Rather, the

---

[121] As Murdoch suggests, "what we really are seems much more like an obscure system of energy out of which choices and visible acts of will emerge at intervals in ways that are often unclear and often dependent on the condition of the system in between the moments of choice" (Murdoch 1971, 53).

question is whether perceiving differently is a requisite feature of morality. And, according to Murdoch,

> goodness is connected with knowledge: not with impersonal quasi-scientific knowledge of the ordinary world ... but with a refined an honest perception of what is really the case, a patient and just discernment and exploration of what confronts one, which is the result not simply of opening one's eyes but of a certainly perfectly familiar kind of moral discipline.
>
> (1971, 37)

Moreover,

> the authority of the Good seems ... necessary because the realism (ability to perceive reality) required for goodness is a kind of intellectual ability to perceive what is true, which is automatically at the same time a suppression of the self.
>
> (1971, 64)

What Murdoch describes as "the checking of selfishness in the interest of the real" (1971, 63), then, is an important aspect of morality founded in the process of trying to perceive the world more clearly— a process that arguably necessitates *thinking from* the concepts we use, creatively applying our imagination to what confronts us, without resorting to preconceived notions or values associated with the concepts we use. Indeed, to merely use the words you have been taught, as Clov protests to do in *Endgame,* is to give up, not merely on intellectual freedom, but also on morality.

A new paradigm for interpretation

So, what happens when we do not understand what we experience, for example, in performance? Do we unnecessarily complicate the 'skeleton simple' in a process of selection aimed at filling in the blanks? Or do we resort to the public domain, to someone else's understanding, to received opinions of the stature or relevance of the work? That is, do we give up on our capacity to think from experience? Or do we take such experiencing as an invitation to search deeper into our own responses to identify the limits of our perceptive powers? Perhaps, these are questions that cannot be answered with any degree of certainty. Some may perhaps even deem them irrelevant on account of the difficulties to account for the inner life of felt sense, or on account of the impossibility to verify the answers to such questions. Still, I maintain, the activity of making judgements about works of art more broadly, or about Beckett's drama specifically, is not merely a matter of rational discernment, it is also a matter of responsivity that has ethical implications. Homed in perception, memory, and attention are guided by curiosity. As Beckett explains in "Proust":

> Curiosity is the hair of our habit tending to stand on end. It rarely happens that our attention is not stained in a lesser or greater degree by this element. ... The more interested our interest, the more indelible must be its record of impressions.
>
> (Beckett 1999, 30).

Whether we are aware of it or not, perception panders to the needs of curiosity, and since curiosity easily wanes, the mood of curiosity is never separate from context. In this chapter, I have therefore suggested that the use of mis-movements in performance affords a heuristic solution to the predicament of expression, that the nature of this predicament is related to our habitual tendencies to settle for linguistic meanings rather than exercising our imaginative faculties, and that the linguistic meanings stated in words and concepts mean *more than* we usually take them to mean. Finally, I have assumed that, to *think from* embodied experience and to carry the implied intricacies of felt meanings forward is to entrain the poetic logic of mis-movements.

The questions that I have been grappling most with throughout this third chapter are thus questions of whether (a) the paradigm for interpretation could include *more than* words, and (b) how the kind of "poetisizing" that makes something new, something that we only with hindsight may relate to old, familiar meanings (Gendlin 1985, 384), happens in the context of Beckett's drama? If Beckett's drama creates something new, something not immediately recognizable, the likes of which we may never have seen before, then what Beckett said about the inexpressibility of van Velde's art is an important point of entry into his own aesthetic practice.[122] And yet, as Edouard Morot-Sir maintains, "to seek meaning for a group of phrases is to accept the fact of allegory" (Morot-Sir 1976, 25). Could there therefore not be literary criticism without an implicit recognition of literary language:

> if there is justification for a critic's adding a new projection to a given language, is not for because he thinks that the first language contains within it another hidden language which it is his responsibility as a critic to extract from or expatiate upon?
>
> (1976, 27)

Moreover, Morot-Sir continues, to approach literature as allegory is to approach it within a republic of letters (cf. Casanova) that subsumes everything to "this creeping disease of any literature in any genre: the *allegorical sin*" (Morot-Sir 1976, 25). In a similar vein, David Lloyd maintains that "Beckett's very deliberately 'allegorical' mode of approach to the literary by way of the painterly", should not be reduced to, or merely transferred to, the visual paradigm as opposed to the writerly (2018, 87). Such reduction of Beckett's effort to "speak through another medium" risk missing what "this allegory … uncovers for this most expressly anti-symbolist of writers" (Lloyd 2018, 87). While I do not question Lloyd's descriptions of literary

---

[122] "For what is that coloured plane, that was not there before. I don't know what it is, having never seen anything like it before." (Beckett 1983, 145)

criticism, I confess to share Morot-Sir's ambivalence about the project of seeking to understand Beckett's drama as an allegory of human situatedness. In this chapter, I have thus addressed Beckett's aesthetics of gesture as an essentially anti-symbolical, anti-allegorical practice, even as it acknowledges the spectator's complicity in imaginatively producing symbolic meanings of their own. In so doing, I have built on the argument in the previous chapters', namely that Beckett's drama is ecological (in that it understands the significance of interaction for communication,) and phenomenological (in that it recognizes the specificity of lived experience for the creation of meaning,) to finally arrive at the suggestion that it is ethical, in that it links judgement to perception as an imaginative act. I have maintained that Beckett seems to have seized upon the medium of theatre as a fruitful context for such aspirations. Based on the assumption that expressions are medium-and context-specific, I have also proposed that the theatre afforded Beckett a new mode of expression, one that could be seen to answer to his effort to avoid the effort to intellectualize or pigeonhole experience by grasping for meanings that match preconceived ideas, *viz*. 'the allegorical sin'. Indeed, even if literature, in its broadest sense, is exemplary when it comes to helping us understand ourselves and our fellow human beings, this is not because literature explains the world to us, but because it invites us to approach things within a mood of curiosity. Taking off from this insight, I have arrived to conclude that the aesthetics in Beckett's drama safeguard an ethics of knowing that takes Gendlin's *more than* (…..) as the starting point for creative, imaginative interaction between spectator and performance. Indeed, Beckett's drama reveals our complicity in the meanings we create, and so it seems more important than ever.

Conclusion

As Sarah Ahmed reminds us, "[t]hose who are 'in place' also must arrive; they must get 'here', but their arrival is more easily forgotten" (Ahmed 2006, 9–10).[123] Here, in the conclusion, I would therefore want to acknowledge that the arrival of the ideas presented in this book would be difficult to trace. They result from a process of thinking that has progressed over many years, often interrupted by the arrival of new ideas. My thinking about mis-movements and the aesthetics of gesture in Beckett's drama has therefore been moving vertically and horizontally, spiralling onwards, not necessarily needing a point of arrival. Yet, even in moments of being stuck, there are openings for moving on. Just as dancers often come to realize that injuries are guides that help them move differently rather than merely adversaries that block movements, we all need to dare to let go of what we are most committed to, namely our beliefs and convictions, to find routes or ways to communicate with each other. To think with experience, Schoeller and Dunaetz point out, is "to ask not only what it is that matters when something matters, but also how it matters and why is it important that it matters" (2011, 130). It is to take "that which emerges freshly in the embodied process of thinking, speaking or reading— [to be emerging] ... with precision even if it is also richly unfinished" (Schoeller and Dunaetz 2018, 131). Thinking from experience, we may leave off thinking based on concepts that are already defined and come up with new ones. Admittedly, this is not an easy task, as evidenced by the often-convoluted terminology derived from phenomenological and new materialist accounts. Yet, in actual practice is not a matter of abandoning language or concepts. Rather, it is about attuning to what we mean when we speak and calling our own assumptions into question. It is about acknowledging the

---

[123] Admittedly Ahmed makes this comment in relation to migrant orientations, but I see it as pertinent also to the form of 'migrant thinking' generated by trying to figure out how I arrived to take an interest in the body in performance, and why it seems still worth my time.

'perhaps' that frames human situatedness, and Gendlin's process model of thinking here provides a model for understanding how we move in, and are changed by, the relations that we are. On such an account, identity is no longer a relation between distinct entities, but emerges from interaction yet "[i]n these interactively responsive processes there is something surprising to be discovered: with Stanley Cavell one might describe this as 'finding one's own voice." [unquote] (Schoeller and Dunaetz 2018, 125). Language is therefore as important as ever. That is, the emphasis on embodied cognition does not deny the significance of language, despite Barad's catchphrase: "Language has been granted too much power" (2003, 802). Only, we need to rethink our processes of sense-making. Attuning to embodied cognition reveals our mode of being in the world as intrinsically incomplete: we cannot create meaning on our own (Gendlin), nor can we speak a private language (Wittgenstein), but we emerge from interaction, as do meanings, concepts, and identities. Embodied cognition is therefore an important potential resource for thinking, but also for communicating with the other.

In this book, then, I have taken off from perspectives that could be seen to blur the Cartesian distinction between self and other, to suggest that Beckett's drama calls us to examine our lives, and that the knowledge we stand to gain from becoming involved in such activity is the kind of insights needed to regain a sense of what it means to be a human being, not in the rational sense associated with western philosophy, but in the sense afforded by recognising that we are interaction. My discussions of mis-movements have been informed by theoretical perspectives that conventionally fall under the remits of epistemology and hermeneutics. Yet while essentially phenomenological, the discussions have not begun in pure description, and my approach to the body in performance has not in this sense been objective. Rather, as my interest in the body in performance testifies, I have arrived at Beckett's drama from a certain perspective and there is no escaping the fact that my discussions in this book are tainted by my personal experiences, as well as guided by my discoveries. Thus, my interest in the body in Beckett's drama has led me to consider perception, and my interest in perception has led me to consider time, not primarily as a psychological experience but as a primordial structure for experience within which change appears, and my interest in how change appears has led me to consider performance as ecology, and my interest in performance as ecology has led me to consider performance as a system within which change can happen anywhere, and so on. Moreover, the process of struggling to express my ideas, has made me realize that I need a new syntax capable of capturing the complexity of perspectives that interact in Beckett's aesthetics of gesture, a syntax that does not look *at* mis-movements as objects, but as experiences and encounters that take place in a context. The process of thinking about the body in performance has thus entailed zigzagging from one idea to another, spiralling upwards, sideways, and downwards, turning and returning to the question of Beckett's corporeal turn (and its potential implications). In so doing, I have arrived to suggest that Beckett's aesthetics of gesture safeguards ethics through creating presentations that are vague, abstract, and ambiguous and which invite spectators to pay attention to how such phenomena appears for perception as openings to acknowledge our complicity in producing meaning in the context of Beckett's drama. In short, in probing the issue of mis-movements in Beckett's drama, I have been receiving ideas, stumbled upon insights that I have subsequently merged into an already an existing web of ideas, and this book implicitly gives an account for the arrival of such insights.

My aim to take a closer look at the phenomenology of mis-movements has therefore not resulted in an exhaustive analysis of what mis-movements in Beckett's drama mean. Still, I hope to have indicated the relevance of mis-movements for Beckett's aesthetics of gesture, which seems more to resemble the kind of 'inner revolution' "that van Gogh saw as necessary to counteract the rise of nihilism" (see Griffin 2017, ix). In the preface to *Modernism and Phenomenology: Literature, Philosophy, Art,* Roger Griffin refers to Vincent van Gogh's letter to his brother Theo on "the impact of 'modern progress'" (2017, ix). According to Griffin Leo Tolstoy's account of the principle of revolution in Christianity (*My Religion*), inspires van Gogh to envision modernism as similarly driven by a "revolutionary force … in a sense only distantly related to the one made familiar by standard accounts of the (political or social) revolutions on which modern historians cut their teeth" (*ibid.*) The disenchantment of the world brought about by the social and political effects of modernity is in this sense revolutionary, but the outer revolution of modernity is also paralleled by an inner, hidden revolution, "out of which a new religion will be born, or rather, something completely new which will be nameless, but which will have the same effect of consoling, of making life possible, as the Christian religion used to" (Tolstoy qtd in Griffin 2017, ix). Such a 'hidden' revolution seems also to be at work in Beckett's theatre, which sets the stage for a more open-ended encounter between audience and work, one that takes aesthetic experience, *both* as foundational *and* revelatory. Correspondingly, Ackerley observes, "[e]piphanic moments abound in Beckett's writings, but they are invariably attended by frustration, scepticism and uncertainty" (2014, 18).[124] The characters in Beckett's drama are invariably engaged in processes that invalidate previous moments of

---

[124] According to Ackerley "the aesthetic of failure" is already "a presence in Beckett's writing in the early 1930s" but finds a solution in *Murhpy* (1938) where Beckett weds Carl Jung's tripartite diagram of the psyche (the ego, the personal unconscious, and the collective unconscious), to Leibnitz's monadology, specifically to reconcile Murphy's desire for a unity of mind, body, and soul (Ackerley 2014, 19). This tripartite structure of consciousness was subsequently mapped in the series of novels conventionally known as *The Three Novels*: *Molloy* (1951), *Malone Dies* (1951) and *The Unnamable* (1953). Working his way towards "the dark zone of the Unnamable's inner being" Beckett can finally do justice to the deeper structures of the unconscious mind (Ackerley 2014, 19). The aesthetic of failure thus runs deeper than merely comic relief. Nonetheless, as Ulrika Maude observes, in *Murphy*, the tripartite monad fails: "The protagonist of Beckett's first novel …, strives for a life of the mind, but ends up with his 'body, mind and soul, […] freely distributed over the floor' of a Dublin pub" (2015, 170). Thus, the novel could be seen to end with an image that suggestively conjures up the intermingling of these parts into a larger imagined whole.

clarity, and they tersely comment on this situation. Thus, Krapp concludes at the end of *Krapp's Last Tape* (1958): "Perhaps my best years are gone. When there was a chance of happiness. But I wouldn't want them back. Not with the fire in me now. No, I wouldn't want them back" (*TN III*, 10, 275–277). Ostensibly, Krapp holds on to his new insights, even as letting go is a prerequisite for moving on, and even as acknowledging ignorance is a prerequisite for acquiring knowledge. Perhaps, then, it is Krapp's stubborn persistence to hold on to what he has become that makes him so pitiful. His refusal to let go, his pathetic reassurances of insight, ringing hollow, as testified by the tapes. Yet, only by yielding to the intrinsic otherness that proposes itself as an intrinsic dimension of the present, as it were, could he possibly move on.

Indeed, to acknowledge ignorance is to widen the purview of knowledge, to see more and more dimensions of knowing and being. There is always something more to be known about the world, something *other than* conventional belief allows us to see, yet this something more or other does not make our beliefs and creeds relativist. Rather, the fact that knowledge is context-specific means that each context possesses what Dewey terms "pervasive qualities" (qtd in Johnson 2008, 72–73). And *"pervasive qualities* [that] *are not properties of objects"* (Dewey qtd in Johnson 2008, 72, emphasis in original), define our experience of the whole situation before we arrive to select details for analysis. It is merely that habit frequently prevents us from noticing what goes on. Conventionally we "learn to understand and to experience our world as consisting of pre-given, mind-independent objects that have discrete properties and stand in various external relations to each other" (Johnson 2008, 73). But this is not how the world appears to us in experience. Rather than discrete units, we perceive "unified wholes", pervaded by "all-encompassing" qualities that make them what they are (Johnson 2008, 73). Those unified wholes may be atmospheric, which is to say they may reveal themselves in moods or appear in various states of organization (chaotic, structured etc.). They reveal themselves as wholes that guide us in the process of selection that enfolds interpretation. Thus, we see the whole before we see the parts, rather than the other way around. Quoting Dewey, Johnson therefore maintains that nobody "could mistake a Nolde for a Picasso or a Vermeer" (2008, 73). By analogy, nobody would mistake Beckett, for example, for Pinter, Ionesco, or Artaud.

As human beings, then, we consistently discover things that we did not previously know, and which cast a different light on the known and the pragmatist aesthetic perspective, adapted in this book on Beckett's aesthetics of gesture, has revealed a set of correspondences with philosophers like James, and Dewey, who emphasize the continuity between embodied experience and thinking. Beckett's work is marked by somatic qualities that readers and spectators are invited to attend to, even as they seem irrelevant, and the fact that Beckett's pervasive wholes always comprise more than we are accustomed to acknowledging is thus key to the process of interpreting his work. That is, the aesthetic dimension of experience is key to how we approach Beckett's drama, and my claim in this book has been that such qualities speak to us as human beings, regardless of context and that the enormous response that Beckett's drama has generated testifies to this situation. There is simply no escaping the processes of meaning-making into which we are immersed, and which are intrinsically linked to aesthetic experience, but unless we arrive at a challenge for habitual perception, at least momentarily, the opportunity for moving on, for seeing things differently, for carrying our felt sense forward etc., inevitably slips through our fingers. Beckett's creative solution to this predicament spells mis-movements, which could be described as technical devices that invite spectators to counter the deadening effects of habit. That said, what mis-movements show is not that we cannot know but that we cannot *not* know. Even as ignorance is exponential—the more we know, the more we realize how little we know—we cannot stop interacting and participating in creating meaning, an insight which can be both painful, humbling, and liberating.

The oft-cited declaration 'know thyself' attributed to Socrates, implies that unexamined life is somehow "lost" (see Cavell 1997, 25).

In fact, "Socrates believed that one could have ALL the other kinds of knowledge, and be totally lost – totally aimless – if one didn't have the other kind of knowledge, which was knowledge of one's self." (Lecture, "101 Socrates and the Life of Inquiry"). Curiously, however, none of Beckett's characters, from Vladimir and Estragon in *Waiting for Godot* (1953) to Dreamer (A) and his dreamt self (B) in *Nacht und Träume* (1982), lay any claim to linguistic knowledge. When it comes to the possibility of knowing, they seem more fallibilist than sceptical, a stance that affiliates them with Socrates's attitude to knowledge, which entails denying "any knowledge except the knowledge of his ignorance" (McEvilley 2002, 193). Yet, to affirm one's ignorance is already to admit the possibility of truth, at the very least the truth of one's ignorance, and so it seems paradoxically to establish the possibility that truth exists. Importantly, therefore, failure to know (or being wrong) does not exclude the potential for knowing (or being right) any more than the fact that our arrival at seeing things differently must lead to relativism. Indeed, it safeguards that potential. Because, if being wrong would not be an option, then there would be no failure to speak about, just as there would be no possibility of being right, and nor would there be multiple perspectives on the same. In *Theaetetus*, Socrates criticizes Protagoras for "making every individual self-sufficient in wisdom" (2003, 77). That is, even as "Socrates turns the investigation of philosophy towards human concerns, and away from the cosmos", he is not a relativist:

> Socrates' position was that the relativists had to be wrong, but it didn't follow from that that Socrates himself had to know the absolute truth. In other words, Socrates thought that he absolutely knew there must be some truths that were absolutely important for human beings, without making the further claim that he knew what they were.
>
> (Roderick, Lecture "101 Socrates and the Life of Inquiry", transcript, 15.53–16.18)

Unlike his main antagonists, the Sophists, Socrates does not accept the individualist notion that "man is the measure of all things" (Roderick "101 Socrates and the Life of Inquiry", 13.19–13.45). Because "[o]n this argument by the Sophists ... knowledge is impossible. Because each individual will have—just like a nose—an opinion, and a right to it, and no-ones' will be more right than the other." (Roderick "101 Socrates and the Life of Inquiry", 14.08–14.22).[125] Notably, Beckett's attitude to knowledge, as reflected in his drama, resembles Socrates's attitude to knowledge in that it maintains that there is at least the possibility to glimpse truth, even as this possibility is framed by anxiety. Again, the fact that there are moments of clarity does not mean that thinking stops short or that new moments of clarity cannot be experienced that revoke previous moments of insight—correspondingly anxiety does not exclude the possibility of knowledge, any more than it safeguards a morality linked to action.

My claim that Beckett's drama is Socratic should be read in this light. It is a serious effort to rob spectators of their habitual strategies of interpretation, specifically to produce the necessary conditions of possibility for perceiving clearly, even as the nature of knowledge under scrutiny in Beckett's drama does not tend towards Socratic dialogue, nor Platonic purity. Yet, as Thomas McEvilley explains, the purpose of Socrates's "*elenchus*—the trial or ordeal by dialectic—is to awaken people from their dogmatic slumber into intellectual curiosity (2002, 189), and this is a claim that I find suggestively paralleled in Beckett's claim that "habit is a great deadener" (Beckett *TN I*, 82: 2756–2773). The question pertains to the nature of the knowledge that one may hope to gain (McEvilley 2002, 189–190). Notably, the kind of knowledge that Socratic seeks is of the highest order, namely a knowledge that corresponds to the One.

---

[125] According to Roderick, "[a]nother, more sophisticated way to understand Protagoras is for him to be saying something like this: "Each tribe or cultures' standards of knowledge will be the standards that will hold for that tribe or that culture". That's a more sophisticated version of what some philosophers like to call relativism" ("101 Socrates and the Life of Inquiry", 14.24–14.48).

A purification, rebirth, which according to Plato "[i]s unlike intellectual knowledge that is requires a redirecting of the entire being" (McEvilley 2002, 190).[126] The "organ of knowledge" that Plato writes about in the Republic (qtd in McEvilley 2002, 192), "has become blind", yet "when purified, [it] 'is worth more than ten thousand physical eyes for by it alone is reality seen'" (Plato qtd in McEvilley 2002, 192). The "wisdom-eye of which Plato's Socrates speaks can only be turned to the light by turning the whole body away from the darkness (the world of phenomena)" (McEvilley 2002, 192). Paradoxically, then, the intuition that sustains seeing must be separate from the world of phenomena, in a move that seems to approximate a phenomenological reduction. By analogy—and even if the possibility of arriving at the kind of purified wisdom envisioned by Plato's Socrates seems openly refuted in Beckett's emphasis on ignorance— questions of whether knowledge, truth and beauty exist, and whether such values could be expressed, and if so, how, nevertheless loom large in Beckett's drama.

In this book, I have therefore argued that the reconfiguration of the context of performance approximates what could be described as an inward turn, towards the embodied reservoirs of sense-making, a situation that also has ethical implications. Structurally, Beckett's drama is characterized by incompleteness. It does not tell us what to understand or think. In other words, it is not didactic, at least not in any conventional sense. Yet, it invites spectators to pay attention to aesthetic aspects of performance, by means of mis-movements as paths to aesthetic experience, and to engage imaginatively and creatively in thinking from such experiencing. If Beckett's drama has a black box character to it, then anything or nothing may be read into the vague and ambiguous situations staged, a fact that makes the actual

---

[126] "It is like 'an eye that could not be converted to the light from the darkness except by turning to the whole body. Even so this organ of knowledge must be turned away from the world of becoming along with the entire soul, like the scene-shifting *periactus* in the theatre, until the soul is able to endure the contemplation of essence and the brightest region of being" (McEvilley 2002, 190).

contexts (historical, cultural, social, or otherwise) even more important, not less. The conditions for ethical discernment that emerge in Beckett's drama do so because they are vague about meaning, not despite this fact. Since "it matters how we arrive at the places we do" (Ahmed 2006, 2), spectators will also approach the context of performance within their own perceptual horizons, always limited by habit, bias and preconceived notions about meaning. Indeed, as Beckett observed, people love to 'dig' (qtd in Craig et al. 2008, 540), and they dig where they stand. Yet it is precisely to the effect of transcending such perceptual horizons in the context of performance that mis-movements serve to home in on aesthetic experience as a path to reconnect with embodied cognition and so as a path to escape the prison house of language built by old concepts and meanings.

Thus, Beckett's dramatic enquiry into what it means to live under the auspices of such authorities as truth and meaning comprises an ethical call. It calls the observer to pay attention to how the world is constituted in perception. Indeed, the function of mis-movements, and the rationale of the aesthetics of gesture, are to guide the spectator's perception towards interaction as the bedrock of communication. More than merely conspicuous, therefore, mis-movements are important frames for staging a different mode of perception. Mis-movements prompt spectators to look for meaning beyond the limits of language, but they also prompt spectators to acknowledge their complicity in producing linguistic meaning. Taking the embodied foundation for meaning-making into consideration therefore does not abolish interpretation. It merely reconfigures it, and my aim in this book has been to address the implications of this situation in Beckett's drama.

In this book, then, I have been mining the reservoirs of embodied cognition, specifically to outline a tentative list of features that seem to characterize the aesthetics of gesture in Beckett's drama. The aesthetics of gesture in Beckett's drama is phenomenological in its emphasis on the senses, rhetorical in its capacity to generate new perspectives, and ethical in its capacity to generate discernment and self-reflection. But it does not abolish language. Rather, is reveals the continuity between the sense and sense-making intrinsic to perception and embodied cognition. Thus, both the poetic logic of mis-movements, and the rationale for the aesthetics of gesture in Beckett's drama, predicate on a 'carnal hermeneutics' aimed at redirecting the spectators' attention away from language towards sensation. Indeed, the corporeal turn paves the way for thinking with *more than* language, which is also how it affords a route to intellectual freedom.[127] Both the emphasis on ignorance and the invitation to recognize that there are things one cannot state are therefore key to understanding the function of mis-movements in Beckett's drama. Arguably, you do not have to understand to listen and see. You do not have to think to encounter that which appears. In a sense, the more intently you watch something, the more focused your gaze becomes, the more silent your mind will go.[128] It is a matter of yielding before the approaching object, which in the context of Beckett's drama are mis-movements as they appear in the context of performance. It is also about getting in touch with one's own ignorance, recognizing that not even words are forms that hold but words move with the body and evolve, as Gendlin explains (1986, 269).[129] Thus, language is "never alone, [but] it is implied by the body in situations" (Gendlin 1986, 269).

---

[127] Thus, for instance its capacity to generate conflicts between individual and social perspectives, or its capacity to generate new metaphors of embodied cognition, seemingly afford relevant perspectives to investigate.

[128] I am indebted to Emelie Hallgren, yoga teacher, for framing this insight so clearly.

[129] As, Gendlin explains we are inherently part of every context, and every context is inherently part of us.[129] Yet, "Each of us [also] believes, correctly, that he or she surely is *more than* lump of pulsating flesh" (2008, 163). Our phenomenal body, then, is *more than* the hand that grasps or the feet that fall—it is an ongoing interaction between the object grasped and the ground that is being walked upon. Consequently, we must not make the mistake of leaving out "large parts of what makes meaning and mind possible", nor the "sources of, and constraints on, meaning and mind that come from the character of our corporeal rootedness in the biological–ecological processes of life" (Johnson 2008, 166).

As the discussions in this book hope to have shown, there are no specific meanings attached to mis-movements, only the messy, inchoate, ongoing processes of interaction that mis-movements invite, and through which spectators may arrive to use words in new ways. Perhaps, the secret allure of Beckett's drama is simply that it affords the opportunity for intellectual freedom through showing us the structures that hold us captive. Arguably, to experience the event of Beckett's drama is to perceive change. Yet, as discussed in chapter one, it is also to perceive the hierarchies of meaning created as mis-movements shifts logical typing as part of producing change. Indeed, the goal of Beckett's art seems epitomized in an aesthetics of gesture that challenges or undermines habitual perceptions of the world, not to establish meaning as unattainable, but to re-examine those perceptions on which our values and meanings are founded, *viz.* the perceptive act itself. And if the ways in which we arrive to valorize and make sense of experience, our modes of thinking as it were, conventionally tend to move from parts to wholes in processes of inductive reasoning, then mis-movements disrupt such conventional modes of interpretation.

Mis-movements, then, invite us to take up more holistic approaches to interpretation. Put differently, Beckett's aesthetics of gesture invites audiences to re-examine the ineffable fullness of experience, which acts as a ligature between private and public meanings. Yet, ultimately, the notion that directors should be obliged to follow Beckett's stage directions to the letter seems redundant. What the stage directions reveal is not the final key to Beckett's drama but Beckett's development as director and the aesthetics of gesture resulting from this process. It therefore need not be the case that a production staging Beckett's drama must perform to the letter the mis-movements described in the stage directions. Rather, in reconfiguring the aesthetic image from object to experience, Beckett affords a simple and highly complex solution to the predicament of expression; and any staging of mis-movements that figures the theatrical sign as kinetically and experientially significant, thereby retaining the intellectual freedom opened out by mis-movements, would therefore be carrying the torch of Beckett's creative solution forward.

Bibliography

Ackerley, C. J., and S. E. Gontarski. *The Grove Companion to Samuel Beckett: A Reader's Guide to His Works, Life, and Thought*. First edition. New York: Grove Press, 2004.

Ackerley, C. J. "'Deux Besoins': Samuel Beckett and the Aesthetic Dilemma." In *The Edinburgh Companion to Beckett and the Arts*. Ed. S. E. Gontarski. Edinburgh University Press, 2014, pp. 17–24.

Adorno, Theodore. *Aesthetic Theory*. 1970. London: Continuum. 1997.

Ahmed, Sara. *Queer Phenomenology: Orientations, Objects, Others*. Durham and London: Duke University Press, 2006.

Asmus, Walter. "Practical Aspects of Theatre, Radio and Televison". *Journal of Beckett Studies*, No. 2, Summer 1977.

Attridge, Derek. "Taking Beckett at His Word: The Event of *The Unnamable*". *Journal of Beckett Studies*, Vol. 26, No. 1 (2017), pp. 10–23. DOI: 10.3366/jobs.2017.0184.

Au, Susan. *Ballet and Modern Dance*. London: Thames & Hudson, 1997.

Balaam, Annette, C. *Samuel Beckett in Virtual Reality*. A dissertation submitted to the University of Bristol in accordance with the requirements for award of the degree of PhD in the Faculty of Arts, Graduate School of Arts and Humanities, October 2019.

Bachelard, Gaston. *Intuition of the Instant*. Translated by Eileen Rizo-Patron, Northwestern University Studies in Phenomenology and Existential Philosophy. Eds. James M. Edie, Anthony Steinbock, and John McCumber. Evanston: Northwestern University Press, 2013.

Barthes, Roland. "The Third Meaning: Research Notes on Some Eisenstein Stills". *Image, Music, Text*. New York: Hill and Wang: New York, 1978.

Barad, Karen. *Meeting the Universe Half-Way*. Durham and London: Duke University Press, 2007.

Bateson, Gregory. (1979) *Mind and Nature: A Necessary Unity*. Cresskill: Hampton Press, 2002.

—. *Steps to an Ecology of Mind*. Foreword by Mary Catherine Bateson. Chicago and London: Chicago University Press, 2000.

—. *A Sacred Unity: Further Steps to an Ecology of Mind*. Ed. Rodney E. Donaldson. New York: A Cornelia & Michael Bessie Book. *An imprint of* Harper Collins *publishers*, 1991.

—. And Mary Catherine Bateson. *Angels Fear: Towards and Epistemology of the Sacred*. New York: Macmillan, 1987.

Buchanan, Ian. *Assemblage: Theory and Method*. London, New York, Dublin: Bloomsbury Academic, 2021.

Beckett, Samuel. *Murphy* (1938). New York: Grove Weidenfeld, 1957.

—. *Watt* (1953). New York: Grove Press, 1959.
—. *Molloy* (1951), *Malone Dies* (1951), *The Unnamable* (1953): *Three Novels by Samuel Beckett*. 1955. New York: Grove Weidenfeld, 1991.
—. and Georges Duthuit. *Proust and Three Dialogues*. 1965. London: Calder, 1999.
---. and Ruby Cohn. *Disjecta: Miscellaneous Writings and a Dramatic Fragment*. 1983. London: Calder, 2001.
—. and James Knowlson. Ed. *Happy Days: Samuel Beckett's Production Notebook*. London: Faber, 1984.
—. *The Complete Dramatic Works*. 1986. London: Faber, 2006.
—. and James Knowlson and Dougal Macmillan Eds. *The Theatrical Notebooks of Samuel Beckett: Vol. I, Waiting for Godot*. London: Faber, 1993.
—. and S.E. Gontarski and James Knowlson. Eds. *The Theatrical Notebooks of Samuel Beckett: Vol. II, Endgame*. London: Faber, 1992.
—. and James Knowlson and S.E. Gontarski. Eds. *The Theatrical Notebooks of Samuel Beckett: Vol. III, Krapp's Last Tape*. London: Faber, 1992.
—. and S.E Gontarski and James Knowlson. Eds. *The Theatrical Notebooks of Samuel Beckett: Vol. IV, The Shorter Plays*. 1994. London: Faber, 1999.
—. and Fehsenfeld, Martha Dow, Lois More Overbeck et al. *The Letters of Samuel Beckett, Vol I*. Cambridge, UK; New York: Cambridge University Press, 2009.
Begam, Richard. *Samuel Beckett and the End of Modernity*. California: Stanford University Press, 1996.
Beloborodova, Olga. *Postcognitivist Beckett*. Cambridge: Cambridge Elements, 2020.
Bergson, Henri. *Matter and Memory* (1896). New York; London: Zone; Distributed by MIT Press, 1988.
Birkett, Jennifer, and Kate Ince, editors. *Samuel Beckett*. Routledge, 1999.
Brooks, Peter. "Aesthetics and Ideology: What Happened to Poetics?" *Critical Inquiry*, Vol. 20, No. 3 (1994), pp. 509-523.
Brown, Llewellyn. "Samuel Beckett, Quickening the 'dead voices': From *Waiting for Godot* to *That Time*". *Beckett's Voices / Voicing Beckett*, Themes in Theatre, Volume: 12, Brill, 2021, pp. 67–84.
Browne, Sarah. *Echo's Bones: A Parallel Play*. Fingal County Council, 2023.
Bryden, Mary. *Samuel Beckett and the Idea of God*. Basingstoke; New York: Macmillan; St. Martin's Press, 1998.
Buber, Martin. *I and Thou*. (1970). Translation, with a prologue and footnotes by Walter Kauffmann. Simon & Schuster, 1997.
Calder, John. *The Philosophy of Samuel Beckett*. London: Calder, 2001.
Carney, James. "Thinking avant la lettre: A Review of 4E Cognition." *Evol Stud Imaginative Cult*. Vol., 4, No. 1 (Spring 2020), pp. 77-90. doi: 10.26613/esic/4.1.172. PMID: 32457930; PMCID: PMC7250653.
Cavell, Stanley. *Must We Mean What We Say?* (1969). New York: Cambridge University Press, 2003.

—. "Something out of the Ordinary". Presidential Address delivered before the Ninety-Third Annual Eastern Division Meeting of the American Philosophical Association in Atlanta, Georgia, December 29, 1996.

Chabert, Pierre. "The Body in Beckett's Theatre", *Journal of Beckett Studies*, No. 8, pp. 23–28 (Autumn 1982).

Cohn, Ruby. *Back to Beckett*. Princeton University Press, 1973.

—. *Just Play: Beckett's Theater*. Princeton, N.J.: Princeton University Press, 1980.

—. *The Comic Gamut*. New Brunswick, N.J.: Rutgers University Press, 1962.

—. *Beckett: Waiting for Godot, A Casebook*. London: MacMillan, 1987.

—. "Philosophical Fragments in the Works of Samuel Beckett." *Criticism*, Vol. 6, No. 1 (Winter 1964), pp. 33-43, (11 pages). URL: https://www.jstor.org/stable/23094159 .

Connor, Steven. *Samuel Beckett: Repetition, Theory and Text* (1988). Oxford: Basil Blackwell, 2007.

—. *Beckett, Modernism and the Material Imagination*. Cambridge: Cambridge University Press, 2014.

Craig George, with Martha Dow Feshenfeld, Dan Gunn and Lois More Overbeck, Eds., *The Letters of Samuel Beckett, Vol II*. Cambridge, UK; New York: Cambridge University Press 2009.

Critchley, Simon. "Tragedy." Public open lecture for the students of the Division of Philosophy, Art & Critical Thought. The European Graduate School / EGS. Valletta, Malta, Thursday October 19, 2017. URL: https://www.youtube.com/watch?v=2QOMx1kMngo

Dearlove, Judith. *Accommodating the Chaos*. Durham: Duke University Press, 1982.

Dewey, John. *Art as Experience*. Perigree (Penguin), 2005.

Dolezal, Luna. "Thinking through the Body with Richard Shusterman." *International Journal of Philosophical Studies*, 2014. DOI: 10.1080/09672559.2013.873240.

Dowd, Garin. "PROLEGOMENA TO A CRITIQUE OF EXCAVATORY REASON: Reply to Matthew Feldman." *Samuel Beckett Today / Aujourd'hui*, 2008, Vol. 20, Des éléments aux traces: Elements and Traces (2008), pp. 375-388.

Dufrenne, Mikel. *The Phenomenology of Aesthetic Experience*. Foreword Edward E. Casey. Northwestern University Press, 1973.

Durantaye, de la, Leland. *Beckett's Art of Mis-Making*. Harvard University Press, 2016.

Einarsson, P. Charlotta. "The significance of mis-movements in Samuel Beckett's Endgame." *Lectures de Endgame, Fin de partie de Samuel Beckett*. Eds. Geneviève Chevallier, Delphine Lemonnier-Texier and Brigitte Prost, Rennes: Presses Universitaires de Rennes, 2009, s. 105–122.

—. "Mis-Movements: The Aesthetics of Gesture in Samuel Beckett's Drama." PhD Thesis. Stockholms universitet, Humanistiska fakulteten, Engelska institutionen. ORCID-id: 0000-0002-0918-899X.

—. *A Theatre of Affect: The Corporeal Turn in Samuel Beckett's Drama*. Stuttgart: ibidem Press, 2017.

Emerson, Ralph, Waldo. "Self-Reliance" (1841). *Essays and English Traits*. The Harvard Classics edited by Charles W. Eliot. P. F. Collier & Son Corporation, 1965. Accessed at the Internet Archive.org.

Elliott, Brian. *Phenomenology and Imagination in Husserl and Heidegger*. London: Routledge, 2005.

Esslin, Martin. *The Theatre of the Absurd* (1965). New ed. London: Methuen, 2001.

—. "The Universal Image". *Beckett: Waiting for Godot,. A Casebook*, Ed. Ruby Cohn, London: MacMillan, 1987.

Feldman, Matthew, and Ulrika Maude. *Beckett and Phenomenology*. London: Continuum, 2009.

—. "Returning to Beckett Returning to the Presocratics, or, 'All their balls about being and existing.'" *Genetic Joyce Studies* 6, Spring 2006, pp. 1-11. URL; https://www.geneticjoycestudies.org/articles/GJS6/GJS6 Feldman .

—. *Falsifying Beckett: Essays on Archives, Philosophy, and Methodology in Beckett Studies*. Foreword by Eric Tonning. Ibidem Verlag, 2015.

Felski, Rita. *The Limits of Critique*. Chicago University Press, 2015.

Feshenfeld, Martha Dow, and Lois Overbeck. Eds. *The Letters of Samuel Beckett: 1929–1940*, Cambridge: Cambridge University Press, 2009.

Fletcher, John, "Samuel Beckett and the Philosophers." Comparative Literature, Vol. 17, No. 1 (Winter, 1965), pp. 43-56 (14 pages). URL: https://www.jstor.org/stable/1769742#:~:text=%E2%80%A2-,https,-%3A//www.jstor.org .

Floyd, Juliet. Lecture at "Why Does the Claim of Reason Matter? A Symposium in Memory of Stanley Cavell". Duke Franklin Humanities Institute, November 1, 2019. URL: https://www.youtube.com/watch?v=zYgUg9WuKLc .

Forster, E. M. *Howards End*. 1910. Dover Thrift Editions, 2002.

Frost, Everett. "BECKETT AND GEULINCX'S ETHICS: '...my Geulincx could only be a literary fantasia'." *Samuel Beckett Today / Aujourd'hui*, Vol. 24, Early Modern Beckett / Beckett et le début de l'ère moderne: Beckett Between / Beckett entre deux. Brill, 2012 pp. 171-186.

Früchtl, Josef. "For here there is no place that does not see you: 'Minority Report' and art as de/legitimization." *NECSUS*, Vol. 5, No. 2 (Autumn 2016), pp. 73–88. URL: https://necsus-ejms.org/for-here-there-is-no-place-that-doesnot-see-you-minority-report-and-art-as-delegitimisation/

Garner, Stanton B. *Bodied Spaces: Phenomenology and Performance in Contemporary Drama*. New York: Cornell University Press, 1994.

Gendlin, Eugene. "The new phenomenology of carrying forward." *Continental Philosophy Review* 37. Kluwer Academic Publishers, 127–151, 2004.

—. *A Process Model*. Foreword by Robert. A. Parker. Northwestern University Press, 2018.

—. "How Philosophy Cannot Appeal to Experience", *Language beyond Postmodernism: Saying and Thinking in Gendlin's Philosophy*, Illinois: Northwestern University Press, 1997.

—. *Experiencing and the Creation of Meaning: A Philosophical and Psychological Approach to the Subjective*. Northwestern University Press, 1997.

—. "Process ethics and the political question". In A-T. Tymieniecka (Ed.), *Analecta Husserliana. Vol. XX. The moral sense in the communal significance of life*, 1986, pp. 265-275.

—. "Nonlogical moves and nature metaphors." In A-T. Tymieniecka (Ed.), *Analecta Husserliana. Vol. XIX. Poetics of the elements in the human condition: the sea.* 1985, pp. 383-400. Dordrecht: Reidel. https://www.focusing.org/gendlin/docs/gol_2134.html .

—. *Focusing*. Everest House, 1978.

—. "Interaction First: A Process Model." Online Lecture. URL: YouTube: https://www.youtube.com/watch?v=xaopap6K_JQ .

Genetti, Stefano. "Filiations Chorégografiques: Winnie selon Béjart et chez les Dupuy." *Samuel Beckett Today / Aujourd'hui*, Vol. 23, Filiations & Connexions/ Filiations & Connecting Lines (2011), pp. 49-62, 2011.

Gontarski, S. E., "Beckett and Performance". Ed. Oppenheim, L. *Palgrave Advances in Samuel Beckett Studies*. London: Palgrave, 2004.

—. "Beckett and Performance". In *Journal of Irish Studies*, Vol. 17, Japan, and Ireland. 2002, pp. 89–97.

—. *Creative Involution: Bergson, Beckett, Deleuze*. Edinburgh: Edinburgh University Press, 2015.

Graver, Lawrence, and Raymond Federman. Eds. *Samuel Beckett: The Critical Heritage*. London: Routledge, 1979.

Griffin, Roger. "Preface." *Modernism and Phenomenology: Literature, Philosophy, Art*. By Ariane Mildenberg. Palgrave Macmillan, 2017.

Gumbrecht, Hans Ulrich. *Production of Presence: What Meaning Cannot Convey*, Stanford, California: Stanford University Press, 2004.

—. *Atmosphere, Mood, Stimmung: On a Hidden Potential of Literature* (2011). Translated by Erik Butler. Stanford, California: Stanford University Press, 2012.

Harmon, Maurice (ed.), *No Author Better Served: The Correspondence of Samuel Beckett and Alan Schneider.* Cambridge, Massachusetts, London: Harvard University Press, 1998.
Hart, Kevin. "Preface." Bourne-Taylor, Carole J. A (Volume editor) and Ariane Mildenberg (Volume editor). *Phenomenology, Modernism and Beyond.* Peter Lang, 2010.
Husserl, Edmund. *Cartesian Meditations: An Introduction to Phenomenology.* The Hague: Nijhoff; Dordrecht: Kluwer, 1973.
—. *The Idea of Phenomenology.* Transl. Lee Hardy. Ed. Rudolf Bernet. Dordrecht: Kluwer Academic Publishers, 1999.
Ihde, Don. *Experimental Phenomenology: An Introduction* (1977). Albany, NY: State University of New York Press, 1986.
Johnson, Mark. *The Meaning of the Body: Aesthetics of Human Understanding.* Chicago: University of Chicago Press, 2007.
—. "Mind Incarnate: From Dewey to Damasio." *Daedalus*, Vol. 135, No. 3, On Body in Mind (Summer, 2006), pp. 46-54.
Juliet, Charles. *Conversations with Samuel Beckett and Bram van Velde.* Transl. Tracy Cooke, Axel Nesme, Janey Tucker, Morgaine Reinl and Aude Jeanson (Champaign and London: Dalkey Archive Press, 2009).
Kalb, Jonathan. *Beckett in Performance.* Cambridge: Cambridge University Press, 1989.
Kane, Leslie. *The Language of Silence.* London: Associated University Press, 1984.
Kearney, Richard. "What is Carnal Hermeneutics?", *New Literary History*, Vol 46, No. 1 (Winter 2015), pp. 99–124.
—. *Poetics of Modernity: Towards a Hermeneutic Imagination.* New York: Humanity Books, 1999.
Kenner, Hugh. *Samuel Beckett: A Critical Study.* New ed. Berkeley, Calif.: University of California Press, 1973.
Knowlson, James. *Damned to Fame.* New York: Grove Press. 1996.
—. and Pilling, John. *Frescoes of the Skull: The Later Prose and Drama of Samuel Beckett.* London: John Calder, 1979.
—. and John Haynes. *Images of Beckett.* Cambridge: Cambridge University Press, 2003.
Lawrence, Tim. *Samuel Beckett's Critical Aesthetics.* Cham: Palgrave Macmillan, 2018.
Leder, Drew. *The Absent Body.* Chicago: University of Chicago Press, 1990.
Leitch, Vincent B., et al. Eds. *The Norton Anthology of Literary Criticism.* London: Norton, 2001.
Lloyd, David. *Beckett's Thing: Painting and Theatre.* (2016) Other Becketts. Edinburgh: Edinburgh University Press, 2018.
Locatelli, Carla. *Unwording the Word: Samuel Beckett's Prose Works After the Nobel Prize.* Pennsylvania: Pennsylvania UP, 1990.

Lockton, Dan. (PDF) Exploring Bateson's Syllogism in Grass in systemic design. Available from: https://www.researchgate.net/publication/363670718_Exploring_Bateson's_Syllogism_in_Grass_in_systemic_design [accessed Jul 12, 2023].

Loesberg, Jonathan. *A Return to Aesthetics.* Stanford: Stanford University Press, 2005.

Massumi, Brian. "The Autonomy of Affect", *Cultural Critique*, No. 31, The Politics of Systems and Environments, Part II (Autumn, 1995), pp. 83-109.

McDonald, Rónán. *The Cambridge Introduction to Samuel Beckett.* Cambridge University Press, 2006.

McEvilley, Thomas. *The Shape of Ancient Thought: Comparative Studies in Greek and Indian Philosophies.* New York: Allworth Press, 2002.

McKaughan, Daniel, J. "From Ugly Duckling to Swan: C. S. Pierce, Abduction, and the Pursuit of Scientific Theories." *Transactions of the Charles S. Peirce Society*, Vol. 44, No. 3 (Summer, 2008), pp. 446-468 (23 pages). URL: https://www.jstor.org/stable/40321321. Accessed: July 28, 2023.

McNaughton, James. "'Choose Your Horror': An Introduction to Beckett's Political Aesthetic on the International Stage." *Samuel Beckett Today / Aujourd'hui*, Vol. 31 (2019), pp.183–199.

—. *Samuel Beckett and the Politics of Aftermath.* Oxford University Press, 2018.

McMullin, Ernan and Leon Pompa. "Vico's Theory of Science". *Social Research.* Vol. 43. No. 3 (1976), pp. 450-483.

McMullan, Anna. *Theatre on Trial: Samuel Beckett's Later Drama.* New York and London: Routledge, 1993.

—. *Performing Embodiment in Samuel Beckett's Drama.* London: Routledge, 2010.

—. *Samuel Beckett Today / Aujourd'hui*, Vol. 6, Samuel Beckett: Crossroads and Borderlines / L'ŒUVRE CARREFOUR/L'ŒUVRE LIMITE. 1997, pp. 353-364.

Maude, Ulrika. "Beckett, Body and Mind." *The New Cambridge Companion to Samuel Beckett.* Cambridge, UK: Cambridge University Press, 2015.

—. *Beckett, Technology and the Body.* Cambridge, UK; New York: Cambridge University Press, 2009.

—. and Matthew Feldman. *Beckett and Phenomenology.* London: Continuum, 2009.

Meadows, Donella. "Leverage Points: Places to Intervene in a System", "Donella Meadows Archives", *The Donella Meadows Project: Academy for Systems Change.* Accessed Sep. 15, 2023. URL: https://donellameadows.org/archives/leverage-points-places-to-intervene-in-a-system/ .

Mercier, Vivian. "The Uneventful Event". *Critical Essays on Samuel Beckett*, Ed. Lance St. John Butler, Critical Thought Series, Vol. 4, Aldershot: Scolar Press, 1994.

Merleau-Ponty, Maurice. *Phenomenology of Perception* (1945). London: Routledge, 2005.

Mildenberg, Arianne. *Modernism and Phenomenology: Literature, Philosophy, Art.* Palgrave MacMillan, 2017.

Moran, Dermot. *Introduction to Phenomenology.* New York: Routledge, 2000.

—. "Beckett and Philosophy." *Samuel Beckett – One Hundred Years.* Ed. Christopher Murray, New Island Press, 2006, pp. 93–110.

Morot-Sir, Edouard. "Samuel Beckett and Cartesian Emblems." *Samuel Beckett: The Art of Rhetoric.* Eds. Howard Harper, Douglas McMillan III, and Edouard Morot-Sir. Chapel Hill, 1976.

Moorjani, Angela. *Abysmal Games in the Novels of Samuel Beckett.* Chapel Hill: University of North Carolina, 1982.

Murdoch, Iris. *The Sovereignty of Good.* Routledge & Kegan Paul, 1971.

Mykhailyuk, O.Yu., and H.Ya. Pohlod "The Languages We Speak Affect Our Perceptions of the World". *Journal of Vasyl Stefanyk.* Vol. 2, No. 2–3 (2015). DOI:10.15330/jpnu.2.2-3.36-41.

Oppenheim, Lois. Ed. *Directing Beckett.* (1994). Michigan: U Michigan P. 1997.

—. *The Painted Word: Samuel Beckett's Dialogue with Art* (2000). Ann Arbor: University of Michigan Press, 2003.

—. *Palgrave Advances in Samuel Beckett Studies.* New York: Palgrave Macmillan, 2004.

Pattie, David. *The complete Critical Guide to Samuel Beckett.* London: Routledge, 2000.

Phelan, James. *Somebody Telling Somebody Else: A Rhetorical Poetics of Narrative.* Ohio State Press, 2017.

Peirce: C.P. Editorial Introduction to Electronic Edition Membra Ficte Disjecta (A Disordered Array of Severed Limbs) Editorial Introduction by John Deely to the electronic edition of *The Collected Papers of Charles Sanders Peirce.* URL: chrome-extension://efaidnbmnnnibpcajpcglclefindmkaj/https://coloryse miotica.files.wordpress.com/2014/08/peirce-collectedpapers.pdf [accessed Jul 12, 2023].

Plato. *Theatetus.* Transl. Robin H. Waterfield. New York: Penguin, 1987.

—. *Meno.* URL: http://classics.mit.edu/Plato/meno.html .

Polanyi, Michel. *The Tacit Dimension* (1966). Foreword Amartya Sen. Chicago and London: The University of Chicago Press, 2009.

—. And Harry Prosch. *Meaning.* Chicago and London: The University of Chicago Press, 1977.

—. *Personal Knowledge: Towards a Post-Critical Philosophy.* Chicago: Chicago University Press, 1974.

Pountney, Rosemary. *Theatre of Shadows.* New Jersey: Barnes and Noble. 1988.

Price, David W. "Vico and Nietzsche: On Metaphor, History, and Literature." *The Personalist Forum*, Fall1994, Vol. 10, No. 2, *Vico and Nietzsche* (Fall 1994), pp. 119-132. Published by: University of Illinois Press on behalf of the Society for the Advancement of American Philosophy.

Purves, Alex, C. *Homer and the Poetics of Gesture.* New York: Oxford University Press, 2019.

Rosch, Eleanor. "Introduction to the Revised Edition". *The Embodied Mind: Cognitive Science and Human Experience.* With Francisco Varela, Evan Thompson. Foreword by Jon Kabat-Zinn. Massachusetts: Massachusetts Institute of Technology Press, 2016.

Sansonese, Nigro, J. *The Body of Myth: Mythology, Shamanic Trance, and the Sacred Geography of the Body.* Rochester, Vermont: Inner Traditions International, 1994.

Sartre, Jean-Paul. *Search for a Method.* Translated by Hazel E. Barnes. Vintage Books, 1968.

Seel, Martin. *Aesthetics of Appearing.* Stanford, California: Stanford UP, 2005.

Sheets-Johnstone, Maxine. *The Corporeal Turn: AN Interdisciplinary Reader.* Imprint Academic, 2009.

Shellekens, Elisabeth. *Aesthetics & Morality.* Continuum, 2007.

Schoeller, Donata and Neil Dunaetz. "Thinking emergence as interaffecting: approaching and contextualizing Eugene Gendlin's Process Model". Continental Philosophy Revview, Vol. 51 (2018), pp. 123–140. DOI: https://doi.org/10.1007/s11007-018-9437-9 .

Schusterman, Richard. *Pragmatist Aesthetics: Living Beauty, Rethinking Art.* (1992) 2nd edition. Lanham; Boulder; New York; Oxford: Rowman and Littlefield Publishers, 2000.

Simpson, Hannah. "Tics in the Theatre: The Quiet Audience, the Relaxed Performance, and the Neurodivergent Spectator." *Theatre Topics*, Johns Hopkins University Press, Volume 28, Number 3 (November 2018), pp. 227-238. DOI: 10.1353/tt.2018.0046.

—. "Samuel Beckett and Disability Performance." *Journal of Beckett Studies.* Vol. 30, No. 1 (2021), pp. 26-44.

—. *Samuel Beckett and Disability Performance.* Cham: Palgrave MacMillan, 2022.

Tonning, Eric. *Samuel Beckett's Abstract Drama: Works for Stage and Screen 1962-1985.* Oxford: Land, 2007.

Tolle, Eckhart. *Stillness Speaks.* Novato, California: New World Library, and Vancouver, Canada: Namaste Publishing2003.

Tengelyi, László. "On the Border of Phenomenology and Theology." *Phenomenology and Religion: New Frontiers.* Edited by Jonna Bornemark & Hans Ruin. Södertörn Philosophical Studies, Vol. 8 (2010), pp.17–35.

Trezise, Thomas. *Into the Breach: Samuel Beckett and the Ends of Literature.* Princeton: Princeton University Press, 1990.

Vico, Giambattista. *New Science*. (1744). Penguin Books, 2013.
Verene, Donald, Phillip. *Vico's "New Science": A Philosophical Commentary*. Ithaca, New York: Cornell University Press, 2015.
Walsh, Richard. *The Rhetoric of Fictionality: Narrative Theory and the Idea of Fiction*. Ohio State Press, 2007.
Wynands, Sandra. *Iconic Spaces: The Dark Theology of Samuel Beckett's Drama*. Indiana: Notre Dame, 2007.
Wittgenstein, Ludwig. *The Blue and Brown Books*. Harper Torch Books, 1958.

Index

A

abduction, 122, *See* Pierce, Charles S.
Ackerley, C. J., 194
Ackerley, C. J. and Gontarski, S. E., 15, 16, 72
Adorno, Theodore, 43
aesthetic experience, 12, 44, 47, 49, 54, 80, 89, 97, 129, 130, 132, 140, 143, 147, 148, 152, 153, 154, 159, 168, 170, 182, 194, 196
    and perception, 156
    performance as a context for, 60
    value of, 160
aesthetics, 7
aesthetics of gesture, 27, 30, 31, 41, 142, 169, 170, 172, 173, 176, 182, 193, 196, 202
Ahmed, Sara, 3, 61, 66, 98, 119, 120, 133, 152, 191, 200
    Queer Phenomenology, 92
Alexander Technique,™, 169
Alexiou, Nikos, 28
Arnold, Matthew, 24
Asmus, Walter, 57
Attridge, Derek, 153, 154, 155, 157
Au, Susan, 135

B

Bachelard, Gaston, 116
Badiou, Alain, 154
Balaam, Anette, 27, 49, 50
Barad, Karen, 65, 89, 175, 192
Barnes, Hazel E., 35
Barthes, Roland, 159
    obtuse meaning, 159
    third meanings, 156
Bateson, Gregory, 32, 34, 53
    billiard-ball physics, 55
    binocular vision, 127
    difference which makes a difference, 58
    double bind, 50, 120
    ecological perspective on mind, 149
    ecological theory of mind, 137
    habit, 44
    logical typing, 54, 168
    patterns that connect, 88, 154
    perception, 81
    sacred unity, 128
    six criteria for mental processes, 31, 46, 67, 70, 71, 79
    stability, 68
    syllogism in Barbara, 123
    syllogism in grass, 123, 124
    syntax, 68
    tautology, 4, 68
Bateson, Mary Catherine, 127
Beckett, Samuel
    "Dante ... Bruno .. Vico . Joyce", 172
    "Les Deux Besoins", 70
    "Recent Irish Poetry", 2
    Complete Dramatic Works, 16, 114
    Disjecta, 68
    Embers, 113, 115, 117
    Endgame, 1, 49, 78, 125, 145, 186
    Footfalls, 1, 37, 54, 56, 57, 124, 134

Happy Days, 124, 125, 126
Krapp's Last Tape, 109
Krapp's Last Tape, 1, 15, 105, 107, 108, 124, 134, 152, 195
Malone Dies, 194
Molloy, 194
Murphy, 194
Nacht und Träume, 197
Proust and Three Dialogues with Georges Duthuit, 187, See Habit
Rockaby, 16, 54
The Complete Dramatic Works, 37, 165
The Theatrical Notebooks Vol. I–IV, 146
The Unnamable, 153, 194
Waiting for Godot, 8, 26, 49, 52, 139, 140, 144, 146, 165, 197
Watt, 63
Whoroscope, 10
Beckett's drama
 analogy with Wagner's gesamtkunstwerk. See Wagner
 and body-en#2, 115
 and Cartesianism, 9
 and interaction en#2. See Gendlin
 and phenomenology, 98
 and philosophy, 8
 and stage directions, 57
 and the body, 5, 10
 as performing ecology, 46, 132
 body–en#2. See Gendlin, Eugene
 function of, 12, 89
 poetry of, 1
 Socratic, 34, 198
 the atmospheric phase, 25, 26
 the corporeal turn, 27
 the material phase, 25, 26
 the organic phase, 25, 26
 Waiting for Godot, 119
 zone of being, 117, 181

Begam, Richard, 17
Bell, Michael, 70
Beloborodova, Olga, 10, 11, 12, 13, 22, 23
Bennett, Jane, 6, 7
Bergson, Henri, 8, 42, 43
Berkeley, George, 8
Biesta, Gert, 98
binocular vision, 127, See Bateson, Gregory
Blake, William, 122
Blin, Roger, 145
body
 and environment, 99
 and mis-movements. See mis-movements
Bourdieu, Pierre, 43, 91
bracketing. See epoché
Brooks, Peter, 154
Brown, Llewellyn, 182
Browne, Sarah, 142
Bryden, Mary, 24
Buber, Martin, 115
 'I and Thou', 112
 'I–It', 116
 experiencing, 113
 twofold attitude of man, 87, 111
Butho, 135
Butler, Lance St. James, 14

C

Calder, John, 42, 85, 179
Camus, Albert, 8
Caracciolo, Marco, 174, See Kukkonen, Karin
carnal hermeneutics, 160, 163, 168, 201
Carney, James, 11
Cartesian dualism, 33, 192
Cartesianism, 9, 10, 11, 13, 91, 103, 104, 136
Casey, Edward S., 89
Cavell, Stanley, 19, 65, 77, 90, 192

ordinary language use, 64
Chabert, Pierre, 40, 48
change
   and levels of complexity, 68
   and mis-movements, 50, *See* mis-movements
   as coded effects, 49
   as event, 32, 34
chronos, 109
Cluchey, Rick, 107
Cohn, Ruby, 9, 10, 21, 24, 28, 40
Coleridge, Samuel
   willing suspension of disbelief, 91
Connor, Steven, 14, 17, 63
Craig, George et al., 70, 139, 140, 200
Critchley, Simon, 181
curiosity, 5, 20, 42, 187, 189

D

dance, 28, 41, 110
   and interaction, 89
Dante, Alighieri, 8, 172
Dearlove, Judith, 179
Deleuze, Gilles, 14
Deleuze, Gilles and Guattri, Felix, 62
Democritus, 8, 13, 72
Dennis, Amanda, 11, 12, 22, 23, 125
Derrida, Jacques, 14
Descartes, René, 8, 10, 12
Dewey, John, 77, 162, 168, 169, 195, 196
Dolezal, Luna, 169
doting, 6, 7, *See* Bennett, Jane
Dowd, Garin, 18
Duchamp, Marcel, 134
Dufrenne, Mikel, 89, 91
Durantaye, de la, Leland, 179, 181
Duthuit, Georges, 67, 68, 70

E

Elliott, Brian, 133
embodied cognition
   4E cognition, 10
   and Beckett's drama, 10
embodied experience, 12, 23, 95, 141, 149
embodiment
   in Beckett's work, 10
Emerson, Ralph, Waldo, 77, 80, 131
energy
   flow, 56
environment
   as part of events, 99
epoché, 96
   phenomenological reduction, 91
Esslin, Martin, 8, 28, 51
ethics, 193
existentialism, 10
experience
   and felt sense, 186
   and interaction, 102
   and phenomenology, 78
   embodied aspects of, 86

F

fabula and sujet, 39
Feldenkrais™, 169
Feldman, Matthew, 13, 16, 18, 19
Felski, Rita, 10, 144, 160
Fletcher, John, 8
Flexner, Abraham, 20
flow, 49, 59
   of performance, 57, 110
Floyd, Juliet, 65
Forster, E.M., 137
Fracci, Carla, 28
Frost, Everett, 16
Früchtl, Joseph, 148

G

Garner, Stanton B., 8, 14, 64, 74
Gendlin, Eugen
    subjectivity, 178
Gendlin, Eugene, 3, 160
    authentic decision-making
        process, 178
    carrying forward, 31, 118, 120,
        137
    ethics, 177
    excess, 98
    felt sense, 31, 96, 115
    interaction, 201
    interaction body-en#0, 100
    interaction body-en#1, 99, 111
    interaction body-en#2, 100,
        102, 109, 111
    interaction body-en#3, 100
    new phenomenology, 95
    occurring and implying, 102
    process model of thinking, 101,
        192
    subjectivity, 119
    thinking with *more than* words,
        8, 31, 75, 78, 79, 80, 88, 95,
        109, 164
Genetti, Stefano, 28
Geulincx, Arnold, 15
Gontarski, S. E., 25, 28, 41, 49, 62,
    145, 151, 152, 153, 155, 157
Graver, Lawrence and Federman,
    Raymond, 135
Griffin, Roger, 193
Gumbrecht, Hans-Ulrich, 29

H

habit, 44, 47, 52, 70, 73, 93, 108,
    117, 143, 187, 196, 200
habitual linguistic appropriation of
    meaning, 130
habitual modes of thinking, 131
habitual strategies of sense-
    making, 93, 125, 126, 181

habitus, 43, 91, 181
Hart, Kevin, 132
Heidegger, Martin, 94, 177
Heron, Jonathan, 23, *See* Johnson,
    Nicholas E.
Hesla, David H., 14
Hill, Leslie, 70
Hoffman, Frederick J., 10
holistic
    images, 147
    perspective on lived
        experience, 150
    perspective on performance,
        47, 137, 144
Husserl, Edmund, 78, 90, 91, 92, 94

I

Idhe, Don, 132, 133
imagination, 30, 35, 183
    and meaning, 65
    and phenomenology, 132
    and poeticizing, 172
instability, 73
interaction, 11, 19, 21, 101, 109,
    167
    and communication, 189
    and environment, 99
    and logical typing, 59
    and mental process, 32
    and phenomenology, 189
    as a mode of thinking, 95
interpretation
    and aesthectic experience, 141
    and aesthetic experience, 60,
        62, 79, 80, 132, 143, 148
    and Beckett's corporeal turn, 47
    and complexity, 140
    and embodied experience, 167
    and ethics, 32
    and habit, 44, 108
    and interaction, 37, 105, 133,
        149
    and language, 65

and mis-movements, 49, 66, 170, 174, 180, 195, *See* mis-movements
and phenomenology, 93
and responsivity, 156
and the body, 174
as an act of creation, 39
crisis of, 98
performance as a context for, 12, 51, 53, 67, 131, 177, 179, 186, 188, 198
intuition, 93, 199

J

James, William, 129, 149, 161, 196
Johnson, Mark, 141, 149, 164, 165, 166, 169
Johnson, Nicholas E., 23, *See* Heron, Jonathan
Joyce, James, 180

K

Kaelin, Eugene F., 14
kairos, 109
Kalb, Jonathan, 22, 37, 48
Kane, Leslie, 17
Kant, Immanuel, 166
Karr, Jean-Baptiste Alphonse, 69
Kaun, Axel, 2, 70, 76, 173
Kearney, Richard, 164, 169
 carnal hermenutics, 167
Kenner, Hugh, 9, 10, 13, 16
Knowlson, James, 8, 28, 41, 51, 52, 76, 85, 106, 140, 144, 145, 146, 180, 181
kōans, 133
Koczy, Daniel, 4
Kotzamani, Marina, 28
Kukkonen, Karin, 173, *See* Caracciolo, Marco

L

language
 medium for thinking, 171
 ordinary use of, 86
 thinking from experience, 86
 using it 'thinkingly', 6, 7, 11, 15, 78, 81, 163, 182, 183
 value of, 169
Lawrence, Tim, 4, 24, 27, 69, 70, 171
Leder, Drew, 87
 dys-appearance, 103
 the absent body, 103
Leitch, Vincent B. et al., 24
linguistic turn, 160
Lloyd, David, 188
Locatelli, Carla, 17
Lockton, Dan, 124
Loesberg, Jonathan, 158, 161

M

Masson, André, 67
Massumi, Brian, 167
Maude, Ulrika, 11, 21, 22, 23, 142, 194
McDonald, Rónán, 139
McEvilley, Thomas, 199
McKaughan, Daniel J., 122, 124
McMullan, Anna, 10, 11, 22, 23, 40, 64, 72, 142, 147, 164
McMullin, Ernan and Pompa, Leon, 171
McNaughton, James, 35
Meadows, Donella, 149
memory, 21, 42, 43, 74, 85, 152, 161, 176, 187
Merleau-Ponty, Maurice, 94, 104
 experience error, 90
Mildenberg, Ariane, 166
mis-movements
 and aesthetic experience, 79, 199
 and binocular vision, 127

and body-en#2, 104
and change, 50, 53, 59
and *dys*-appearance, 104
and felt sense, 169
and interaction, 176
and interpretation, 29, 49, 53, 105
and language, 78, 174
and mood, 159
and ordinary language use. *See* Cavell, Stanley
and patterns that connect, 127, *See* Gendlin, Eugene, *See* Batseson, Gregory
and perception, 1, 5, 7
and phenomenology, 1
and representation, 1
and the body, 1
and thinking with *more than words*, 159
and time. *See* time
and unpredictability, 54
as coded effects of change, 62, 71
as information, 58
as interaction. *See* interaction
as metamessages, 79
context of, 66
definition of, 1, 104
function of, 1, 4, 7, 12, 39, 54, 56, 77, 79, 81
phenomenological analysis of, 99
rhetorical use of, 2, 12, 148
strategic use of, 1, 73, 143, 175
thinking with *more than* words. *See* Gendlin, Eugene
Mitchell, Pamela, 139
mood, 10
Mooney, Michael E., 13
Moran, Dermot, 8, 91, 92
Morin, Emelie, 34, 35
Morot-Sir, Edouard, 9, 10, 188, 189
Murdoch, Iris, 182, 183, 185, 186
introspectabilia, 183

Mykhailyuk, O. Yu and Pohlod, H. Ya., 163

N

natural attitude, 90, 97, 116, 122, 133, 181
Navridis, Nikos, 28

O

Oppenheim, Lois, 28, 39, 117, 139

P

Page, Anthony, 145
pathology
  and description, 103
  dys-appearance. *See* Leder
Pattie, David, 8, 17
performance
  and interaction, 151
  as a context for aesthetic experience, 66
  as ecology, 108
  ecology of, 8, 149
  logic of, 12
  phenomenology of, 90
Phelan, James, 75, 170
phenomenological attitude, 91, *See* phenomenology
phenomenology
  and experience, 78
  carrying forward. *See* Gendlin, Eugene *carrying forward*
  intentionality, 91
  natural attitude. *See* natural attitude
  phenomenological attitude, 92
Pierce, Charles S., 121
  abduction, 88
  pursuitworthiness, 122
Pilling, John, 28
Pinter, Harold, 135, 136
Plato, 199

Meno, 96
Theaetetus, 197
Polanyi, Michel, 93, 96, 98, *See* Prosch, Harry
    personal knowledge, 94, *See* Gendlin, Eugene thinking with *more than* words
    personal knowlegde, 78
    tacit knowledge, 94, 96, 98
Popper, Karl, 18
Pountney, Rosemary, 22
predicament of expression, 79
presocratic philosophy, 13
Price, David, 171
Prosch, Harry. *See* Polanyi, Michel
Protagoras, 197
Psychoulis, Alexandras, 28
Purves, Alex C., 42
Pythagorean terror, 67

R

relevance
    the criterion of, 16
resistance, 69
    and interaction, 101
rhythm
    of performance, 110, 146
Roderick, Rick, 35, 177, 184, 198
Rorty, Richard, 160
Rosch, Eleanor, 23

S

Sansonese, Nigro J., 134
Sartre, Jean-Paul, 14, 35, 94, 177, 182
Schellekens, Elisabeth, 141
Schenker, Israel, 117
Schneider, Alan, 145
Schoeller, Donata and Dunaetz, Neil, 88, 191
Schopenhauer, Arthur, 8
Schusterman, Richard, 93, 129, 143, 161

Seel, Martin, 149, 157, 158
Shenker, Israel, 180
Shusterman, Richard, 149, 169
Simpson, 21, 22, 151
Simpson, Alan, 145
Simpson, Hannah, 23, 142, 151
Socrates, 196, 198
Sokolowski, Robert, 118, 182
    natural attitude, 97
    phenomenological attitude, 91
stability, 68, 69, *See* Bateson, Gregory
Starte, Josephine, 28
Stevens, Wallace, 129
subject and object relation, 68

T

Tajiri, Yoshiki, 22
Tal Coat, Pierre, 67
Tengelyi, László, 92
The Ring of the Nibelung
    The Ring of the Nibelung, 83
Thobo-Carlsen, John, 73, 74
time, 118, *See chronos* and *kairos*
timing. *See* rhythm
Tolle, Eckart, 115
Trezise, 14, 17
Tudor, David, 134

V

van Gogh, Vincent, 193
van Hoecke, Micha, 28
van Velde, Bram, 67, 68, 70
Verene, Donald Phillip, 172
Vico, Giambattista, 171, 173
von Hofmannsthal, Hugo, 132

W

Wagner, Richard
    and Beckett's drama. *See* Beckett's drama
waiting

Waiting for Godot, 75
walking, 41, 60, 102
   Footfalls, 75
   interaction body-en#2, 101
Walsh, Richard, 37, 38, 39
Warstellen

waiting points in *Godot*, 110
Whitman, Walt, 6, 7
Wittgenstein, Ludwig, 192
   ordinary language use. *See* Cavell, Stanley
Wynands, Sandra, 21